COMMITTEE FOR THE STUDY
OF ECONOMIC AND MONETARY UNION

1. Report on economic and monetary union in the European Community

2. Collection of papers submitted to the Committee for the Study of Economic and Monetary Union

This report has been prepared in response to the mandate of the European Council 'to study and propose concrete stages leading towards economic and monetary union'.

Luxembourg: Office for Official Publications of the European Communities, 1989

ISBN 92-826-0655-4

Catalogue number: CB-56-89-401-EN-C

Articles and texts appearing in this document may be reproduced freely.

Printed in the Federal Republic of Germany

Foreword

At its meeting in Hanover on 27 and 28 June 1988 the European Council recalled that, 'in adopting the Single Act, the Member States of the Community confirmed the objective of progressive realization of economic and monetary union'. The Heads of State or Government therefore decided to examine at the European Council meeting in Madrid in June 1989 the means of achieving this union. To that end they decided to entrust to a Committee, chaired by Mr Jacques Delors, President of the European Commission, 'the task of studying and proposing concrete stages leading towards this union'.

In response to this request, the Committee has the honour to submit the attached Report. The ideas expressed and the proposals contained in the Report are put forward by the members of the Committee in their personal capacity.

Contents

1. The Report

	Page
Chapter I — Past and present developments in economic and monetary integration in the Community	11
1. The objective of economic and monetary union	11
2. The European Monetary System and the ECU	12
3. The Single European Act and the internal market programme	13
4. Problems and perspectives	14
Chapter II — **The final stage of economic and monetary union**	17
1. General considerations	17
2. The principal features of monetary union	18
3. The principal features of economic union	20
4. Institutional arrangements	25
5. Economic and monetary union in the context of the world economy	29
Chapter III — **Steps towards economic and monetary union**	31
1. Principles governing a step-by-step approach	31
2. The ECU	33
3. The principal steps in stage one	34
4. The principal steps in stage two	37
5. The principal steps in stage three	39
6. One or several Treaties	40
7. Suggested follow-up procedure	42
Annex — Excerpts from the Conclusions of the Presidency presented after the meeting of the European Council in Hanover on 27 and 28 June 1988	43

2. Collection of papers

		Page
I — Introductory note		47
II — The Werner Report		51
G. D. Baer and T. Padoa-Schioppa:	The Werner Report revisited (September 1988)	53
III — Papers relating to economic union		61
J. Delors:	Economic and monetary union and relaunching the construction of Europe (September 1988)	63
M. F. Doyle:	Regional policy and European economic integration (December 1988)	69
J. Delors:	Regional implications of economic and monetary integration (January 1989)	81
A. Lamfalussy:	Macro-coordination of fiscal policies in an economic and monetary union in Europe (January 1989)	91
IV — Papers relating to monetary union		127
K. O. Pöhl	The further development of the European Monetary System (September 1988)	129
N. Thygesen:	A European central banking system — Some analytical and operational considerations (October 1988)	157
J. de Larosière:	First stages towards the creation of a European Reserve Bank — The creation of a European Reserve Fund (October-December 1988)	177
W. F. Duisenberg:	The ECU as a parallel currency (October 1988)	185
J. Godeaux:	The working of the EMS: A personal assessment (November 1988)	191
A. Lamfalussy:	The ECU banking market (December 1988)	201

		Page
G. D. Baer and T. Padoa-Schioppa:	The ECU, the common currency and the monetary union (January 1989)	209
A. Lamfalussy:	A proposal for stage two under which monetary policy operations would be centralized in a jointly-owned subsidiary (January 1989)	213
P. Jaans:	The basic difference between the frameworks for policy decision-making provided by the EMS and EMU (March 1989)	221
C. A. Ciampi:	An operational framework for an integrated monetary policy in Europe (April 1989)	225

V — List of members of the Committee 233

1. The Report

Chapter I

Past and present developments in economic and monetary integration in the Community

Section 1

The objective of economic and monetary union

1. In 1969 the Heads of State or Government, meeting in The Hague, agreed that a plan should be drawn up with a view to the creation, in stages, of an economic and monetary union within the Community. This initiative was taken against the background of major achievements by the Community in the 1960s: the early completion of the transition period leading to a full customs union, the establishment of the common agricultural policy and the creation of a system of own resources. At the same time the Bretton Woods system was showing signs of decline. The *Werner Report*, prepared in 1970, presented a plan for the attainment of economic and monetary union. In March 1971, following the Werner Report, Member States expressed 'their political will to establish an economic and monetary union'.

2. Several important *moves followed*: in 1972 the 'snake' was created; in 1973 the European Monetary Cooperation Fund (EMCF) was set up; and in 1974 the Council Decision on the attainment of a high degree of convergence in the Community and the Directive on stability, growth and full employment were adopted. Yet, by the mid-1970s the process of integration had lost momentum under the pressure of divergent policy responses to the economic shocks of the period.

3. In 1979 the process of monetary integration was relaunched with the creation of the *European Monetary System* (EMS) and the European Currency Unit (ECU). The success of the EMS in promoting its objectives of internal and external monetary stability has contributed in recent years to further progress, as reflected in the adoption, in 1985, of the internal market programme and the signing of the Single European Act.

Section 2

The European Monetary System and the ECU

4. The *European Monetary System* was created by a Resolution of the European Council followed by a Decision of the Council of Ministers and an Agreement between the participating central banks.

5. Within the framework of the EMS the participants in the exchange rate mechanism have succeeded in creating *a zone of increasing monetary stability* at the same time as gradually relaxing capital controls. The exchange rate constraint has greatly helped those participating countries with relatively high rates of inflation in gearing their policies, notably monetary policy, to the objective of price stability, thereby laying the foundations for both a downward convergence of inflation rates and the attainment of a high degree of exchange rate stability. This, in turn, has helped moderate cost increases in many countries, and has led to an improvement in overall economic performance. Moreover, reduced uncertainty regarding exchange rate developments and the fact that the parities of the participating currencies have not been allowed to depart significantly from what is appropriate in the light of economic fundamentals have protected intra-European trade from excessive exchange rate volatility.

The EMS has served as the focal point for improved monetary policy coordination and has provided a basis for multilateral surveillance within the Community. In part, its success can be attributed to the participants' willingness to opt for a strong currency stance. Also important has been the flexible and pragmatic way in which the System has been managed, with increasingly close cooperation among central banks. Moreover, the System has benefited from the role played by the Deutschmark as an 'anchor' for participants' monetary and intervention policies. The EMS has evolved in response to changes in the economic and financial environment, and on two occasions (Palermo 1985 and Basle/Nyborg 1987) its mechanisms have been extended and strengthened.

At the same time, the EMS has not fulfilled its full potential. Firstly, a number of Community countries have not yet joined the exchange rate mechanism and one country participates with wider fluctuation margins. Secondly, the lack of sufficient convergence of fiscal policies as reflected in large and persistent budget deficits in certain countries has remained a source of tensions and has put a disproportionate burden on monetary policy. Thirdly, the transition to the second stage of the EMS and the establishment of the European Monetary Fund, as foreseen by the Resolution of the European Council adopted in 1978, have not been accomplished.

6. In launching the EMS, the European Council declared in 1978 that '*a European Currency Unit (ECU) will be at the centre of the EMS*'. Apart from being used as the numeraire of the exchange rate mechanism and to denominate operations in

both the intervention and credit mechanisms, the ECU serves primarily as a reserve asset and a means of settlement for EMS central banks. Although it is an integral part of the EMS, the ECU has for a number of reasons played only a limited role in the operating mechanisms of the EMS. One reason is that central banks have preferred to intervene intra-marginally; therefore, compulsory interventions and the build-up of intervention balances to be settled in ECUs have remained rather limited.

By contrast, the ECU has gained considerable popularity in the market place, where its use as a denominator for financial transactions has spread significantly. It ranks fifth in international bond issues, with a 6% market share. The expansion of financial market activity in ECUs reflects in part a growing issuance of ECU-denominated debt instruments by Community institutions and public-sector authorities of some member countries, and in part the ECU's attractiveness as a means of portfolio diversification and as a hedge against currency risks.

International banking business in ECUs grew vigorously in the first half of this decade, but has moderated since then, although the creation of an ECU clearing system has contributed to the development and liquidity of the market, as has the issue of short-term bills by the UK Treasury. The lion's share of banking business represents interbank transactions, whereas direct business with non-banks has remained relatively limited and appears to have been driven primarily by officially encouraged borrowing demand in a few countries. ECU-denominated deposits by the non-bank sector have stagnated since 1985, suggesting that the ECU's appeal as a near money substitute and store of liquidity is modest. In addition, in the non-financial sphere the use of the ECU for the invoicing and settlement of commercial transactions has remained limited, covering at present only about 1% of the Community countries' external trade.

Section 3

The Single European Act and the internal market programme

7. In January 1985 the Commission proposed realizing the objective of a market without internal frontiers by the end of 1992. The detailed measures for the removal of physical, technical and fiscal barriers were set out in a White Paper, which specified the precise programme, timetable and methods for creating a unified economic area in which persons, goods, services and capital would be able to move freely. This objective was embodied in December 1985 in the *Single European Act*.

8. The Single European Act marked the first significant revision of the Treaty of Rome. It introduced *four important changes* in the Community's strategy for advancing the integration process. Firstly, it greatly simplified the requirements of harmonizing national law by limiting harmonization to the essential standards and by systematic adoption of mutual recognition of national norms and regulations.

Secondly, it established a faster and more efficient decision-making process by extending the scope of qualified majority voting. Thirdly, it gave the European Parliament a greater role in the legislative process. Fourthly, it reaffirmed the need to strengthen the Community's economic and social cohesion, to enhance the Community's monetary capacity with a view to economic and monetary union, to reinforce the Community's scientific and technological base, to harmonize working conditions with respect to health and safety standards, to promote the dialogue between management and labour and to initiate action to protect the environment.

9. Over the last three years considerable progress has been made in implementing the internal market programme. In particular, it has been decided that eight member countries will have fully liberalized capital movements by 1 July 1990 and that the other member countries will follow suit after a period of transition.

In December 1988 the European Council, meeting in Rhodes, noted that 'at the halfway stage towards the deadline of December 1992, half of the legislative programme necessary for the establishment of the large market is already nearly complete' and underlined 'the *irreversible nature* of the movement towards a Europe without internal frontiers'. There is, indeed, widespread evidence that the objective of a single market enjoys the broad support of consumers and producers and that their economic decisions are increasingly influenced by the prospects of 1992. The anticipation of a market without internal frontiers has generated a new dynamism and has contributed to the recent acceleration of economic growth in the Community.

Section 4

Problems and perspectives

10. The completion of the single market will link national economies much more closely together and significantly *increase the degree of economic integration* within the Community. It will also entail profound structural changes in the economies of the member countries. These changes offer considerable opportunities for economic advancement, but many of the potential gains can only materialize if economic policy — at both national and Community levels — responds adequately to the structural changes.

By greatly strengthening economic interdependence between member countries, the single market will reduce the room for independent policy manoeuvre and amplify the cross-border effects of developments originating in each member country. It will, therefore, necessitate a more effective coordination of policy between separate national authorities. Furthermore, Community policies in support of a broadly balanced development are an indispensable complement to a single market. Indeed, the need to back up the removal of market barriers with a strengthening of common regional and structural policies was clearly recognized in the Brussels package of measures agreed in February 1988.

11. Although substantial progress has been made, the process of integration has been uneven. *Greater convergence of economic performance is needed.* Despite a marked downward trend in the average rate of price and wage inflation, considerable national differences remain. There are also still notable divergences in budgetary positions and external imbalances have become markedly greater in the recent past. The existence of these disequilibria indicates that there are areas where economic performances will have to be made more convergent.

12. With full freedom of capital movements and integrated financial markets incompatible national policies would quickly translate into exchange rate tensions and put an increasing and undue burden on monetary policy. The integration process thus requires *more intensive and effective policy coordination*, even within the framework of the present exchange rate arrangements, not only in the monetary field but also in areas of national economic management affecting aggregate demand, prices and costs of production.

A tighter coordination of economic policy-making is required. In the monetary field, the problems of the EMS referred to above continue to exist. In the economic field, policy coordination remains insufficient. Especially in the area of fiscal policy, the 1974 Decision on economic convergence has not succeeded in establishing an effective foundation for policy coordination. The pressure for mutually consistent macro-economic policies has stemmed from the growing reluctance to change exchange rate parities. Such pressure has hitherto been lessened to some extent by the existence of capital controls in some countries and by the segmentation of markets through various types of non-tariff barriers, but as capital movements are liberalized and as the internal market programme is implemented, each country will be less and less shielded from developments elsewhere in the Community. The attainment of national economic objectives will become more dependent on a cooperative approach to policy-making.

13. Decision-making authorities are subject to many pressures and institutional constraints and even best efforts to take into account the international repercussions of their policies are likely to fail at certain times. While *voluntary cooperation* should be relied upon as much as possible to arrive at increasingly consistent national policies, thus taking account of divergent constitutional situations in member countries, there is also likely to be a need for more binding procedures.

14. The success of the internal market programme hinges to a decisive extent on a much closer coordination of national economic policies, as well as on more effective Community policies. This implies that in essence a number of the steps towards economic and monetary union will already have to be taken in the course of establishing a single market in Europe.

Although in many respects a natural consequence of the commitment to create a market without internal frontiers, the move towards economic and monetary union represents a quantum jump which could secure a significant increase in economic welfare in the Community. Indeed, *economic and monetary union implies far more than the single market programme* and, as is discussed in the following two chapters of this Report, will require further major steps in all areas of economic policy-making. A particular role would have to be assigned to common policies aimed at developing a more balanced economic structure throughout the Community. This would help to prevent the emergence or aggravation of regional and sectoral imbalances which could threaten the viability of an economic and monetary union. This is especially important because the adoption of permanently fixed exchange rates would eliminate an important indicator of policy inconsistencies among Community countries and remove the exchange rate as an instrument of adjustment from the member countries' set of economic tools. Economic imbalances among member countries would have to be corrected by policies affecting the structure of their economies and costs of production if major regional disparities in output and employment were to be avoided.

15. At its meeting on 27 and 28 June 1988 the European Council confirmed the objective of economic and monetary union for the Community. In accordance with its mandate, the Committee has focused its attention on the task of studying and proposing concrete stages leading towards the *progressive realization of economic and monetary union.* In investigating how to achieve economic and monetary union the Committee has examined the conditions under which such a union could be viable and successful. The Committee feels that concrete proposals towards attaining this objective can only be made if there is a clear understanding of the implications and requirements of economic and monetary union and if due account is taken of past experience with and developments in economic and monetary integration in the Community. Hence, Chapter II of this Report examines the principal features and implications of an economic and monetary union. Chapter III then presents a pragmatic step-by-step approach which could lead in three stages to the final objective. The question of when these stages should be implemented is a matter for political decision.

Chapter II

The final stage of economic and monetary union

Section 1

General considerations

16. *Economic and monetary union* in Europe would imply complete freedom of movement for persons, goods, services and capital, as well as irrevocably fixed exchange rates between national currencies and, finally, a single currency. This, in turn, would imply a common monetary policy and require a high degree of compatibility of economic policies and consistency in a number of other policy areas, particularly in the fiscal field. These policies should be geared to price stability, balanced growth, converging standards of living, high employment and external equilibrium. Economic and monetary union would represent the final result of the process of progressive economic integration in Europe.

17. Even after attaining economic and monetary union, the Community would continue to consist of individual nations with differing economic, social, cultural and political characteristics. The existence and preservation of this *plurality* would require a degree of autonomy in economic decision-making to remain with individual member countries and a balance to be struck between national and Community competences. For this reason it would not be possible simply to follow the example of existing federal States; it would be necessary to develop an innovative and unique approach.

18. The Treaty of Rome, as amended by the Single European Act, provides the legal foundation for many of the necessary steps towards economic integration, but does not suffice for the creation of an economic and monetary union. The realization of this objective would call for new arrangements which could only be established on the basis of *a Treaty change* and consequent changes in national legislations. For this reason the union would have to be embodied in a Treaty which clearly laid down the basic functional and institutional arrangements, as well as provisions governing their step-by-step implementation.

19. Taking into account what is already provided for in the EC Treaties, the need for a *transfer of decision-making power* from Member States to the Community as a whole would arise primarily in the fields of monetary policy and macroeconomic management. A monetary union would require a single monetary policy and responsibility for the formulation of this policy would consequently have to be vested in one decision-making body. In the economic field a wide range of decisions would remain the preserve of national and regional authorities. However, given their potential impact on the overall domestic and external economic situation of the Community and their implications for the conduct of a common monetary policy, such decisions would have to be placed within an agreed macroeconomic framework and be subject to binding procedures and rules. This would permit the determination of an overall policy stance for the Community as a whole, avoid unsustainable differences between individual member countries in public-sector borrowing requirements and place binding constraints on the size and the financing of budget deficits.

20. An essential element in defining the appropriate balance of power within the Community would be adherence to the *'principle of subsidiarity'*, according to which the functions of higher levels of government should be as limited as possible and should be subsidiary to those of lower levels. Thus, the attribution of competences to the Community would have to be confined specifically to those areas in which collective decision-making was necessary. All policy functions which could be carried out at national (and regional and local) levels without adverse repercussions on the cohesion and functioning of the economic and monetary union would remain within the competence of the member countries.

21. Economic union and monetary union form *two integral parts of a single whole* and would therefore have to be implemented in parallel. It is only for reasons of expositional clarity that the following sections look separately at an economic and a monetary union. The description begins with monetary union, chiefly because the principal features of an economic union depend significantly on the agreed monetary arrangements and constraints. But the Committee is fully aware that the process of achieving monetary union is only conceivable if a high degree of economic convergence is attained.

Section 2

The principal features of monetary union

22. A *monetary union* constitutes a currency area in which policies are managed jointly with a view to attaining common macroeconomic objectives. As already stated in the 1970 Werner Report, there are three necessary conditions for a monetary union:

— the assurance of total and irreversible convertibility of currencies;

THE PRINCIPAL FEATURES OF MONETARY UNION

— the complete liberalization of capital transactions and full integration of banking and other financial markets; and

— the elimination of margins of fluctuation and the irrevocable locking of exchange rate parities.

The first two of these requirements have already been met, or will be with the completion of the internal market programme. The single most important condition for a monetary union would, however, be fulfilled only when the decisive step was taken to lock exchange rates irrevocably.

As a result of this step, national currencies would become increasingly close substitutes and their interest rates would tend to converge. The pace with which these developments took place would depend critically on the extent to which firms, households, labour unions and other economic agents were convinced that the decision to lock exchange rates would not be reversed. Both coherent monetary management and convincing evidence of an effective coordination of non-monetary policies would be crucial.

23. The three abovementioned requirements define a single currency area, but their fulfilment would not necessarily mark the end of the process of monetary unification in the Community. The adoption of *a single currency,* while not strictly necessary for the creation of a monetary union, might be seen — for economic as well as psychological and political reasons — as a natural and desirable further development of the monetary union. A single currency would clearly demonstrate the irreversibility of the move to monetary union, considerably facilitate the monetary management of the Community and avoid the transactions costs of converting currencies. A single currency, provided that its stability is ensured, would also have a much greater weight relative to other major currencies than any individual Community currency. The replacement of national currencies by a single currency should therefore take place as soon as possible after the locking of parities.

24. The establishment of a monetary union would have far-reaching implications for the formulation and execution of monetary policy in the Community. Once permanently fixed exchange rates had been adopted, there would be a *need for a common monetary policy,* which would be carried out through new operating procedures. The coordination of as many national monetary policies as there were currencies participating in the union would not be sufficient. The responsibility for the single monetary policy would have to be vested in a new institution, in which centralized and collective decisions would be taken on the supply of money and credit as well as on other instruments of monetary policy, including interest rates.

This shift from national monetary policies to a single monetary policy is an inescapable consequence of monetary union and constitutes one of the principal institutional changes. Although a progressively intensified coordination of national monetary policies would in many respects have prepared the way for the move to a single

19

monetary policy, the implications of such a move would be far-reaching. The permanent fixing of exchange rates would deprive individual countries of an important instrument for the correction of economic imbalances and for independent action in the pursuit of national objectives, especially price stability.

Well before the decision to fix exchange rates permanently, the full liberalization of capital movements and financial market integration would have created a situation in which the coordination of monetary policy would have to be strengthened progressively. Once every banking institution in the Community is free to accept deposits from, and to grant loans to, any customer in the Community and in any of the national currencies, the large degree of territorial coincidence between a national central bank's area of jurisdiction, the area in which its currency is used and the area in which 'its' banking system operates will be lost. In these circumstances the effectiveness of national monetary policies will become increasingly dependent on cooperation among central banks. Indeed, the growing coordination of monetary policies will make a positive contribution to financial market integration and will help central banks gain the experience that would be necessary to move to a single monetary policy.

Section 3

The principal features of economic union

25. *Economic union* — in conjunction with a monetary union — combines the characteristics of an unrestricted common market with a set of rules which are indispensable to its proper working. In this sense economic union can be described in terms of four basic elements:

— the single market within which persons, goods, services and capital can move freely;

— competition policy and other measures aimed at strengthening market mechanisms;

— common policies aimed at structural change and regional development; and

— macroeconomic policy coordination, including binding rules for budgetary policies.

In defining specific rules and arrangements governing an economic union, the Community should be guided by two considerations.

Firstly, the economic union should be based on the same market-oriented economic principles that underlie the economic order of its member countries. Differences in policy choices may exist between member countries or, within the same country, in different periods. However, beyond such differences, a distinctive common feature of economic systems in Europe is the combination of a large degree of freedom for market behaviour and private economic initiative with public intervention in the provision of certain social services and public goods.

Secondly, an appropriate balance between the economic and monetary components would have to be ensured for the union to be viable. This would be essential because of the close interactions between economic and monetary developments and policies. A coherent set of economic policies at the Community and national levels would be necessary to maintain permanently fixed exchange rates between Community currencies and, conversely, a common monetary policy, in support of a single currency area, would be necessary for the Community to develop into an economic union.

26. The creation of a single currency area would add to the potential benefits of an enlarged economic area because it would remove intra-Community exchange rate uncertainties and reduce transactions costs, eliminate exchange rate variability and reduce the susceptibility of the Community to external shocks.

At the same time, however, exchange rate adjustments would no longer be available as an instrument to correct economic imbalances within the Community. Such *imbalances might arise* because the process of adjustment and restructuring set in motion by the removal of physical, technical and fiscal barriers is unlikely to have an even impact on different regions or always produce satisfactory results within reasonable periods of time. Imbalances might also emanate from labour and other cost developments, external shocks with differing repercussions on individual economies, or divergent economic policies pursued at national level.

With parities irrevocably fixed, foreign exchange markets would cease to be a source of pressure for national policy corrections when national economic disequilibria developed and persisted. Moreover, the statistical measurement and the interpretation of economic imbalances might become more difficult because in a fully integrated market balance-of-payments figures, which are currently a highly visible and sensitive indicator of economic disequilibria, would no longer play such a significant role as a guidepost for policy-making. None the less, such imbalances, if left uncorrected, would manifest themselves as regional disequilibria. Measures designed to strengthen the mobility of factors of production and the flexibility of prices would help to deal with such imbalances.

27. In order to create an economic and monetary union the single market would have to be complemented with *action in three interrelated areas*: competition policy and other measures aimed at strengthening market mechanisms; common policies to enhance the process of resource allocation in those economic sectors and geographical areas where the working of market forces needed to be reinforced or complemented; macroeconomic coordination, including binding rules in the budgetary field; and other arrangements both to limit the scope for divergences between member countries and to design an overall economic policy framework for the Community as a whole.

THE FINAL STAGE OF ECONOMIC AND MONETARY UNION

28. *Competition policy* — conducted at the Community level — would have to operate in such a way that access to markets would not be impeded and market functioning not be distorted by the behaviour of private or public economic agents. Such policies would not only have to address conventional forms of restrictive practices and the abuse of dominant market positions, but would also have to deal with new aspects of antitrust laws, especially in the field of merger and takeover activities. The use of government subsidies to assist particular industries should be strictly circumscribed because they distort competition and cause an inefficient use and allocation of scarce economic resources.

29. *Community policies in the regional and structural field* would be necessary in order to promote an optimum allocation of resources and to spread welfare gains throughout the Community. If sufficient consideration were not given to regional imbalances, the economic union would be faced with grave economic and political risks. For this reason particular attention would have to be paid to an effective Community policy aimed at narrowing regional and structural disparities and promoting a balanced development throughout the Community. In this context the regional dimension of other Community policies would have to be taken into account.

Economic and monetary integration may have beneficial effects on the less developed regions of the Community. For example, regions with lower wage levels would have an opportunity to attract modern and rapidly growing service and manufacturing industries for which the choice of location would not necessarily be determined by transport costs, labour skills and market proximity. Historical experience suggests, however, that in the absence of countervailing policies, the overall impact on peripheral regions could be negative. Transport costs and economies of scale would tend to favour a shift in economic activity away from less developed regions, especially if they were at the periphery of the Community, to the highly developed areas at its centre. The economic and monetary union would have to encourage and guide structural adjustment which would help poorer regions to catch up with the wealthier ones.

A step in this direction was taken in February 1988 when the European Council decided to strengthen and reorganize the Community's regional and structural policies in several respects: the size of structural funds will be doubled over the period up to 1993, emphasis will be shifted from project to programme financing, and a new form of partnership will be established between the Community and the recipient regions. Depending upon the speed of progress, such policies might have to be strengthened further after 1993 in the process of creating economic and monetary union.

At the same time, excessive reliance on financial assistance through regional and structural policies could cause tensions. The principal objective of regional policies should not be to subsidize incomes and simply offset inequalities in standards of living, but to help to equalize production conditions through investment programmes in such areas as physical infrastructure, communications, transportation and education so that large-scale movements of labour do not become the major adjustment factor. The success of these policies will hinge not only on the size of the available financial resources, but to a decisive extent also on their efficient use and on the private and social return on the investment programmes.

Apart from regional policies, the Treaty of Rome, as amended by the Single European Act, has established the basis for Community policies in areas such as infrastructure, research and technological development, and the environment. Such policies would not only enhance market efficiency and offset market imperfections, but could also contribute to regional development. While respecting the principle of subsidiarity, such policies would have to be developed further in the process towards economic and monetary union.

Wage flexibility and labour mobility are necessary to eliminate differences in competitiveness in different regions and countries of the Community. Otherwise there could be relatively large declines in output and employment in areas with lower productivity. In order to reduce adjustment burdens temporarily, it might be necessary in certain circumstances to provide financing flows through official channels. Such financial support would be additional to what might come from spontaneous capital flows or external borrowing and should be granted on terms and conditions that would prompt the recipient to intensify its adjustment efforts.

30. *Macroeconomic policy* is the third area in which action would be necessary for a viable economic and monetary union. This would require an appropriate definition of the role of the Community in promoting price stability and economic growth through the coordination of economic policies.

Many developments in macroeconomic conditions would continue to be determined by factors and decisions operating at the national or local level. This would include not only wage negotiations and other economic decisions in the fields of production, savings and investment, but also the action of public authorities in the economic and social spheres. Apart from the system of binding rules governing the size and the financing of national budget deficits, decisions on the main components of public policy in such areas as internal and external security, justice, social security, education, and hence on the level and composition of government spending, as well as many revenue measures, would remain the preserve of Member States even at the final stage of economic and monetary union.

However, an economic and monetary union could only operate on the basis of mutually consistent and sound behaviour by governments and other economic agents in all member countries. In particular, uncoordinated and divergent national budgetary policies would undermine monetary stability and generate imbalances in the real and financial sectors of the Community. Moreover, the fact that the centrally managed Community budget is likely to remain a very small part of total public-sector spending and that much of this budget will not be available for cyclical adjustments will mean that the task of setting a Community-wide fiscal policy stance will have to be performed through the coordination of national budgetary policies. Without such coordination it would be impossible for the Community as a whole to establish a fiscal/monetary policy mix appropriate for the preservation of internal balance, or for the Community to play its part in the international adjustment process. Monetary policy alone cannot be expected to perform these functions. Moreover, strong divergences in wage levels and developments, not justified by different trends in productivity, would produce economic tensions and pressures for monetary expansion.

To some extent market forces can exert a disciplinary influence. Financial markets, consumers and investors would respond to differences in macroeconomic developments in individual countries and regions, assess their budgetary and financial positions, penalize deviations from commonly agreed budgetary guidelines or wage settlements, and thus exert pressure for sounder policies. However, experience suggests that market perceptions do not necessarily provide strong and compelling signals and that access to a large capital market may for some time even facilitate the financing of economic imbalances. Rather than leading to a gradual adaptation of borrowing costs, market views about the creditworthiness of official borrowers tend to change abruptly and result in the closure of access to market financing. The constraints imposed by market forces might either be too slow and weak or too sudden and disruptive. Hence countries would have to accept that sharing a common market and a single currency area imposed policy constraints.

In the general macroeconomic field, a common overall assessment of the short-term and medium-term economic developments in the Community would need to be agreed periodically and would constitute the framework for a better coordination of national economic policies. The Community would need to be in a position to monitor its overall economic situation, to assess the consistency of developments in individual countries with regard to common objectives and to formulate guidelines for policy.

As regards wage formation and industrial relations, the autonomous negotiating process would need to be preserved, but efforts would have to be made to convince European management and labour of the advantages of gearing wage policies largely to improvements in productivity. Governments, for their part, would refrain from direct intervention in the wage and price formation process.

In the budgetary field, binding rules are required that would: firstly, impose effective upper limits on budget deficits of individual member countries of the Community, although in setting these limits the situation of each member country might have to be taken into consideration; secondly, exclude access to direct central bank credit and other forms of monetary financing while, however, permitting open market operations in government securities; thirdly, limit recourse to external borrowing in non-Community currencies. Moreover, the arrangements in the budgetary field should enable the Community to conduct a coherent mix of fiscal and monetary policies.

Section 4

Institutional arrangements

31. Management of the economic and monetary union would call for *an institutional framework* which would allow policy to be decided and executed at the Community level in those economic areas that were of direct relevance for the functioning of the union. This framework would have to promote efficient economic management, properly embedded in the democratic process. Economic and monetary union would require the creation of a new monetary institution, placed in the constellation of Community institutions (European Parliament, European Council, Council of Ministers, Commission and Court of Justice). The formulation and implementation of common policies in non-monetary fields and the coordination of policies remaining within the competence of national authorities would not necessarily require a new institution; but a revision and, possibly, some restructuring of the existing Community bodies, including an appropriate delegation of authority, could be necessary.

32. A new monetary institution would be needed because a single monetary policy cannot result from independent decisions and actions by different central banks. Moreover, day-to-day monetary policy operations cannot respond quickly to changing market conditions unless they are decided centrally. Considering the political structure of the Community and the advantages of making existing central banks part of a new system, the domestic and international monetary policy-making of the Community should be organized in a federal form, in what might be called a *European System of Central Banks* (ESCB). This new System would have to be given the full status of an autonomous Community institution. It would operate in accordance with the provisions of the Treaty, and could consist of a central institution (with its own balance sheet) and the national central banks. At the final stage the ESCB — acting through its Council — would be responsible for formulating and implementing monetary policy as well as managing the Community's exchange rate policy *vis-à-vis* third currencies. The national central banks would be entrusted with the implementation of policies in conformity with guidelines established by the Council of the ESCB and in accordance with instructions from the central institution.

The European System of Central Banks would be based on the following principles:

Mandate and functions

— The System would be committed to the objective of price stability;
— subject to the foregoing, the System should support the general economic policy set at the Community level by the competent bodies;

- the System would be responsible for the formulation and implementation of monetary policy, exchange rate and reserve management, and the maintenance of a properly functioning payment system;
- the System would participate in the coordination of banking supervision policies of the supervisory authorities.

Policy instruments

- The policy instruments available to the System, together with a procedure for amending them, would be specified in its Statutes; the instruments would enable the System to conduct central banking operations in financial and foreign exchange markets as well as to exercise regulatory powers;
- while complying with the provision not to lend to public-sector authorities, the System could buy and sell government securities on the market as a means of conducting monetary policy.

Structure and organization

- A federative structure, since this would correspond best to the political diversity of the Community;
- establishment of an ESCB Council (composed of the Governors of the central banks and the members of the Board, the latter to be appointed by the European Council), which would be responsible for the formulation of and decisions on the thrust of monetary policy; modalities of voting procedures would have to be provided for in the Treaty;
- establishment of a Board (with supporting staff), which would monitor monetary developments and oversee the implementation of the common monetary policy;
- national central banks, which would execute operations in accordance with the decisions taken by the ESCB Council.

Status

- Independence: the ESCB Council should be independent of instructions from national governments and Community authorities; to that effect the members of the ESCB Council, both Governors and the Board members, should have appropriate security of tenure;
- accountability: reporting would be in the form of submission of an annual report by the ESCB to the European Parliament and the European Council; moreover, the Chairman of the ESCB could be invited to report to these institutions. Supervision of the administration of the System would be carried out indepen-

dently of the Community bodies, for example by a supervisory council or a committee of independent auditors.

33. In the *economic field,* in contrast to the monetary field, an institutional framework for performing policy tasks was already established under the Treaty of Rome, with different and complementary functions conferred on the European Parliament, the Council of Ministers, the Monetary Committee, the Commission and the Court of Justice. The new Treaty would therefore not have to determine the mandate, status and structure of a new institution but would have to provide for additional or changed roles for the existing bodies in the light of the policy functions they would have to fulfil in an economic and monetary union. It would have to specifically define these changes and determine the areas in which decision-making authority would have to be transferred from the national to the Community level.

General criteria

In order to ensure the flexible and effective conduct of policies in those economic areas in which the Community would be involved, several basic requirements would have to be fulfilled:

— where policies were decided and enacted at the Community level, there would have to be a clear distribution of responsibilities among the existing Community institutions, a distinction being made as to whether decisions related to the setting of broad policy directions or to day-to-day operations. By analogy with the structure of the European System of Central Banks, where the ESCB Council would determine the broad lines of monetary policy and the Board would be responsible for its day-to-day execution, a similar division of responsibilities could be envisaged in the economic field. The Council of Ministers would determine the broad lines of economic policy, while the implementation would be left to the national governments and the Commission in their respective areas of competence;

— in the event of non-compliance by Member States, the Commission, or another appropriately delegated authority as envisaged in paragraph 31, would be responsible for taking effective action to ensure compliance; the nature of such action would have to be explored.

Single market and competition policy

In these two areas, the necessary procedures and arrangements have already been established by the Treaty of Rome and the Single European Act, which confer the requisite legislative, executive and judicial authority on the Community. The completion of the internal market will result in a marked easing of the overall burden of regulation for economic agents, but for the Community institutions it will mean a substantial addition to their executive and policing functions.

Community policies in the regional and structural field

The foundations for a more effective Community role in regional and structural development have recently been established, with both a doubling of the resources of structural funds and a reorganization of policies as described earlier in this Report. These mechanisms would perhaps have to be further extended and made more effective as part of the process leading to economic and monetary union.

Macroeconomic policy

The broad *objective* of economic policy coordination would be to promote growth, employment and external balance in an environment of price stability and economic cohesion. For this purpose coordination would involve defining a medium-term framework for budgetary policy within the economic and monetary union; managing common policies with a view to structural and regional development; formulating in cooperation with the ESCB Council the Community's exchange rate policy and participating in policy coordination at the international level.

New *procedures* required for this purpose would have to strike a balance between reliance on binding rules, where necessary, to ensure effective implementation and discretionary coordination adapted to particular situations.

In particular it would seem necessary to develop both binding rules and procedures for *budgetary policy*, involving respectively:

— effective upper limits on budget deficits of individual member countries; exclusion of access to direct central bank credit and other forms of monetary financing; limits on borrowing in non-Community currencies;

— the definition of the overall stance of fiscal policy over the medium term, including the size and financing of the aggregate budgetary balance, comprising both the national and the Community positions.

34. The new Treaty laying down the objectives, features, requirements, procedures and organs of the economic and monetary union would add to the existing Community institutions (European Parliament, European Council, Council of Ministers, Commission and Court of Justice) a new institution of comparable status, the European System of Central Banks. With due respect for the independent status of the ESCB, as defined elsewhere in this Report, appropriate consultation procedures would have to be set up to allow for effective *coordination between budgetary and monetary policy*. This might involve attendance by the President of the Council and the President of the Commission at meetings of the ESCB Council, without power

to vote or to block decisions taken in accordance with the rules laid down by the ESCB Council. Equally, the Chairman of the ESCB Council might attend meetings of the Council of Ministers, especially on matters of relevance to the conduct of monetary policy. Consideration would also have to be given to the role of the European Parliament, especially in relation to the new policy functions exercised by various Community bodies.

Section 5

Economic and monetary union in the context of the world economy

35. The establishment of an economic and monetary union would give *the Community a greater say in international negotiations* and enhance its capacity to influence economic relations between industrial and developing countries.

36. The responsibility for *external trade policy* has been assigned to the Community in the Treaty of Rome, and the Commission, acting as the Community's spokesman, represents all the member countries in multilateral trade negotiations. This role will be strengthened with the completion of the single market, which has the potential to stimulate multilateral trade and economic growth at the global level. However, this potential can only be exploited to the full in an open trading system, which guarantees foreign suppliers free access to the Community market and, conversely, guarantees exporters from the Community free access to foreign markets. The removal of internal trade barriers within the Community should constitute a step towards a more liberal trading system on a worldwide scale.

37. The creation of an economic and monetary union would increase the role of the Community in the process of *international policy concertation*. In the monetary field this would involve short-term cooperation between central banks in interest rate management and exchange market interventions as well as the search for solutions to issues relating to the international monetary system. In the economic field, the formulation of a policy mix would allow the Community to contribute more effectively to world economic management.

38. The *institutional arrangements* which would enable the Community to fulfil the new responsibilities implied by its increased weight in the world economy are partly in place or would be implemented in the process of creating an economic and monetary union. In the area of external trade policies and, to some extent, in the field of cooperation with developing countries, the responsibilities have already been attributed to the Community. With the establishment of the European System of Central Banks the Community would also have created an institution through which it could participate in all aspects of international monetary management. As far as macroeconomic policy coordination at the international level is concerned, the

Community as such is currently represented only at the summit meetings of the major industrial countries. In order to make full use of its position in the world economy and to exert influence on the functioning of the international economic system, the Community would have to be able to speak with one voice. This emphasizes the need for an effective mechanism for macroeconomic policy coordination within the economic and monetary union.

Chapter III

Steps towards economic and monetary union

39. After defining the main features of an economic and monetary union, the Committee has undertaken the 'task of studying and proposing concrete stages leading towards this union'. The Committee agreed that the *creation of an economic and monetary union must be viewed as a single process*. Although this process is set out in stages which guide the progressive movement to the final objective, the decision to enter upon the first stage should be a decision to embark on the entire process.

A clear political commitment to the final stage, as described in Chapter II of this Report, would lend credibility to the intention that the measures which constitute stage one should represent not just a useful end in themselves but a firm first step on the road towards economic and monetary union. It would be a strong expression of such a commitment if all members of the Community became full members of the EMS in the course of stage one and undertook the obligation to formulate a convergent economic policy within the existing institutions.

Given that background, commitment by the political authorities to enter into negotiations on a new Treaty would ensure the continuity of the process. Preparatory work for these negotiations would start immediately. At the end of this Report suggestions are made regarding the procedures to be followed for the further development of economic and monetary union.

Section 1

Principles governing a step-by-step approach

40. In *designing a step-by-step approach* along the path to economic and monetary union the general principle of subsidiarity, referred to earlier in this Report, as well as a number of further considerations, would have to be taken into account.

41. *Discrete but evolutionary steps*. The process of implementing economic and monetary union would have to be divided into a limited number of clearly defined stages. Each stage would have to represent a significant change with respect to the preceding one. New arrangements coming into force at the beginning of each

stage would gradually develop their effects and bring about a change in economic circumstances so as to pave the way for the next stage. This evolutionary development would apply to both functional and institutional arrangements.

42. *Parallelism.* As has been argued in Chapter II, monetary union without a sufficient degree of convergence of economic policies is unlikely to be durable and could be damaging to the Community. Parallel advancement in economic and monetary integration would be indispensable in order to avoid imbalances which could cause economic strains and loss of political support for developing the Community further into an economic and monetary union. Perfect parallelism at each and every point of time would be impossible and could even be counter-productive. Already in the past the advancement of the Community in certain areas has taken place with temporary standstill in others, so that parallelism has been only partial. Some temporary deviations from parallelism are part of the dynamic process of the Community. But bearing in mind the need to achieve a substantial degree of economic union if monetary union is to be successful, and given the degree of monetary coordination already achieved, it is clear that material progress on the economic policy front would be necessary for further progress on the monetary policy front. Parallelism would have to be maintained in the medium term and also before proceeding from one stage to the next.

43. *Calendar.* The conditions for moving from stage to stage cannot be defined precisely in advance; nor is it possible to foresee today when these conditions will be realized. The setting of explicit deadlines is therefore not advisable. This observation applies to the passage from stage one to stage two and, most importantly, to the move to irrevocably fixed exchange rates. The timing of both these moves would involve an appraisal by the Council, and from stage two to stage three also by the European System of Central Banks in the light of the experience gained in the preceding stage. However, there should be a clear indication of the timing of the first stage, which should start no later than 1 July 1990 when the Directive for the full liberalization of capital movements comes into force.

44. *Participation.* There is one Community, but not all the members have participated fully in all its aspects from the outset. A consensus on the final objectives of the Community, as well as participation in the same set of institutions, should be maintained, while allowing for a degree of flexibility concerning the date and conditions on which some member countries would join certain arrangements. Pending the full participation of all member countries — which is of prime importance — influence on the management of each set of arrangements would have to be related to the degree of participation by Member States. However, this management would have to keep in mind the need to facilitate the integration of the other members.

Section 2

The ECU

45. The Committee investigated *various aspects of the role* that the ECU might play in the process of economic and monetary integration in Europe.

46. Firstly, the Committee examined the role of the ECU in connection with an eventual move to a single currency. Although a monetary union does not necessarily require a single currency, it would be a desirable feature of a monetary union. The Committee was of the opinion that the ECU has the potential to be developed into such *a common currency*. This would imply that the ECU would be transformed from a basket of currencies into a genuine currency. The irrevocable fixing of exchange rates would imply that there would be no discontinuity between the ECU and the single currency of the union and that ECU obligations would be payable at face value in ECUs if the transition to the single currency had been made by the time the contract matured.

47. Secondly, the Committee considered the possibility of adopting a *parallel currency strategy* as a means of accelerating the pace of the monetary union process. Under this approach the definition of the ECU as a basket of currencies would be abandoned at an early stage and the new fully-fledged currency, called the ECU, would be created autonomously and issued in addition to the existing Community currencies, competing with them. The proponents of this strategy expect that the gradual crowding-out of national currencies by the ECU would make it possible to circumvent the institutional and economic difficulties of establishing a monetary union. The Committee felt that this strategy was not to be recommended for two main reasons. Firstly, an additional source of money creation without a precise linkage to economic activity could jeopardize price stability. Secondly, the addition of a new currency, with its own independent monetary implications, would further complicate the already difficult endeavour of coordinating different national monetary policies.

48. Thirdly, the Committee examined the possibility of using the official ECU as an instrument *in the conduct of a common monetary policy*. The main features of possible schemes are described in the Collection of papers submitted to the Committee, which represent personal contributions.

49. Fourthly, the Committee agreed that there should be no discrimination against the *private use of the ECU* and that existing administrative obstacles should be removed.

Section 3

The principal steps in stage one

50. Stage one represents the *initiation of the process* of creating an economic and monetary union. It would aim at a greater convergence of economic performance through the strengthening of economic and monetary policy coordination within the existing institutional framework. In the institutional field, by the time of the transition to stage two, it would be necessary to have prepared and ratified the Treaty change.

51. *In the economic field* the steps would centre on the completion of the internal market and the reduction of existing disparities through programmes of budgetary consolidation in those countries concerned and more effective structural and regional policies. In particular, there would be action in three directions.

Firstly, there would be a complete removal of physical, technical and fiscal barriers within the Community, in line with the internal market programme. The completion of the internal market would be accompanied by a strengthening of Community competition policy.

Secondly, the reform of the structural Funds and doubling of their resources would be fully implemented in order to enhance the ability of Community policies to promote regional development and to correct economic imbalances.

Thirdly, the 1974 Council Decision on economic convergence would be replaced by a new procedure that would strengthen economic and fiscal policy coordination and would, in addition, provide a comprehensive framework for an assessment of the consequences and consistency of the overall policies of Member States. On the basis of this assessment, recommendations would be made aimed at achieving a more effective coordination of economic policies, taking due account of the views of the Committee of Central Bank Governors. The task of economic policy coordination should be the primary responsibility of the Council of Economic and Finance Ministers (Ecofin). Consistency between monetary and economic policies would be facilitated by the participation of the Chairman of the Committee of Central Bank Governors in appropriate Council meetings. In particular, the revised 1974 Decision on convergence would:

— establish a process of multilateral surveillance of economic developments and policies based on agreed indicators. Where performances were judged inadequate or detrimental to commonly set objectives, policy consultations would take place at Community level and recommendations would be formulated with a view to promoting the necessary corrections in national policies;

— set up a new procedure for budgetary policy coordination, with precise quantitative guidelines and medium-term orientations;

— provide for concerted budgetary action by the member countries.

52. *In the monetary field* the focus would be on removing all obstacles to financial integration and on intensifying cooperation and the coordination of monetary policies. In this connection consideration should be given to extending the scope of central banks' autonomy. Realignments of exchange rates would still be possible, but an effort would be made by every country to make the functioning of other adjustment mechanisms more effective. Action would be taken along several lines.

Firstly, through the approval and enforcement of the necessary Community Directives, the objective of a single financial area in which all monetary and financial instruments circulate freely and banking, securities and insurance services are offered uniformly throughout the area would be fully implemented.

Secondly, it would be important to include all Community currencies in the EMS exchange rate mechanism. The same rules would apply to all the participants in the exchange rate mechanism.

Thirdly, all impediments to the private use of the ECU would be removed.

Fourthly, the 1964 Council Decision defining the mandate of the Committee of Central Bank Governors would be replaced by a new Decision. According to this Decision the Committee of Central Bank Governors should:

— formulate opinions on the overall orientation of monetary and exchange rate policy, as well as on measures taken in these fields by individual countries. In particular, the Committee would normally be consulted in advance of national decisions on the course of monetary policy, such as the setting of annual domestic monetary and credit targets;

— express opinions to individual governments and the Council of Ministers on policies that could affect the internal and external monetary situation in the Community, especially the functioning of the EMS. The outcome of the Committee's deliberations could be made public by the Chairman of the Committee;

— submit an annual report on its activities and on the monetary situation of the Community to the European Parliament and the European Council.

The Committee could express majority opinions, although at this stage they would not be binding. In order to make its policy coordination function more effective, the Committee would set up three sub-committees, with a greater research and advisory role than those existing hitherto, and provide them with a permanent research staff:

— a monetary policy committee would define common surveillance indicators, propose harmonized objectives and instruments and help to gradually bring about a change from *ex post* analysis to an *ex ante* approach to monetary policy cooperation;

— a foreign exchange policy committee would monitor and analyse exchange market developments and assist in the search for effective intervention strategies;

— an advisory committee would hold regular consultations on matters of common interest in the field of banking supervision policy.

53. A number of Committee members advocated the creation of a *European Reserve Fund (ERF)* that would foreshadow the future European System of Central Banks. The main objectives of the ERF would be:

— to serve as a training ground for implementing a better coordination of monetary analysis and decisions;

— to facilitate, from a Community point of view, the concerted management of exchange rates and possibly to intervene visibly (in third and participating currencies) on the foreign exchange market at the request of the participating central banks;

— to be the symbol of the political will of the European countries and thus reinforce the credibility of the process towards economic and monetary union.

The resources of the Fund would be provided by the pooling of a limited amount of reserves (for instance 10% at the start) by participating central banks. The Fund would, moreover, require a permanent structure and staff in order to carry out its tasks, namely:

— managing the pooled reserves;

— intervening on the exchange markets as decided by the members;

— analysing monetary trends, from a collective perspective, in order to enhance policy coordination.

All EC central banks would be eligible to join the Fund. However, membership would be subject to their participation in the exchange rate mechanism, the reason being that the EMS implies specific constraints on monetary policy and foreign exchange interventions, both of which require a common approach on the part of the central banks concerned.

The ERF would consist of:

— a Board of Directors, which would comprise, ex officio, the Governors of all the central banks participating in the ERF;

— an Executive Committee, whose members would be selected by the Committee of Governors on the basis of competence. This Executive Committee would be small in size, consisting of three or four members who would have direct responsibility for the different departments of the ERF;

— three committees, namely the Foreign Exchange Policy Committee, the Monetary Policy Committee and the Committee on Banking Supervision Policy;

— two departments: a Foreign Exchange and Reserve Management Department and a Monetary Policy Department.

54. Other members of the Committee felt that the creation of an ERF was not opportune at this stage. Their reservations stem from the following considerations:

— too much emphasis is placed on external considerations; common interventions by such a Fund cannot be a substitute for economic adjustment to correct imbalances within the Community;

— the proposal involves an institutional change which, in accordance with Article 102a of the amended Treaty of Rome, would fall under the procedure stipulated in Article 236 and require a new Treaty; the setting-up of a Fund under the same procedures as those applied in establishing the EMS is not considered possible;

— they consider that some functions of the Fund could be performed by the Committee of Governors if it were given wider powers; thus there is no need to set up a new institution immediately;

— what, in the view of these members, is essential is coordination of intervention policies rather than the technique of common interventions. Such coordination can provide the necessary training ground while avoiding the unnecessary complication of instituting an additional intervention window.

Section 4

The principal steps in stage two

55. The *second stage* could begin only when the new Treaty had come into force. In this stage the basic organs and structure of the economic and monetary union would be set up, involving both the revision of existing institutions and the establishment of new ones. The institutional framework would gradually take over operational functions, serve as the centre for monitoring and analysing macroeconomic developments and promote a process of common decision-making, with certain operational decisions taken by majority vote. Stage two must be seen as a period of transition to the final stage and would thus primarily constitute a training process leading to collective decision-making, while the ultimate responsibility for policy decisions would remain at this stage with national authorities. The precise operating procedures to be applied in stage two would be developed in the light of the prevailing economic conditions and the experience gained in the previous stage.

56. *In the economic field*, the European Parliament, the Council of Ministers, the Monetary Committee and the Commission would reinforce their action along three lines.

Firstly, in the area of the single market and competition policy the results achieved through the implementation of the single market programme would be reviewed and, wherever necessary, consolidated.

Secondly, the performance of structural and regional policies would be evaluated and, if necessary, be adapted in the light of experience. The resources for supporting the structural policies of the Member States might have to be enlarged. Community programmes for investment in research and infrastructure would be strengthened.

Thirdly, in the area of macroeconomic policy, the procedures set up in the first stage through the revision of the 1974 Decision on convergence would be further strengthened and extended on the basis of the new Treaty. Policy guidelines would be adopted by majority decision. On this basis the Community would:

— set a medium-term framework for key economic objectives aimed at achieving stable growth, with a follow-up procedure for monitoring performances and intervening when significant deviations occurred;

— set precise, although not yet binding, rules relating to the size of annual budget deficits and their financing; the Commission should be responsible for bringing any instance of non-compliance by Member States to the Council's attention and should propose action as necessary;

— assume a more active role as a single entity in the discussion of questions arising in the economic and exchange rate field, on the basis of its present representation (through the Member States or the Commission) in the various forums for international policy coordination.

57. *In the monetary field*, the most important feature of this stage would be that the European System of Central Banks would be set up and would absorb the previously existing institutional monetary arrangements (the EMCF, the Committee of Central Bank Governors, the sub-committees for monetary policy analysis, foreign exchange policy and banking supervision, and the permanent secretariat). The functions of the ESCB in the formulation and operation of a common monetary policy would gradually evolve as experience was gained. Some possible schemes for coordinating monetary policies in the course of this stage are discussed in the *Collection of papers submitted to the Committee*. Exchange rate realignments would not be excluded as an instrument of adjustment, but there would be an understanding that they would be made only in exceptional circumstances.

The key task for the European System of Central Banks during this stage would be to begin the transition from the coordination of independent national monetary policies by the Committee of Central Bank Governors in stage one to the formulation and implementation of a common monetary policy by the ESCB itself scheduled to take place in the final stage.

The fundamental difficulty inherent in this transition would lie in the organization of a gradual transfer of decision-making power from national authorities to a Community institution. At this juncture, the Committee does not consider it possible to propose a detailed blueprint for accomplishing this transition, as this would depend on the effectiveness of the policy coordination achieved during the first stage, on the provisions of the Treaty, and on decisions to be taken by the new institutions. Account would also have to be taken of the continued impact of financial innovation on monetary control techniques (which are at present undergoing radical changes in most industrial countries), of the degree of integration reached in European financial markets, of the constellation of financial and banking centres in Europe and of the development of the private, and in particular banking, use of the ECU.

The transition that characterizes this second stage would involve a certain number of actions. For instance, general monetary orientations would be set for the Community as a whole, with an understanding that national monetary policy would be executed in accordance with these global guidelines. Moreover, while the ultimate responsibility for monetary policy decisions would remain with national authorities, the operational framework necessary for deciding and implementing a common monetary policy would be created and experimented with. Also, a certain amount of exchange reserves would be pooled and would be used to conduct exchange market interventions in accordance with guidelines established by the ESCB Council. Finally, regulatory functions would be exercised by the ESCB in the monetary and banking field in order to achieve a minimum harmonization of provisions (such as reserve requirements or payment arrangements) necessary for the future conduct of a common monetary policy.

As circumstances permitted and in the light of progress made in the process of economic convergence, the margins of fluctuation within the exchange rate mechanism would be narrowed as a move towards the final stage of the monetary union, in which they would be reduced to zero.

Section 5

The principal steps in stage three

58. The *final stage* would commence with the move to irrevocably locked exchange rates and the attribution to Community institutions of the full monetary and economic competences described in Chapter II of this Report. In the course of the final stage the national currencies would eventually be replaced by a single Community currency.

59. *In the economic field,* the transition to this final stage would be marked by three developments.

Firstly, there might need to be a further strengthening of Community structural and regional policies. Instruments and resources would be adapted to the needs of the economic and monetary union.

Secondly, the rules and procedures of the Community in the macroeconomic and budgetary field would become binding. In particular, the Council of Ministers, in cooperation with the European Parliament, would have the authority to take directly enforceable decisions, i.e.:

— to impose constraints on national budgets to the extent to which this was necessary to prevent imbalances that might threaten monetary stability;
— to make discretionary changes in Community resources (through a procedure to be defined) to supplement structural transfers to Member States or to influence the overall policy stance in the Community;
— to apply to existing Community structural policies and to Community loans (as a substitute for the present medium-term financial assistance facility) terms and conditions that would prompt member countries to intensify their adjustment efforts.

Thirdly, the Community would assume its full role in the process of international policy cooperation, and a new form of representation in arrangements for international policy coordination and in international monetary negotiations would be adopted.

60. *In the monetary field*, the irrevocable locking of exchange rates would come into effect and the transition to a single monetary policy would be made, with the ESCB assuming all its responsibilities as foreseen in the Treaty and described in Chapter II of this Report. In particular:

— concurrently with the announcement of the irrevocable fixing of parities between the Community currencies, the responsibility for the formulation and implementation of monetary policy in the Community would be transferred to the ESCB, with its Council and Board exercising their statutory functions;
— decisions on exchange market interventions in third currencies would be made on the sole responsibility of the ESCB Council in accordance with Community exchange rate policy; the execution of interventions would be entrusted either to national central banks or to the European System of Central Banks;
— official reserves would be pooled and managed by the ESCB;
— preparations of a technical or regulatory nature would be made for the transition to a single Community currency.

The change-over to the single currency would take place during this stage.

Section 6

One or several Treaties

61. *Legal basis*. The Committee has examined the scope for progress in economic and monetary integration under the present legal provisions in force in each member country. This investigation has shown that under present national legislations no

member country is able to transfer decision-making power to a Community body, nor is it possible for many countries to participate in arrangements for a binding *ex ante* coordination of policies.

As has been pointed out in paragraph 18 of this Report, the Treaty of Rome, as amended by the Single European Act, is insufficient for the full realization of economic and monetary union. There is at present no transfer of responsibility for economic and monetary policy from Member States to the Community. The rules governing the EMS are based on agreements between the central banks concerned and are not an integral part of Community legislation. Without a new Treaty it would not be possible to take major additional steps towards economic and monetary union. The process of integration based on a step-by-step approach requires, however, a clear understanding of its content and final objective, its basic functional and institutional arrangements and the provisions governing its gradual implementation. A new political and legal basis would accordingly be needed. A new Treaty would establish not only the objective but also the stages by which it is to be achieved and the procedures and institutions required to move forward at each stage along the way. Political agreement would be required for each move to be implemented.

A new Treaty would also be required to ensure parallel progress in the economic and in the monetary fields. The appropriate institutional and procedural arrangements to that effect should also be set out in the Treaty.

62. The Committee has not investigated in detail the possible approaches by means of which the objective of economic and monetary union and its implementation would be embodied in the new Treaty. There would be basically two options. One procedure would be to conclude *a new Treaty for each stage*. The advantage of this procedure would be that it would explicitly reaffirm the political consensus at each stage and would allow for modification of the form the following stage should take in the light of experience with the current stage. At the same time, this approach might prove unwieldy and slow, it might not safeguard the overall consistency of the process sufficiently and it might carry the risk that parallel progress on the monetary and non-monetary sides might not be respected. In any event, if this procedure were chosen it would be crucial that the first Treaty laid down clearly the principal features of the ultimate objective of economic and monetary union.

63. Alternatively, it could be decided to conclude *a single comprehensive Treaty* formulating the essential features and institutional arrangements of economic and monetary union and the steps by which it could be achieved. Such a Treaty should indicate the procedures by which the decision would be taken to move from stage to stage. Each move would require an appraisal of the situation and a decision by the European Council.

Section 7

Suggested follow-up procedure

64. If the European Council can accept this Report as a basis for further development towards economic and monetary union, the following procedure is suggested.

65. The Council and the Committee of Governors should be invited to take the decisions necessary to implement the first stage.

66. Preparatory work for the negotiations on the new Treaty would start immediately. The competent Community bodies should be invited to make concrete proposals on the basis of this Report concerning the second and the final stages, to be embodied in a revised Treaty. These proposals should contain a further elaboration and concretization, where necessary, of the present Report. They should serve as the basis for future negotiations on a revised Treaty at an inter-governmental conference to be called by the European Council.

Annex

Excerpts from the Conclusions of the Presidency presented after the meeting of the European Council in Hanover on 27 and 28 June 1988

Monetary union

The European Council recalls that, in adopting the Single Act, the Member States confirmed the objective of progressive realization of economic and monetary union.

They therefore decided to examine at the European Council meeting in Madrid in June 1989 the means of achieving this union.

To that end they decided to entrust to a Committee the task of studying and proposing concrete stages leading towards this union.

The Committee will be chaired by Mr Jacques Delors, President of the European Commission.

The Heads of State or Government agreed to invite the President or Governor of their central banks to take part in a personal capacity in the proceedings of the Committee, which will also include one other member of the Commission and three personalities designated by common agreement by the Heads of State or Government. They have agreed to invite:

— Mr Niels Thygesen, Professor of Economics, Copenhagen;
— Mr Lamfalussy, General Manager of the Bank for International Settlements in Basle, Professor of Monetary Economics at the Catholic University of Louvain-la-Neuve;
— Mr Miguel Boyer, President of Banco Exterior de España.

The Committee should have completed its proceedings in good time to enable the Ministers for Economic Affairs and for Finance to examine its results before the European Council meeting in Madrid.

2. Collection of papers

I — Introductory note

Introductory note

These papers were submitted for discussion by individual members of the Committee for the Study of Economic and Monetary Union. This Committee had been set up by the European Council at its meeting in Hanover on 27 and 28 June 1988 in order 'to study and propose concrete stages leading towards economic and monetary union in Europe'. In response to this mandate the Committee prepared a 'Report on economic and monetary union in the European Community', which was submitted to the Heads of State or Government in April 1989.

The papers were submitted to the Committee as background information and were prepared on the personal responsibility of each author. The views expressed in the papers are therefore those of their authors and not necessarily the views of the Committee.

II — The Werner Report

The Werner Report revisited

Gunter D. Baer
Tommaso Padoa-Schioppa

The Werner Report on the realization by stages of economic and monetary union was drawn up against the background of the end of the transitional period leading to the completion of the customs union and the definition of the common agricultural policy. The Hanover Council has asked that renewed impetus should be given to the objective of economic and monetary union in the light of the adoption of the Single European Act and the fact that the process of completion of the internal market programme has now reached a point at which it is irreversible.

This discussion paper first outlines the main features of the Werner Report and its legislative follow-up. It then gives an assessment of the Report itself and its implementation. Finally it discusses some major developments during the post-Report period.

I — Main features of the Report

The Werner Report gave a comprehensive definition of the *final objective,* which it said should be achieved by stages. A detailed description of the measures needed for implementing the *first stage* was, however, not matched by an examination of the process by which one stage would lead to another and to the final objective. The second stage was essentially to have been a reinforced first stage. The Report also paid relatively little attention to institutional matters.

1. The final objective

Economic and monetary union, the Report said, would make it possible to 'realize an area in which goods and services, people and capital will circulate freely and without competitive distortions, without thereby giving rise to structural or regional disequilibrium'. Equilibrium within this area would be achieved, as in an individual national economy, by the mobility of factors of production and financial transfers by public and private sectors. Hence only the balance of payments of the Community as a whole would be of importance.

Monetary union would imply 'the total and irreversible convertibility of currencies, the elimination of margins of fluctuation in exchange rates, the irrevocable fixing of parity rates and the complete liberation of movements of capital'.

The Report considered that many elements of economic policy-making in this union would have to be centralized or transferred to the Community. 'The creation of liquidity throughout the area and monetary and credit policy will be centralized; monetary policy in relation to the outside world will be within the jurisdiction of the Community; and policies as regards capital markets would have to be unified'. Also, 'the essential features of the whole of the public budgets, and in particular variations in their volume, the size of balances and the methods of financing or utilizing them, will be decided at the Community level. Regional and structural policies will no longer be exclusively within the jurisdiction of the member countries; and a systematic and continuous consultation between the social partners will be ensured at the Community level'.

The Report recognized that the above would require 'the creation or the transformation of a certain number of Community organs to which powers until then exercised by the national authorities will have to be transferred'. It did not, however, give detailed consideration to the institutional structure that would be necessary, but it considered that the following two Community organs would be 'indispensable to the control of economic and monetary policy inside the unions':

(i) *a Centre of decision for economic policy,* which would in itself exercise a decisive influence over Community economic policy, and especially national budgetary policies. It would also have responsibility for changes in the parity of the sole currency or the whole of the national currencies. The Centre would have to be politically responsible to a European Parliament;

(ii) *a Community system for the central banks,* which could be based on the structure for the Federal Reserve. It would conduct the principal elements of internal monetary policy and be responsible for intervention on the foreign exchange markets.

2. The first and second stages

The primary aim of the first and second stages was to reinforce the coordination of economic policies so as to make it possible to decide on guidelines in common. The intention was that constraint on national policy-making should be applied progressively. This was to be achieved by a strong interaction between decision-making at Community and national levels. National decisions were progressively to be made in the light of Community guidelines; and as well as there being a system for prior consultations for budgetary and monetary policy, performances would be closely monitored. A system of indicators would detect the emergence of potentially dangerous situations.

The coordination of general economic policy-making was to be principally the responsibility of the Council, which would fix medium-term objectives and annual programmes on the basis of a detailed procedure which was designed to lead to permanent surveillance of the economic situation.

The Committee of Governors of the Central Banks was to play an increasingly important role in both internal and external monetary policy-making. So as to define the general guidelines of monetary and credit policy, the Committee was to prepare the regular Council meetings which the Governors were to attend.

The Governors would also manage the proposed system for Community exchange rate relations, which would progressively lead to a narrowing of the fluctuation bands.

'Progress in the convergence of economic and monetary policies should be such in the course of the second stage that Member States no longer have to resort on an autonomous basis to the instrument of parity adjustment.'

The creation of a 'European fund for monetary cooperation' would be necessary in the second stage, but it could also be part of the first stage. The fund would take over the short- and medium-term support mechanisms and would progressively manage Community reserves. In the final stage it would be integrated into the system of Community central banks.

II — Follow-up to the Report

1. The Werner Report considered that the first stage could last three years and begin at the start of 1971. In March that year the Council adopted a Decision on the strengthening of cooperation between central banks and a Resolution on the attainment of economic and monetary union by stages. That Resolution accepted the definition of the final objective that had been given in the Report and the need for a broadly-based package of measures to strengthen the coordination of economic policy-making.

Over the following three years, a number of important measures were taken to implement the first two stages:

— 1972: the 'snake' was created, and the Council Directive on regulating international capital flows and neutralizing their undesirable effects on domestic liquidity was adopted;

— 1973: the European Monetary Cooperation Fund (EMCF) was set up;

— 1974: the Council Decision on the attainment of a high degree of convergence of economic policies and the Directive on stability, growth and full employment were adopted.

2. However, the legislative implementation did not fully correspond to the letter or the spirit of the Report.

Firstly, little consideration was given to policies other than monetary or budgetary policies: the initial actions were concerned only with limiting exchange rate fluctuations, and the 1974 Decision on convergence concentrated largely on procedures for the coordination of budgetary policies.

Secondly, interaction between the Community and the Member States in policy-making was not really put into practice. The important prior consultation was lacking, and there was no internal pressure on Member States to follow the guidelines given at the Community level. Procedures were defined for *ex-post* monitoring and giving recommendations, but they were rarely used.

Thirdly, the Committee of Governors was not given extended powers to play an increasingly important role in the coordination of monetary and credit policy as had been called for in the Report. Procedures were not put in place, which had been recommended, for obligatory prior consultations and to allow the Committee to lay down general guidelines for monetary and credit policy for the Community. Moreover, whereas the Report had said that monetary policies should be determined 'having regard' for the guidelines for general economic policy, the 1971 Resolution said that monetary policy should be coordinated while *observing* these guidelines. Furthermore the EMCF was put under the 'observing' control of the Council, whereas the Report had said that it should be under the control of the central bank Governors.

III — An assessment

The Werner Report had concluded that economic and monetary union could be achieved within a decade, provided that the political will existed to realize that objective. However, by the mid-1970s the momentum had been lost and the Werner Report was no longer a driving force in Community developments. This can be attributed to the change in the international environment, but it may be asked whether it was not also due to possible intrinsic weaknesses in the Report. Among these the following could be of special relevance: insufficient constraints on national policies, institutional ambiguities, inappropriate policy conception and lack of internal momentum.

1. *Change in the international environment*

The collapse of the Bretton Woods system, together with the first oil price shock, significantly altered the economic environment in which the Report had been expected to be implemented. However, these unforeseen changes did not pose insurmountable problems of a technical nature. Adjustments to the Report's technical framework would have been possible and, indeed, were to some extent attempted in the context of the 'snake'. Rather, the basis for coordinating economic policy was greatly undermined by disagreements about the appropriate policy response to the oil shock and by expectations that more flexible exchange rates would enlarge the scope for autonomous domestic economic management.

2. Insufficient constraints on national policies

While the Report advocated obligatory prior consultation procedures initially involving existing Community bodies, the impetus for a process of convergence and progressive integration rested basically on voluntary agreement on broad Community objectives which were to be achieved through national policies carried on in accordance with guidelines. These guidelines had the character of recommendations and there was no provision to ensure their observance. Such an approach could work only as long as there was a sufficiently strong policy consensus and willingness to cooperate. However, once that consensus began to weaken, more binding constraints on national policy would have become necessary; in other words, the Report lacked safeguards against (temporary) lapses in policy consensus.

3. Institutional ambiguities

While the Report concentrated on the mechanics of how and when decisions should be made, it left it somewhat unclear who should make the decisions and how responsibilities were to be distributed. For instance, although the Committee of Governors was supposed to be given extended powers, the scope of these powers relative to those of the Council was left ambiguous.

4. Inappropriate policy conception

The procedures for policy coordination detailed in the Report implied a very high degree of confidence in the ability of policy instruments to affect policy goals in a known and predictable way. This over-optimistic view of the efficacy of economic management gave rise to a rather mechanistic and relatively rigid approach to policy coordination (especially in the budgetary field) which left less room for discretionary and flexible policy responses than was needed in the face of changing economic circumstances.

5. A lack of internal momentum

The first stages were self-contained and lacked a dynamic element. They formed a complete process rather than a framework within which there could be growing pressures for policy coordination. This led to both a lack of internal momentum within a given stage and insufficient impetus to move from stage to stage towards the final objective. The report did not envisage an interactive process in which the implementation of certain steps would trigger market reactions that in turn would necessitate further steps towards economic and monetary union. Rather, the Report's method tended more towards stressing the need for parallel progress.

IV — The post-Werner Report period

From the mid-1970s onwards developments in the *economic environment*, the *policy consensus* and the *Community* itself increasingly changed the background against which progress towards economic and monetary union could be considered.

1. *The economic environment*

Two features can be singled out as being of primary importance. Firstly, inflation. The Werner Report was written against the background of a relatively long period of price stability. By contrast, the following decade saw the average inflation rate in the Community rise well above 10%. In the course of the 1980s, the average inflation rate in the Community has again been brought down to levels not seen since the 1960s. The experience of high inflation and of the severity of the measures necessary to curb inflation once it has taken hold in an economic system has emphasized the need for monetary arrangements that promote and preserve stability.

Secondly, international monetary arrangements have also moved through a complete cycle. The Werner Report was written as the dollar-denominated Bretton Woods system was collapsing. There then followed a period of floating exchange rates in which policy coordination was minimal. More recently, there has been an evolution towards a more managed and multi-polar system. Policy coordination has been strengthened through multilateral surveillance procedures and currency arrangements have been developed.

2. *Policy consensus*

Towards the end of the 1960s there was a remarkable consensus on policy-making. The evidence seemed to strongly confirm the effectiveness of medium-term planning and fine-tuning. In the 1970s experience with stagflation destroyed this consensus. Now a new consensus has developed in which attention has shifted towards medium-term financial stability, the supply side of the economy and structural policies. Part of the legacy of the earlier consensus is, however, large budget deficits and a high level of government debt. When the Werner Report was drafted, budgets in the Community were in approximate balance. Deficits subsequently peaked at over 5% of GDP and are still above 4%. Government debt at the beginning of the 1970s averaged less than 40% of GDP, whereas it now averages over 70%.

3. *The Community*

(a) **Significant non-monetary developments**

Although the Community entered a difficult phase as it absorbed new members within an unchanged framework and in an unfavourable economic environment, a number of steps were taken. Among these, as well as enlargement itself, were the following:

— in 1974 the European Council was created to take the place of the earlier summit meetings held at irregular intervals; it became the driving force of the subsequent development of the Community;

— in 1975 the first European Regional Development Fund was set up, representing the beginning of a growing redistributive role for the Community budget;

— in 1977 the Sixth VAT Directive establishing a uniform basis for collection was adopted, marking a major step in the process of tax harmonization;

— in 1979 the first direct elections to the European Parliament were held, broadening the democratic basis of the European structure.

(b) **Monetary developments**

The European Monetary System was created in 1979, with the primary objective of establishing a zone of monetary stability, involving both low inflation and stable exchange rates. The exchange rate constraint has acted as a focal point for improved policy coordination, and the EMS has provided a framework for enhancing multilateral surveillance within the Community. Participants have gradually opted for a strong currency policy stance, so putting the greatest emphasis on domestic adjustment measures. The system has evolved in response to changes in the economic and financial environment, especially improved convergence and increased capital mobility. Most recently, the Basle/Nyborg Agreement of September 1987 made some important modifications to the mechanisms of the system to secure a more balanced implementation of the exchange rate commitment by all participants. The procedures for surveillance were also strengthened.

The use of the ECU within the system has been limited. By contrast, the non-official use of the ECU, especially as a denominator of financial transactions, has increased considerably. International banking business in ECUs has expanded markedly and a significant share of international bond issues is now denominated in ECUs. The non-financial use of the ECU, however, has remained limited although some increase appears to have taken place recently.

(c) **New Community impetus in the 1980s**

The internal market. In 1985 the programme for completing the internal market was proposed by the Commission and adopted by the European Council. It aims, as already stated in the Werner Report, at achieving full freedom of circulation of goods, services, people and capital by 1992, and to this end calls specifically for the removal of all physical, technical and fiscal frontiers.

In November 1987 proposals for the creation of a European financial area, including the full liberalization of capital movements, were tabled. These were adopted by the Ecofin Council of June 1988 and will be implemented by most Member States by 1990. The early implementation of full capital mobility will entail further developments in other areas. For example, since it will increase the potential for exchange rate instability, it will be necessary to further reinforce cooperation within the EMS. Also, as the Werner Report recognized, measures will have to be taken so that differences between tax regimes do not lead to distortions or increased tax evasion.

The Single European Act is the first significant modification to the Treaty of Rome. Its enactment was possible because the internal market programme laid out in the White Paper of 1988 had given the Community a new and concrete objective, together with a more streamlined method of implementation based on mutual recognition rather than full harmonization and a fixed timetable. The Single European Act makes changes that are vital to ensuring that the internal market programme can be completed within the specified time-scale. In particular, it greatly expands the scope of majority voting and lays the basis for an improved institutional balance within the Community with a strengthened role for the European Parliament. The Single European Act not only deals with the internal market but also sets objectives and provides for action in the following related areas: social policy, economic and social cohesion, research and technological development and the monetary capacity of the Community.

Accompanying policies. The Brussels European Council of February 1988 agreed on a package of measures which, as well as putting the Community budget on a solid basis and reinforcing the reform of the common agricultural policy, will lead to a doubling in real terms of the structural Funds. By 1992 Portugal, Greece and Ireland will be receiving inflows of grants and loans from the Community amounting to between 3½ and 6½% of their GDP (and hence 15 to 30% of their gross investments). Transfers to Spain and Italy could amount to something of the order of 1% of GDP.

V — Conclusions

The link between the free movement of goods, services and capital and the need to create an economic and monetary union was the point of departure of the Werner Report; and the mandate from the Hanover Council also comes at a time when significant progress is being made towards completing the internal market. The two processes are self-reinforcing, and the full potential of the single market will only be realized with satisfactory monetary arrangements.

Since the Werner Report was written many of its recommendations have been implemented and there have been significant developments going beyond those that the Report considered to be necessary for the first steps towards economic and monetary union. That ultimate goal, however, still remains unachieved. This is partly because of unfavourable external circumstances, but also because of intrinsic weaknesses in the approach and inadequate implementation. A better understanding of these shortcomings can only increase the chances of future success.

III — Papers relating to economic union

Economic and monetary union and relaunching the construction of Europe

J. Delors

For the first time in almost 15 years, the European Council in Hanover has reopened definite prospects for economic and monetary union. It not only recalled that this objective is now in the Treaty, but also established a procedure to examine ways to achieve this union. This development is based on the spectacular progress made recently in the construction of Europe and especially the 'irreversible' nature of completing the internal market by 1992.

More than ever the Community is now in a position to achieve the fundamental goal, given in Article 2 of the Treaty, which says: 'The Community shall have as its task, by establishing a common market and progressively approximating the economic policies of Member States, the promotion throughout the Community of a harmonious development of economic activities, a continuous and balanced expansion, an increase in stability, an accelerated raising of the standard of living and closer relations between the States belonging to it.'

Prompted by Chancellor Brandt, the Hague Summit in 1969 reaffirmed the political will to establish economic and monetary union. The Werner Report made some concrete recommendations and concluded that the objective could be achieved within the decade. We know what became of the resolutions and decisions taken by the Council between 1971 and 1974. Their implementation was impeded, first by the upheavals in the international economic and monetary environment, and then even more profoundly by Member States turning in on themselves and pursuing divergent economic and monetary policies. The period was characterized by a rising tide of protectionism, declining trade within the Community, unemployment and inflation.

Against this background, the creation of the European Monetary System — based on an intergovernmental agreement rather than on Community law — was a welcome reaction. An exceptional combination of circumstances and the judicious use of a method pioneered by Jean Monnet in the creation of the ECSC, made it possible to overcome strong reservations associated with the deep sense of national sovereignty in the sensitive area of monetary policy.

The success of the EMS has done much to reverse the process of disintegration of the Community by engendering a new process of economic policy convergence. Yet the European Council in Luxembourg, in December 1980, postponed indefinitely the transition to the institutional phase of the EMS.

In retrospect, the first plan for economic and monetary union looks somewhat abstract. It was based on a political design, but was out of phase with the actual state of integration of the European economy of that time. Today, the recent progress towards integration is an incentive to approach the relaunching of Europe in a variety of ways, in addition to the main driving force, which is the dynamic of the internal market. The process initially focused on optimizing the allocation of resources, but unless this is complemented by an awareness of the need for cohesion and balanced development, and for economic growth and stability, this dynamic could fall apart. In other words, the keys to the success of the large internal market are part and parcel of the very logic of economic and monetary union. Moreover, this is evidenced by the Single Act and its implementation.

* * *

The current progress in the construction of Europe must first be set in the context of the crisis experienced by the Community after the successes of the 1960s.

The creeping paralysis of the Community was the result of the Member States calling into question the Community method for the progressive and limited transfer of national powers to common institutions possessing a real power to make decisions. The very ambitious nature of the Community's ultimate objectives — to achieve an economic union and to found a political entity — has been used as a reason for refusing to go too fast in relinquishing sovereignty, since the inevitability of doing so seemed out of proportion with the degree of interdependence of the economies, the social systems, and the cultures of the Member States. In addition, it was sometimes felt that the development of Community powers would deprive Member States of any possibility of supplementing Community action with national measures. The gradualism of the Community method of integration was replaced *de facto* by intergovernmental cooperation based on the search for consensus for even the most trivial decisions.

Despite, or because of, the challenge of the economic crisis, the Community was reduced to its *acquis,* its legacy — that of the ECSC, the customs union and the common agricultural policy. The crisis generated by one Member State's claim for a reduction in its budget contribution exacerbated the problems by paralysing the operation of the Community and by automatically preventing new policies from being launched.

The provisional settlement which the European Council in Fontainebleau devised for the budgetary and agricultural problems made it possible to break the log-jam in the negotiations for Spanish and Portuguese accession and to launch the integrated Mediterranean programmes; nevertheless, it could not conceal the fact that the Community was in danger of relapsing into a state of lethargy without a strategy to give fresh impetus to integration.

**

The central element in the relaunching of Europe was proposed by the Commission of the European Communities in 1985, with the objective of achieving a unified economic area by 1992. The essential part of the measures for the removal of physical, technical and fiscal barriers was set out in a White Paper. It lays down a programme, a timetable and a method (mutual recognition and harmonization of essential standards). The White Paper also notes that there is a link between completing the internal market and the adoption of complementary policies. It states that the 'strengthening of coordination of economic policies and the European Monetary System will be essential factors in the integration of national markets'.

The Milan European Council in June 1985, after adopting the 'detailed programme' and the 'specific timetable' drawn up by the Commission, agreed to undertake the necessary revision of the Treaty of Rome in order to equip the Community with a more effective decision-making process. But the reform which was to be completed six months later with the adoption of the Single Act, goes far beyond a simple institutional adjustment aimed at making it easier to complete the large market by 1992.

The institutional reform is based on three principles: faster decision-making, better decision-making and more democratic decision-making. Extending the scope of qualified-majority voting is a sign of the determination to remove the constraint of the permanent search for consensus. Formerly, the Council merely had the option of relying on the Commission for measures for the implementation of the general rules which the Council lays down: now this is transformed into an obligation. Finally, Parliament is given a genuine part in the legislative process and, in cases where unanimity has been replaced by qualified-majority voting, it is given the power to propose amendments provided that it has the support of the Commission.

But the Single Act, by establishing the objective and the institutional means for creating by 31 December 1992 'an area without internal frontiers in which the free movement of goods, persons, services and capital is ensured' opens up new fields of action which cannot be dissociated from the completion of the large market. The Single Act introduces into the Treaty of Rome the need to strengthen the Community's economic and social cohesion, the recognition of the Community's monetary capacity in the perspective of economic and monetary union, the strengthening of the Community's scientific and technological basis, the harmonization of working conditions and the dialogue between management and labour, and action to protect the environment.

It remained for the Community to give itself the financial resources which would ensure the credibility of the Single Act's overall strategy, and, in particular, of the new objective of economic and social cohesion. This was to be the work of the European Council in Brussels in February 1988 which took the decisions required for the agricultural policy to be better adapted to market conditions, for the resources of the structural Funds to be doubled in order to assist the less-developed regions or those in industrial decline, and for the Community to be provided with sufficient and stable financial resources.

The prospects opened up by the Single Act very quickly led to concrete measures, which, in varying degrees, correspond to the three functions of Community action consistent with the pursuit of economic and monetary union: stabilization, allocation and cohesion.

In September 1987, the Basle and Nyborg Agreements developed certain mechanisms of the EMS and also increased the responsibilities of those important Community bodies, the Committee of Governors and the Monetary Committee, for the surveillance of monetary and economic policies. It remains to be seen whether the new procedures and methods will be sufficient to meet the challenge represented by the forthcoming complete liberalization of capital movements, pursuant to the Directive on that subject adopted by the Council in June 1988. At all events, there remains the problem of the closer coordination of economic and monetary policies, in the framework of some commonly agreed procedures.

In a few months, numerous and important decisions have been taken affecting the free movement of persons, goods, capital and services. Examples are the recent agreement on the new approach to standards, the equivalence of diplomas, the partial opening-up of public procurement, and insurance. This momentum has resulted from the recognition that the process of completing the internal market has become irreversible and from the dynamic force that the objective of 1992 has created at every decision-making level. The anticipation effect is clearly seen in the strategies of European firms: an unprecedented number of mergers foreshadows a strengthening of industrial cooperation. Credibility in the reality of relaunching Europe is restored, as it is in the decision-making capacity of Community bodies.

The imminent implementation of measures ensuring the freedom to provide services has resulted in a quiet revolution taking place. It is likely that fair competition will be guaranteed by certain common disciplines being laid down in the form of Community directives, and no longer mere recommendations. Similarly, the need to take account of the external dimension in the main decisions concerning completion of the internal market gives rise to the principle that the freedom of establishment and the freedom to provide services or the opening-up of public procurement will be applicable to third-country firms under an agreement negotiated by the Community.

The social dimension of the internal market should be one of its important components. There should soon be definite progress in the dialogue between management and labour and the adoption of a minimum core of fundamental worker rights and of a statute for a European company, involving tested methods of employee representation. In order to achieve this, patience will have to be exercised in bringing national positions closer together.

Substantial resources (ECU 13 000 million in 1992) have been set aside for the policy of economic and social cohesion laid down by the Single Act, and the reform of the structural Funds will enable the Community to develop a genuine regional policy. Nevertheless, the relative size of the sums in question will remain modest (three-thousandths of Community 'GNP') and the function of redistribution and of assisting adjustment, which can be exercised by Community action between now and 1992, will remain limited in scope, even if it does achieve macroeconomic significance for the four countries most concerned. The amounts devoted to the development of research (2% of the national research budgets) is similarly modest.

Regional policy and European economic integration

Maurice F. Doyle

Introduction

Progress towards economic and monetary union (EMU) in Europe is usually discussed in terms of achieving the objective of the internal market by the end of 1992 and, beyond that, the closer coordination of policies, leading ultimately to irreversibly fixed exchange rates. The regional dimension receives much less emphasis and is less well defined than other aspects of the process of economic and monetary integration. This paper attempts to introduce more balance. In Section 1, emphasis is placed on the importance of regional policy as an essential part of the integration process. The failure of the market mechanism to guarantee an even distribution of the gains from economic integration and the consequent need for regional policy is elaborated upon in Section 2. A description of what should be viewed as the most desirable features of an effective regional policy is given in Section 3. The final section emphasizes that regional policy must make a real contribution if the peripheral economies are to participate in the benefits of EMU, thereby ensuring that the Europe of the future will have an optimum output and welfare level and the cohesiveness necessary to compete effectively on a global basis.

In the light of the experience of both an economic and monetary union for 100 years and a monetary union for some 50 years with Britain, there are definite views in Ireland on the nature of a viable union, on the principles on which a successful regional policy should be based and, of course, on the pitfalls that should be avoided. In addition, Ireland is in a unique position, being a peripheral economy fully participating in the exchange-rate mechanism of the EMS.

1. Economic and monetary union: Requirements and potential problems

The main elements of EMU are:

— freedom of movement of goods and services, capital and labour;
— a high degree of policy coordination;
— the elimination of regional disparities;
— irreversibly fixed exchange rates.

Clearly, these requirements go far beyond those of the internal market programme, which does not require the close coordination of fiscal and other economic policies or the fixed exchange rates demanded under economic and monetary union.

It is crucial that the important *preconditions* of EMU be recognized at the outset. The process of economic integration requires a number of distinct stages, with monetary union, involving irreversibly fixed exchange rates, being the final stage. Before this can be achieved, all Community countries will need to have reached a broadly similar stage of economic development and be committed to broadly similar economic policies. If this is not the situation, disparities within the Community would cause persistent capital and labour flows from the less prosperous to the richer regions, creating both economic and political tensions that could put the whole process in jeopardy.

The economic union phase of integration requires the removal of restrictions, the elimination of regional disparities and close policy coordination. While Member States would retain the possibility of exchange rate adjustment as a response to external shocks and differences in the evolution of competitiveness, a policy of exchange rate adjustment should be avoided. This is because, firstly, such adjustment would be inconsistent with the degree of exchange rate discipline required for moving towards the ultimate objective of monetary union and, secondly, because any benefits to problem countries would be merely temporary, being quickly reflected in higher inflation and a loss of credibility and would not promote the narrowing of divergences between the richer and poorer countries. Moreover, there is increasing agreement that this principle of avoiding realignments in order to increase credibility and to achieve price stability is appropriate not only for small open economies; other larger ERM participants, through their words and actions, have shown their support for this principle.

Economic union is not something which will suddenly begin after 1992 but, rather, is a process already under way which will continue after 1992 for quite some time before the final stage of EMU is reached. One important element in this process is that, as integration proceeds, Member States will experience an increasing loss of autonomy with increasing coordination of economic and other policies. Without complete political union, Member States will, of course, continue to exist, but there will be growing constraints on their freedom of economic action to deal with their own national regional problems. At the level of the European Community, it is the theory of regional economics, and not the theory of international trade, which will become increasingly relevant in the future. Regional economic theory, confirmed by Ireland's historical experience, suggests that in the absence of appropriate accompanying policies, market forces will not of themselves be sufficient to eliminate divergences and bring about the required degree of economic cohesion within the Community, but rather the reverse. This is because factors such as better infrastructure, lower transport and distribution costs and proximity to bigger markets would almost certainly favour the growth of the stronger regions and the stagnation, or even contraction, of the weaker. The process already occurs in the existing nation-States of Europe. Areas of France south of Lyons, the Mezzogiorno in Italy, and some northern regions of Germany clearly exhibit, although at different absolute levels of income, the process of relative impoverishment — relative, that is, to the richer regions in these countries — even while the national economy as a whole grows richer. According as the barriers to trade, capital and labour movements come down and the freedom for Member States to have independent monetary, fiscal and exchange rate policies diminishes, exactly the same process will take hold throughout the European Community, since economies will no longer be definable simply by reference to national boundaries. The Community as a whole can be expected to fare better in the aggregate from moves towards EMU, but there is a need, already urgent, to tackle the issue of regional imbalances directly; otherwise, the weaker peripheral regions of Europe such as Ireland could suffer, rather than benefit, from the process of economic integration. This can only be achieved through the development of a comprehensive Community regional policy with adequate resources for the task.

While a convincing case can be made for significant regional support in a more integrated Europe, it tends nevertheless to be viewed as a national demand based on national self-interest, rather than a requirement of a sound regional policy framed in the interests of the Community as a whole. The history of the European Regional Development Fund since 1975, with its rigid adherence to national quotas to which each Member State was 'entitled', bears this out. The Fund was viewed not so much as a means of dealing with Community regional problems but rather as Community assistance to Member States to deal with their own, internal, regional problems. The fact that Ireland was recognized as a single region for the purposes of the Fund was more a reflection of the political process than an acknowledgement that Community problems had to be dealt with on a Community scale. There are signs that these attitudes are changing — the doubling of the structural Funds by 1992 and the institution of a 'quota-free' component of the Regional Fund are obvious examples — but there is some way to go yet before it is fully accepted that the backward regions of Europe, whether they are so because of geography, trade patterns or the decline of once-prosperous industries, must get special assistance if they are to remain attractive places in which to live and areas which have an economic future. Regional policy needs to be seen as an essential element in the policy mix necessary to achieve EMU, but equally all members must recognize that regional policy is not simply a question of financial grants for specific projects, or even for programmes, still less does it comprise subsidies to prop up non-viable ways of life; rather it is the continuing application of a regional dimension to *every* European policy.

2. Costs and benefits of economic integration

The establishment of the European Regional Development Fund (ERDF) in 1975 was the first major recognition of the need for an active regional policy at Community level. When outlining the Community decision the Commission noted that:

'... not only do the less-developed regions fail to integrate fully within the Community, but the problems to which they give rise become an increasingly heavy burden on national economies and thus increase the pressure on the public authorities concerned to refuse the constraints inherent in the mechanism of Community integration. It is, moreover, an illusion to hope for the convergence of Member States' economies so long as regional problems continue to weigh so heavily on certain economies... It follows from this situation that Community regional policy must be strengthened and its field of application expanded. This is not only desirable: it is now one of the conditions of continuing European economic integration.' ('Community regional policy — New guidelines', *Bulletin of the European Communities, Supplement 2/77*)

These considerations are even more relevant today than they were in 1975. There is still no guarantee that the benefits of market integration will be evenly distributed among all Member States. Indeed, these concerns increase as economic integration proceeds towards EMU in that the availability of policy instruments to deal with the problems arising from further integration are reduced and thus regional disparities could become more permanent. For these reasons there is an urgent need to establish a strong regional policy before proceeding to EMU. Before outlining in more detail the particular factors likely to give rise to problems, it is worth looking at the case for the complete freeing of trade and the furthering of market integration.

The case for free trade is usually based on the principle that there are efficiency gains from the removal of trade restrictions which are welfare-increasing for the Community as a whole. These gains are generally seen as being of two types. Firstly, there are those resulting from comparative advantage which, in turn, can be classified into gains from increased specialization and gains from an increased volume of trade. These gains increase the welfare of *all parties* engaged in trade and arise primarily from trade involving the output of different industries in the trading countries (that is, interindustry trade). Secondly, there are gains arising from the existence of economies of scale in some industries whereby as a result of the removal of trade restrictions, firms can expand and thus produce more efficiently. This trade involves the output of similar industries in different countries (that is, intra-industry trade). Many of the gains from freer trade within the Community have been of the latter type though, in this case, *only some parties* may gain.

One must take a number of considerations into account, however, when considering the likely distribution of both types of gains in the context of increasing market integration in the Community. Firstly, while the principle of comparative advantage is generally seen as providing a compelling justification for a policy of opening up markets, there are a number of qualifications which need to be considered. These relate to the fact that the basic assumptions underlying the comparative advantage model, i.e. free competition, full employment of factors of production, full mobility of capital and labour and zero transportation costs, are unlikely to be fulfilled in reality. Thus one of the predictions of the model, that trade liberalization leads to the equalization of factor prices and hence to a convergence of incomes and living standards is not borne out in practice, largely because of incomplete factor mobility. Moreover, the forces which give rise to the second type of gains, that is, those arising from the phenomenon of intra-industry trade, that is from the operation of economies of scale in production, suggest that the convergence of incomes and living standards is even less likely. Other considerations such as the non-uniformity of transport costs, the effect of demand factors and the existence of external economies would, in fact, reinforce this conclusion.

The existence of economies of scale in production has been the most important factor giving rise to intra-industry trade in the Community. This provided important efficiency gains in the early days of the Community of Six when economic structures were relatively similar. However, in the present enlarged Community there are much greater differences in economic structures and thus the effect of economies of scale will most likely be to favour the further development of the stronger central regions. This arises because the existence of these economies of scale will create market structures that are oligopolistic, being dominated by a few firms located, for the most part, in the stronger central regions. The effect of other factors will also tend to work in this direction. The level of transport costs will tend to be higher in the peripheral regions of the Community than in the central regions, reflecting the rather obvious fact that it costs more to bring goods to a distant market than to a neighbouring one. This will tend to attract firms to central rather than peripheral regions. The effect of demand factors is likely to be similar — because central regions tend to be densely populated and peripheral regions do not, the largest and most dynamic markets will be found at the centre of the Community and not at the periphery. The central regions will also tend to benefit to a greater extent from external economies, such as a highly developed infrastructure, closer contact with suppliers and access to a larger labour market.

The combination of all these considerations strongly suggests that the attraction of central regions is much stronger than peripheral regions for both the location and growth of new firms. Moreover, the strength of a region is of itself likely to create further external economies and thus one faces the possibility of creating a spiral effect, whereby the relative strength of the central region is an important factor in ensuring its continued growth. This growth, however, is to some extent achieved at the expense of the peripheral regions which find it increasingly difficult to catch up on the more developed regions.

In sum, therefore, while economic theory suggests that the Community as a whole should gain from the integration process, the considerations just outlined strongly indicate that this gain will be concentrated in the stronger regions and will be achieved at the cost of major adjustment on the part of the weaker economies. As a result, the efficiency gap between the weaker and the stronger regions may actually be widened. This suggests that if left to itself the market process would increase divergences between regions rather than lead to convergence.

Another important point which must be borne in mind is that the movement of factors of production from the periphery to the centre may be determined by private rather than social cost considerations. For instance, significant movements of labour into already densely-populated areas may lead to some problems of congestion while, from the point of view of the less-densely populated regions, the outflow of labour will mean that the cost of maintaining the economic and social infrastructure will increase. This latter problem is likely to be compounded because, as Irish experience indicates, the migration of labour tends to come from the younger, more skilled and more enterprising sections of the population; thus, those remaining behind are reduced not only in numbers but also in competitive ability, thereby exacerbating the initial disadvantage.

The above reasons indicate not only why there is a need for a regional policy within the Community *but also why, as integration proceeds, there is a need for that policy to play a greater role.* The requirements of EMU go a considerable distance beyond the 1992 programme in terms of the constraints which they place on policy autonomy in individual countries. For EMU to be sustainable, the economies of the countries forming the union must be similarly competitive or else some countries would be faced with the equivalent of a constant balance-of-payments deficit which, in EMU, would be reflected in terms of stagnation and unemployment. Obviously, the only way in which countries in such a union can compete on similar terms is for the burden of problem regions to be tackled. Otherwise, pressures on national governments would be likely to force them to abandon the commitment to EMU and to take autonomous action to solve their regional problems. This danger, presented by regional imbalances, is the greatest threat to the realization of economic and monetary union.

3. Principles of regional policy in the context of moving towards EMU

Regional policy, which refers not simply to regional fund expenditure but rather to all policies affecting the development of the regions, must be an essential element in the policy mix necessary to achieve economic and monetary union. In its absence, the Community may well fare better on aggregate than before embarking on the process, but it would have created problems associated with highly concentrated industry and populations.

3.1. *The role of regional policy in reducing disparities*

The objective of Community regional policy should be to correct imbalances by contributing to the development and the structural adjustment of the regions. Eliminating regional disparities should not be confused with equalizing income per head between regions. Differences in income could, of course, be greatly reduced by some transfer mechanism, but a mechanism based primarily on income subsidies would not contribute to the achievement of sustainable growth. Rather, it could act as a disincentive to effort in the region receiving the transfers, while possibly damaging the dynamism of the stronger regions. It would, at best, merely subsidize the continuation of the problem; it would not help to solve it.

Instead, it is more constructive to think in terms of equalizing the conditions needed for the production of goods and services. Here, the main difficulty faced by problem regions is a lack of adequate infrastructure. This is true both of peripheral regions and declining regions. Peripheral regions have inferior infrastructure largely because they are both poorer and less densely populated and the per capita cost of providing the infrastructure becomes prohibitive. Declining regions, on the other hand, tend to suffer because decaying infrastructure is not being replaced. The lack of good infrastructure discourages new firms from locating in either type of region and results in higher costs for existing firms. In order to overcome this problem, peripheral regions need assistance to bring their infrastructure up to a similar level as that obtaining in the stronger regions of the Community.

Here, one of the key areas is transport. For example, in Ireland, it is estimated that industry spends approximately IRL 1 billion annually in transporting materials and distributing finished products. Though geography and a lack of producer goods industries will always mean that transport costs in Ireland will represent a significant proportion of total manufacturing costs, it has been calculated that these costs could be reduced by almost half through significant improvements in the road network. The recent decision to expand the Community regional programme to include infrastructural projects undertaken by the private sector is, therefore, welcome.

Even if physical disparities were considerably reduced, however, there remain other locational disadvantages — not merely the demand factors mentioned earlier, but also the existence of economies of scale in the central regions arising from, for example, proximity to research institutes, major financial centres and other services and an abundant supply of skilled labour. The importance of these disadvantages could, however, be reduced as more firms locate in the periphery and as the problems of communication over long distances are reduced by new technology.

3.2. *Regional policy and labour mobility*

Economic theory tells us that in an economic and monetary union, disparities between regions will produce movements of labour and capital. While such mobilitiy is obviously a requirement of any dynamic economy, large-scale mobility, particularly in the case of labour, would hardly be politically acceptable as a major adjustment factor in an integrated Europe. Indeed, from an Irish point of view, the extent of labour mobility might well be regarded as a *measure* of regional disparities and of the lack of success in overcoming them. While disparities cannot be totally eliminated, they must be reduced to a level where labour mobility, in particular, is largely voluntary. It is recognized that migration and emigration today are complex issues and it can be misleading to classify emigration in simple terms such as voluntary or involuntary, but Ireland has long experience of the effects of large-scale involuntary emigration and it has very few positive features. In a more integrated Europe, it is essential that the weaker regions do not become mere suppliers of labour. Regional policy must be structured in such a way as to induce enterprises to locate and labour to stay in the peripheral regions. It is worth bearing in mind that the education and training of individuals who, in the event, emigrate to take up employment elsewhere in the Community represents an outright benefit for the receiving region while, for the region of emigration, it is an investment from which it obtains little or no return. This is a non-trivial example of the way in which the richer regions may benefit from integration at the expense of the weaker areas.

Another aspect of the impact of regional policy on labour is that there should be a move away from providing labour-intensive low-pay projects for peripheral regions. With rapid changes in technology, such projects tend to be short-lived as competition increases from some of the newly industrialized countries with even lower wage levels. Such a policy would not seem likely to bring about the objective of reducing disparities in living standards in the EC.

3.3. Structure of regional policy

The difficulties posed by the 'national quotas' approach to the Regional Fund were mentioned earlier. In the context of European integration, a basic principle must be that aid should be determined on the basis of regions and not of countries. The adoption of this principle should help to reduce the political friction in regional policy, with aid being allocated to approved programmes within the designated regions, regardless of the country in which they happen to be located. This implies a major increase in funding for programmes with specific objectives in mind, a process already under way. It means a shift of emphasis towards setting overall objectives for infrastructure at Community level and providing funds to achieve them, rather than engaging in piecemeal project financing. The recent Council Regulation on the use of the structural Funds commits the Community increasingly to concentrate on programme funding, which by end-1987 was targeted to account for only 20% of regional policy expenditure. This development clearly has much further to go.

A truly European regional policy in the context of EMU should not become another open-ended drain on Community resources and should eventually become self-sustaining. As some regions become self-supporting and able to compete without assistance, there could be greater concentration of resources on the remaining problem areas. A point would eventually be reached where the amount of Community resources needed would decline. A properly-framed regional policy would not become an ever-expanding part of the Community budget; a policy that did so would contain the seeds of its own destruction.

The corollary of a policy for the less-favoured regions is a policy for the more-advanced regions. The other side of the coin of a policy that encourages growth where it now lags is a conscious discouragement of growth where it is not merely unnecessary, but brings great social and economic costs in terms of congestion, pollution, social problems and even destruction of the environment. If transfers of much-needed resources to the peripheral areas are acknowledged as necessary for the cohesion of European integration, then it is surely beyond argument that the case for subsidies to industries operating in the richest and most polluted areas in Europe is open to serious question. A subsidy given to industry to locate in developed Europe has an inevitable and negative effect on underdeveloped Europe. Indeed, the external costs imposed on society by locating an industry in an already overcrowded and polluted environment would justify the imposition of a tax rather than the granting of a subsidy. It is not only the peripheral regions that need to justify subventions for their development.

3.4. *Financing and composition of expenditure*

There should be a move away from a policy of widely dispersing regional aid towards one of concentrating that aid on programmes, projects and activities in regions. This would ensure the maximum return for a given transfer expenditure. Moreover, in designing regional programmes it is important to guard against the problem of 'fatigue' on the part of the richer countries. This tends to arise in the context of debates on annual allocations of national contributions to a central budget and reflects an unduly static analysis of the costs/benefits of regional policy. By focusing mainly on the costs of providing transfers to the poorer regions and taking insufficient account of the less-quantifiable opportunities provided by the opening-up of these countries' markets, an unbalanced picture of the integration process emerges. One way of overcoming the problem of fatigue is by ensuring that a major portion of Community financing is on an 'own resource' basis; that is, that it accrues to the Community budget automatically. From the point of view of the recipient regions, there is a need to ensure that funding would continue to be available for programmes until divergences between the objectives and actual achievements of a regional plan are either eliminated or reduced to acceptable levels.

An essential aspect of a Community regional policy must be that regional transfers should be earmarked for specific purposes rather than taking the form of general purpose funding which, due to fungibility with other uses, can be used to maintain public consumption at unrealistic levels. Thus, the use of specific-purpose transfers would be geared directly towards reducing the impact of locational disadvantages and towards mitigating the adverse effects in the disadvantaged regions of economies of scale arising elsewhere. It would also be desirable that such grants be flexible in their time-frame of application so as to provide an incentive for a country or region to reduce regional disparities in infrastructural facilities at a rapid rate. If Community spending cannot be expanded to match accelerated investment by a national government, it effectively means that national quotas in terms of regional transfers operate in practice; these would not provide any incentive for Member States to undertake ambitious development programmes.

There must also be full appreciation and acceptance of the fact that the Community budgetary funds must be large enough to be effective in reducing regional disparities. In this regard, it is instructive to compare the allocation of structural Funds amounting to ECU 8 billion in 1988 (not all of which is earmarked for the least-favoured regions) to the gains expected from the single market. The Cecchini Report estimated the direct gains from the move to the single market to be of the order of ECU 216 billion in 1988 prices. Even on this basis, there is clearly a need for a greater volume of transfers to the least-favoured regions; otherwise they are likely to contribute more to the gains from the single market than they would receive. An examination of existing federal States demonstrates that the amount of funds as a proportion of GDP devoted to the elimination of regional disparities within these States is considerably greater than it is as between the Member States of the Community. It is not unrealistic to suppose that this may explain why the extent of disparities within existing federal States (at least in the industrial world) is much less than it is within the Community.

3.5. *Administration*

The Community budgetary system should be as democratic and efficient as possible. It is clear from experiences of highly centralized administrations that, in the interests of both democracy and efficiency, the principle of decentralization should be espoused. As much planning and execution as possible should be made and carried out in the regions. There is, however, also a need for much more coordination of policies at a Community level to ensure that there is not a wasteful duplication of projects in the Community. These two opposing needs could be satisfied by the regions developing medium-term plans of say three to five years which they would submit to the Council for discussion, negotiation and approval or, as the case may be, rejection. It is encouraging to note that this type of approach is advocated in the Council Regulation on the use of the structural Funds. Once the medium-term plan and funds (or means of raising the funds) to carry it out is approved and synchronized with other Community plans, administration should be carried out in the region. A Community authority should be empowered to carry out regular audits to ensure that the conditions of the plans were being adhered to.

4. Contribution of regional policy to a stronger Europe

Conclusions

In an economic and monetary union, there would be no *national* policy instruments available to offset the tendency for poorer regions to suffer from the effects of market integration. It is essential, therefore, to be clear on the basic principles that should inform a European regional policy. Among the more important principles on which regional policy should be based are:

— the need to eliminate the locational disadvantages of the poorer regions in the production of goods and services;

— large-scale movements of labour must not become a major adjustment factor;

— regional transfers should be sufficiently large to effect the necessary reduction in disparities between Member States;

— the need for aid should be determined on the basis of regions, not of countries, and aid should be concentrated in the poorer regions;

— the composition of regional transfers should be weighted in favour of programme financing rather than project financing; moreover, it should be designed, as far as possible, to catalyse private-sector investment in the regions so that they become self-sustaining;

— Community regional transfers should be financed from the own resources of the Community and be complemented by macroeconomic policies directed towards financial stability in the medium term;

— a sizeable Community budget.

Regional policy must be directed at enabling the peripheral areas to compete, not at subsidizing them in continued deprivation; it must be far more than financial transfers, and those transfers should be directed towards reducing costs and raising productivity; it should mean a regional dimension to every European policy, and not simply a fund, however well-spent; and it must encompass the richer regions too — both to discourage undesirable development and to acknowledge that the losses of the poor are often the gains of the rich. EMU involves surrendering a high degree of national autonomy in economic policy-making. This should take place in an environment in which the interests of the peripheral regions are protected. Central economies should not gain the benefits of integration at the expense of the peripheral economies. Rather, EMU should mean that all share in the decision-making process and in the benefits that accrue. Commitment to EMU must involve a corresponding commitment to ensuring that the integration process is beneficial to all. In particular, the stronger economies in the Community cannot pick and choose the elements of EMU that are favourable and disregard the rest. EMU must be a package representing a sharing of costs and benefits that is equitable and acceptable to all member countries. The achievement of economic and monetary union on these terms would result in a much more cohesive Europe than is the case at present. This would guarantee not only the sustainability of EMU but also a Europe that would have a more decisive influence in its dealings with the other major economic blocs.

Regional implications of economic and monetary integration

J. Delors

Summary

Since monetary integration progressively eliminates the instrument of exchange rate adjustment between the regions of the economy, this raises a number of issues concerning regional adjustment and convergence, notably:

(i) the question whether the processes of market and monetary integration are likely to be progressive or regressive in their impact on income distribution between regions.

The economic literature points to the presence of several conflicting paradigms, which is why it seems not justified to make any simple predictions, such as that the geographic core will profit at the expense of high-wage areas. It seems necessary to adopt a rather agnostic overall view, unless one is prepared to undertake an extensive and complex multi-factor analysis of the determinants of the evolution of individual regions. Actual trends of comparative regional developments in the industrialized countries would seem to confirm this call for caution;

(ii) the degree of convergence of regional economic performance that may be judged normal or desirable in a double programme of market and monetary integration, or even as a pre-condition to embarking upon such a programme.

It is observed that disparities within the EC at present are considerable, but not incomparably greater than in some mature federations such as the United States, Canada or Switzerland. The political tolerance level for these disparities may be relatively high when language and cultural barriers result in a low propensity to migrate, as is the case in much, but not all (namely Ireland), of the Community. Therefore, the problem of regional disparities, while calling for a serious regional policy effort, would not seem to be an obstacle to a furthering of the EC's economic and monetary integration;

(iii) the lessons of regional policy, as revealed in part by how the public authorities have in recent times been adapting their policy instruments or strategies.

Regional policies of the industrialized countries have been evolving in the light of experience (in the Community and elsewhere) in the direction of a lesser emphasis on automatic, generalized and larger-scale transfers, and with more emphasis on incentives for decentralized local development efforts. Such thinking is also reflected in the current reform of the EC's structural Funds. However, regional policy in the EC is also addressed to specific problems such as cross-frontier infrastructure networks and easing the adjustment costs caused by EC policies such as 1992;

(iv) how the mature federal monetary unions have handled these issues and whether this is helpful in thinking about the future needs of a European monetary union.

The experience of all federal economic and monetary unions is that a diversity of budgetary mechanisms combine in assuring an important 'shock-absorber' function between regions and states with respect to the impact of cyclical and structural shocks. However, the degree to which such shocks are absorbed, and the type of mechanisms used (budget equalization transfers, specific-purpose grants, automatic regional effects of federal taxes and social security) is quite diverse. There is no apparent model on which all integration efforts seem destined to converge. It would thus seem plausible to expect a substantial development of the budgetary function of the EC in the case of a monetary union, but the mechanisms would need to be chosen as a function of the specific needs of the Community at that time.

(i) *The impact of integration on regional convergence.* Economic analysis is currently more agnostic than has sometimes been argued about whether the process of economic integration should lead to regionally regressive or progressive outcomes. Both theoretical and empirical evidence contribute to this new view.

A traditional view, that predicts a regressive concentration of prosperity on rich regions at the geographic centre at the expense of a poorer periphery relies on two arguments: firstly, the locational disadvantage in terms of transport costs of the periphery, and, secondly, the cumulative advantages of economies of scale in large-scale production (in the enterprise, and in the wider economic advantages of large urban agglomerations).

While these arguments have a certain weight, a more qualified view is obtained when a number of newer arguments are introduced. One relates to changes in technology and demand, which witness a faster growth of demand now in the industrialized countries for commodities that have a high value per unit of weight (electrics, electronics, office and data-processing products, chemical and pharmaceutical products, high-quality foods and clothing), with low growth seen in the case of many commodities that have low value per unit of weight (metal products, ores and metals, basic textiles, construction materials). [1] This means that transport costs are becoming, on average, less important in the location of industrial production.

Developments in telecommunications and capital mobility also make it less evident where enterprises will choose to locate their different facilities. The factors just mentioned enhance the sensitivity of investment decisions to the relative levels of costs other than transport and the quality of the business environment in competing locations. In addition, EC initiatives in the 1992 programme and accompanying policies should have a beneficial impact on the transport and telecommunications facilities of the periphery. All the main transport services will be rendered more competitive by the 1992 programme, which will further erode, without of course eliminating, the locational disadvantages of the periphery.

Also relevant to the issue at hand, there has been a fundamental change of emphasis in the economic literature in the analysis of international trade and industrial organization. [2]

The new view gives less importance to the paradigm of comparative advantage as an explanation of trade. While for some sectors the distribution of comparative advantages remain relatively fixed (agriculture, tourism), for much of industry natural endowments are not so important. The alternative paradigm is that trade increasingly consists of a complex pattern of intra-industry specializations between regions and countries of the industrialized world, especially in Western Europe. Competitive advantages are increasingly to be attributed to deliberate strategies of the public authorities relating to market conditions and investments in human capital, R&D and economic infrastructure, and the reactions of mobile corporations to these strategies. The likelihood of systematic imbalances in the impact of market integration is reduced thus diminishing the predictability of winners or losers.

This complex set of influences seems to be consistent with the uncertain pattern of regional economic trends in the industrialized economies. It may be observed, for example, that the United States economy has in recent years seen pronounced economic growth at its geographic edges rather than favouring any dominant centre. There have also been striking changes in the relative economic performance of certain regions: the emergence of much of the south of the United States from economic backwardness, and the recovery of New England. Extreme locational disadvantage in the Far East Asian economies has not prevented spectacular advances in their market shares in North America and Europe.

---

[1] For data, see Table 1.1.3. of 'The economics of 1992', *European Economy*, No 35, March 1988.
[2] See Chapter 8 of 'The economics of 1992' for a fuller presentation of these arguments and further references.

Within Europe, much of the periphery has been growing faster in recent years than the geographic core of the EC. During the present decade, the UK, Spain, Portugal and Italy have grown on average 0.55% per annum faster than the average of Germany, France and the Benelux. Within the larger EC countries the picture is also complex, but one in which some of the arguments advanced above can be recognized. Within Germany the traditional core regions (for example, the Ruhr) have slipped behind, as also have other traditional regions such as Wallonia and North-East France, which are centrally placed in a Community perspective. Meanwhile, new centres of growth have emerged, as in Bavaria and the Rhone valley where these trends are associated with the technological shifts mentioned. Within Italy the problems of the Mezzogiorno have been gradually changing, with prosperity spreading down the Adriatic coast, and the deep problems of Calabria, Campania and Sicily manifestly influenced by non-economic factors. Within the United Kingdom, one has seen parts of Wales and Scotland, whose industrial structures had much in common with Wallonia and North-East France, make rather striking recoveries, in spite of their geographic peripherality.

(ii) *Regional inequality in economic and monetary unions.* A related question is to ask whether the experience of existing monetary unions points to certain minimum standards of regional convergence, which would be implicitly required for viability of the union. Put more strongly still, the question may be put whether there are preconditions of this kind to be met before unions should be formed.

Comparisons of regional GDP or income levels per capita call for care over the comparability of the unit sizes, since the smaller the units the larger the differences tend to be. In comparing the EC and the US, one may observe that the 12 Member States' GDP per capita ranges from 47 in Portugal to 129 in Luxembourg, whereas, in the US, of nine census regions the range of per capita incomes is from 77 in the South-East to 111 on the West Coast. If one looks for a closer comparison with the US census regions, thus merging small units into larger ones, one may note a range between 66 for the Iberian peninsula to 122 for north-eastern Europe (Germany and Denmark).[1]

At the level of small units, one observes a range of 66 for Mississippi to 131 for Alaska and Washington DC, which compares with 45 for the poorest regions of Greece to 237 for Groningen, followed by 195 for Hamburg, 159 for the Ile de France and 155 for Greater London. Both top groups include regions which are conspicuous for their hydrocarbon production, which is a reminder of how these interregional comparisons may be of uncertain policy significance when small units are compared.

---

[1] Detailed regional data are given in *Efficiency, stability and equity* (Annexes D and E), Report of a group of experts presided by T. Padoa-Schioppa, Oxford University Press, 1987.

Other federations have considerable intra-regional differences. In Canada, Newfoundland at one extreme has a GDP per capita of 60, compared to Alberta at 123. In Switzerland, Obwald has a GDP per capita of 76, compared to Zug at 160. In the Federal Republic of Germany, the Saarland has a GDP per capita of 91, compared to Hamburg at 165.

Among the unitary countries, France and the United Kingdom experience disparities which are of the same broad proportions as in Germany, whereas Italy experiences wider disparities, comparable to those of Canada or Switzerland.

Overall these data suggest that the regional disparities in the EC are somewhat greater than in the United States, but not incomparably so. Considerable regional disparities are observed in many economic and monetary unions. However, these simple statistical comparisons have to be qualified by a number of socio-political considerations, of which one of the most important is the propensity for people to migrate between regions and the political system's attitude to migration. Assuming a legal freedom to migrate between States, the important issues are whether the populations have a high propensity to migrate across political frontiers and whether such migration is considered negative, positive or neutral in terms of political values. In the United States the propensity to migrate is high. Across the language frontiers of the EC, the propensity to migrate is today rather low but, politically, mass migratory movements would also be viewed more critically.

A given degree of regional income disparity would call for a more prompt or powerful policy response where the propensity to migrate was high and its political acceptability was low. In practice, the US sees a high propensity but also a high acceptability of migration: therefore there is a relatively relaxed view of interregional disparities. Within the EC, the political acceptability may be lower, but the propensity to migrate is also lower on the whole. It might be expected therefore that the EC could tolerate as great, if not somewhat wider regional disparities than the US. For these reasons the present level of disparities within the EC, while actually the target of policies to reduce them, need not be regarded as a road-block on the path to further integration: especially when it is observed that quite a few backward areas are now catching up or recovering.

Ireland is today the only EC country experiencing a politically uncomfortable rate of emigration. The larger part of this emigration goes to other English-speaking countries (60% to the UK, 25% to North America). This may explain a high propensity to emigrate in the Irish case, but of course it does not ease the economic problem of loss of educational investment in human capital.

The case of Turkey, comparable in some ways to Mexico in relation to the United States, offers a further perspective on these issues. Turkey's income per capita is one third lower than that of Portugal. Turkey's population shows a high propensity to migrate when the regulations of the countries of immigration permit it, no doubt influenced by the extremely low wage levels in Turkey and the almost non-existent social security provisions for much of the population. If the EC labour market were opened to Turkey, that country's potential emigration would appear to be very substantial. In this case it is realistic to discuss the issue of preconditions to joining a European economic and monetary union whereas, among the present members of the EC this debate seems to be much less relevant.

(iii) *Evolution of regional policies.* To identify the essence of new trends in regional policy in the industrialized countries, it is useful to characterize three types of strategy. Practice does not correspond to any of these types in a pure way, but the evolution of their relative importance is significant. The three types are:

(a) Policies that are designed to compensate for institutional rigidities in factor prices or mobility. These are illustrated, on the side of labour, by the reduced social security taxes applied in the South of Italy since 1971 or the regional employment premium system of the United Kingdom of the 1960s (ended in 1977). On the side of capital, there is the widespread tendency to differentiate investment grants regionally, although here also there is nowadays a tendency to apply such subsidies more selectively. These may be called 'neo-classical' regional policies.

(b) Policies that are designed to sustain income and demand in the regions, that for structural or cyclical reasons, may be economically weakened. The main mechanisms here are budget equalization transfer systems, often found in federations, and the automatic interregional redistributive effect of central tax and social security systems. The Reagan Administration in the United States, for example, reduced the importance of these mechanisms, abolishing the federal revenue-sharing system. These may be called 'Keynesian' or 'demand-side' regional policies.

(c) Policies designed to improve the resource base of the region, not only through subsidized investments in physical infrastructure and human capital, but also through incentives to encourage local initiative, even new institutions, to mobilize efforts for the regeneration of weakened regions or communities. The financial flows in these cases may be less than under the first two categories. Policies in several countries, in North America as well as Europe, and in the EC itself, have been heading more in this direction. These may be called 'decentralized supply-side' regional policies.

There are some reasons why an attempt to move more in the direction of the first two types of policy would not seem advisable for the EC in its next phase of systematic development. Regional employment subsidies, on a macroeconomic scale, would risk giving an inappropriate signal to those responsible for labour competitiveness. With the reduction of exchange rate variability, it is important for the wage system to become more responsive to considerations of competitiveness. To suggest that deficiencies in this respect would be compensated by subsidies would be dangerous. As regards the subsidization of capital, the risks to be averted are also those of encouraging inefficient investment, and in particular a capital-intensive bias that may exacerbate employment problems. Experience in some European countries shows this to be not just a theoretical possibility.

As regards the Keynesian type of transfer policies, these are justified basically by one of two arguments, one political and the other economic, neither of which, however, is strongly represented in the EC at the present time. The political case is where a country chooses to write into its constitution, explicitly or implicitly, the objective of having nearly equal standards of public welfare and services in all regions, as seen in Germany or Australia for example. The economic case is where labour mobility is so fluid that moderate differences in public welfare service and tax systems may be sufficient to induce migration which has no other economic justification. (However, in the United States the fluidity of migration between jurisdictions is, to some degree, perceived as a control on the efficiency of local or state public administrations. This is an extreme extension of the paradigm of 'competition between rules.')

In much of the industrialized world considerable scepticism has developed over the effectiveness of the first two categories of centrally developed and financially rather massive systems of regional transfers. This is certainly the case when the policy objective goes beyond purely distributional issues and is addressed to helping weak regions improve their relative economic performance. As a result there has been some shift in favour of policies that rely more on decentralized initiative and a more selective availability of central subsidies. In the United States some striking success stories have been seen in some states — such as Massachusetts, Ohio, Michigan and Pennsylvania — which organized their own revitalization programmes, and succeeded in achieving dramatic reductions in local unemployment levels. In general in the United States, regional income disparities have reduced greatly over the last 50 years, with the South-East moving up from 53 to 86 in relation to the national average, the South-West moving up from 69 to 94 and the Plains from 76 to 96. Federal subsidies can hardly be regarded as the key to this convergence.

In Europe, there have been only hesitant moves in the direction of more decentralized forms of regional policy, although political regionalization has been important in some countries: Spain, Italy, to a lesser degree France, and more emphatically now Belgium. The United Kingdom has seen considerable change in the organization and powers of local government, and this has shown up in the emergence of regional development efforts with new organizational forms. An interesting example is seen in the Strathclyde area of Scotland, where there have been considerable achievements to the credit of the Scottish Development Agency and the Strathclyde Regional Council. These have been supported by the EC structural Funds, including an integrated development programme. The main points here have been a reduced emphasis on grants for large inward investment projects, with more emphasis on the encouragement of local entrepreneurship and labour training, environmental improvement of old urban areas and local institutional developments favouring policy innovation and local initiative. This has features in common with some of the US success stories.

Current reforms of the EC's structural Funds also push in some of these directions. The new regulations entering into force in 1989, applicable until 1993, by which time the real level of annual expenditure will have doubled to ECU 14 billion, call for the preparation of regional development plans, including a regional dimension even in the smaller Member States such as Ireland, Portugal and Greece. For these three countries, and to a lesser degree for Spain also, the Funds will permit a qualitative improvement in economic infrastructure, such as transport and telecommunications; also the expansion, in some cases the establishment for the first time, of extensive manpower training schemes. Another point of emphasis in the reforms is to support the needs of industrial areas defined at the level of quite small regional units, hit by serious problems of restructuring. This should help overcome, *inter alia,* the adjustment problems posed by the 1992 programme.

The budgetary grants of the structural Funds, combined with loans from the European Investment Bank, are due to rise, as a share of the beneficiaries' GNP, to around 5 % in the case of the three smaller countries, and 1½ % in the case of Spain. These amounts will represent substantial percentages of the total financing of these countries' economic infrastructure and manpower training programmes. In terms of the absorptive capacity of the countries concerned, either managerial or from the standpoint of avoiding inflation bottlenecks in sectors such as construction, the funds are on a scale that already represents a considerable challenge for the beneficiaries. The Commission also has particular responsibilities for evaluating the experiences of this new phase of EC structural policy.

(iv) *The case of economic and monetary union.* As and when the system in the Community moves to a fully developed economic and monetary union, one might expect the Community's budgetary mechanisms to develop. The existing systems of the advanced federations have some common features, but it is not evident that between them they offer anything like an ideal model towards which all integration processes must converge.[1]

As regards the most explicit forms of interregional distribution, three federations (Australia, Canada and Germany) have budgetary equalization mechanisms which raise the fiscal capacity of weak states to federally determined minimum standards. However, two federations (United States and Switzerland) have, in contrast, relied more upon specific-purpose grant mechanisms for pursuing policy objectives such as health, education and investment in economic infrastructure. These programmes have a far weaker interregional redistributive power

---

[1] These mechanisms were documented in detail in *The role of public finances in European integration* (Vols I and II), Report of a group of experts presided by Sir D. MacDougall, Commission of the European Communities, 1975.

than the equalization systems. The pattern in these cases is more like a much extended version of the Community's structural Funds and its instruments for pursuing technology policy objectives.

Of course, the central responsibility for defence is a common feature of all the federations, together with its financing by federal taxation, usually including a heavy income-tax component. This always results in a significant degree of automatic and implicit fiscal redistribution between rich and poor states.

Social security systems may also have an important role in automatic interregional redistribution, and this is certainly the case in Germany. However, social security in several cases has strongly decentralized features. Indeed, in the United States social security regimes, especially for health care, probably differ more between the states than is the case between the Member States of the EC.

A common feature, none the less, is that in all federations the different combinations of federal budgetary mechanisms have powerful 'shock-absorber' effects, dampening the amplitude either of economic difficulties or of surges in prosperity of individual states. This is both the product of, and source of the sense of national solidarity which all relevant economic and monetary unions share.[1]

---

[1] 'Relevant' here is meant to exclude the frequently observed cases where very small units voluntarily enter into economic and monetary union with much larger neighbours, sometimes exploiting tax-haven advantages in preference to fiscal integration.

Macro-coordination of fiscal policies in an economic and monetary union in Europe [1]

A. Lamfalussy

Contents

		Page
I —	**Introduction**	93
II —	**Why coordination?**	93
	Argument 1: An appropriate fiscal policy for the EMU	94
	Argument 2: Undue appropriation of EMU savings by one country	95
	Argument 3: Bias towards lack of fiscal restraint in an EMU	97
	Argument 4: Convergence during the transition period to EMU	99
III —	**Conclusions**	100
Appendix I: The experience of federal states and the EEC		102
I —	Introduction and summary of factual findings	102
II —	Federal states	103
	1. Autonomy with respect to expenditure and revenue	103
	2. Constraints on borrowing	104
	3. Size and distribution of expenditure and net borrowing	104
	4. Medium-term control and coordination problems	105
	5. Short-term coordination and macro-management	106
III —	The situation in the Community	107
	1. The Community budget	107
	2. Expenditure and net borrowing concentration	107

---

[1] I would like to thank Claudio Borio for valuable assistance in the preparation and drafting of this paper.

3. Dispersion of net borrowing 107

4. Budgetary transfers 108

IV — How relevant is the experience of federal states? 108

Tables 1-16 109

Appendix II: Market forces and budgetary discipline 125

Tables

Table 1: The expenditure of federal and regional governments, 1987

Table 2: The structure of regional governments' revenue

Table 3: Fiscal indicators of regional governments in the United States, 1985

Table 4: Fiscal indicators of regional governments in the Federal Republic of Germany, 1987

Table 5: Fiscal indicators of regional governments in Canada, 1982

Table 6: Fiscal indicators of regional governments in Australia, 1986-87

Table 7: Fiscal indicators of regional governments in Switzerland, 1986

Table 8: Regional dispersion of fiscal indicators in the United States, 1985

Table 9: Regional dispersion of fiscal indicators in the Federal Republic of Germany, 1987

Table 10: Regional dispersion of fiscal indicators in Canada, 1982

Table 11: Regional dispersion of fiscal indicators in Australia, 1986-87

Table 12: Regional dispersion of fiscal indicators in Switzerland, 1986

Table 13: Fiscal indicators of federal and regional governments in the United States, the Federal Republic of Germany and Canada, 1970-87

Table 14: Fiscal indicators of federal and regional governments in Australia and Switzerland, 1970-87

Table 15: Fiscal indicators of national governments in the EEC, 1988

Table 16: National dispersion of fiscal indicators in the EEC, 1988

I — Introduction

This note attempts to provide a basis for the discussion of the degree of macro-fiscal coordination that might be needed after the establishment of economic and monetary union (EMU) in Europe and during the period of transition towards it.

The note examines several arguments that have been put forward in support of fiscal coordination. Their assessment is based partly on theoretical considerations and partly on lessons drawn from the experience of federal states. As the arguments overlap somewhat, the conclusions bring together the various strands of the analysis.

The note is complemented by two appendices. The first contains a brief review of fiscal arrangements and coordination in federal states, compares the fiscal structure of these states with the current and prospective situation in the EEC and assesses the relevance of their experience for the Community. The second appendix discusses in more detail the question whether market forces can be expected to exert disciplinary effects on fiscal policy and thereby lessen, at least in part, the need for explicit fiscal policy coordination.

The main conclusion of the analysis is that fiscal policy coordination appears to be a vital component of a European EMU. Such coordination would have to be conceived and implemented with two objectives in mind:

— to allow the determination of a global fiscal policy in a way that is sufficiently responsive to evolving domestic and international requirements; and

— to avoid tensions arising from excessive differences between the public sector borrowing requirements of individual member countries.

II — Why coordination?

Basically three partly overlapping arguments have been put forward in support of macro-fiscal coordination in a European EMU, while a fourth one focuses on the difficulties during the transition period:

— the need for an appropriate fiscal policy for the union as a whole;

— the need to avoid disproportionate use of Community savings by one country;

— a possible bias towards lack of fiscal restraint;

— the need for convergence in budgetary positions during the transition period.

Argument 1: An appropriate fiscal policy for the EMU

Description. An economic and monetary union transforms the Community into a single economy. Both for the purpose of internal macroeconomic objectives and in order to be able to participate in the process of international policy coordination, the Community will require a framework for determining a coherent mix of monetary and fiscal policies. The creation of a single currency area implies, by definition, the adoption of a single monetary policy for the Community as a whole. By contrast, if it is assumed that fiscal policy is not centralized, the Community's fiscal stance would merely be the result of the aggregation of unilaterally decided budgetary positions in individual member countries. Consequently, without an explicit coordination of fiscal policies, the Community would not be able to formulate a common fiscal policy, be this with a short-term or longer-term orientation. Monetary policy would be the only instrument available for pursuing macroeconomic objectives.

Assessment. The essential theoretical foundation of this argument is that policy coordination is beneficial to countries whose economies are closely intertwined. Strong linkages between real and financial markets across countries imply that the policies pursued by one country have significant repercussions on economic developments in others. If this interdependence is not taken into account in the policy setting, there is a danger that independent national policy decisions lead to an outcome inferior to that which could have been achieved by a cooperative approach. [1]

A simple illustrative example of the desirability of a jointly decided policy stance in an EMU could run as follows. Even if domestic conditions in the Community called for a fiscal stimulus, each country (region) on its own might have little incentive to shift to a more expansionary fiscal policy (for instance through tax cuts). Each would fear that the policy change would lead to a deterioration in its budgetary position with little gain in output, since a large part of the induced income effect would be transferred via higher 'imports' to other Community countries. If, by contrast, all countries decided jointly to lower taxes, the expansionary income effects would reinforce each other and stimulate economic activity

---

[1] The benefits deriving from coordination in the presence of interdependence are in general supported by the theoretical literature. This is what in game-theory terms is known as the 'cooperative' solution, where every player (e.g. a country) can be better off relative to the 'non-cooperative' solution where each one acts in isolation. For some examples see P. R. Krugman (1987), 'Economic integration in Europe', Annex A to *Efficiency, stability and equity* (Padoa-Schioppa Report), EC, especially page A-19; or, with particular reference to the present EMS arrangements, P. De Grauwe (1985), *Fiscal policies in the EMS: A strategic analysis*, International economics research paper No 53. These studies also make it clear that, while establishing the need for coordination is relatively simple, specific rules depend critically on detailed assumptions about national objectives, the workings of the economy and, implicitly, the ability to control budgetary variables. While the existence of benefits is beyond dispute, there has recently been some scepticism about their magnitude — see, e.g. G. Oudiz and J. Sachs (1984), 'Macroeconomic policy coordination among the industrial economies', *Brookings papers on economic activity*. Note also that the specific question of fiscal policy coordination in an EMU has not as yet been examined within this analytical framework.

with smaller adverse effects on budgetary positions. The creation of a single market and a single currency area greatly strengthens the linkages between individual member countries, thereby heightening the importance of such common decisions within the Community. [1]

The above example illustrates how the need for coordination in a European EMU would arise from a possible misalignment of national (i.e. regional) fiscal policies. There are in principle two types of solution. One would be to use the Community budget to correct any distortions in the aggregate fiscal policy resulting from independent national decisions; the other would be to intervene at the source, by limiting the scope of national discretion in determining budgetary positions.

The problem is clearly analogous to that faced by federal states where regional governments have sizeable budgets. [2] With the exception of Australia, all the federal states examined have tended to discard the second solution. Their macro-fiscal policy is conducted in the context of their sizeable federal budgets, while budgetary policies of individual states are left primarily to the discretion of their governments. This type of solution seems to avoid unnecessary friction with regional authorities. This solution, however, is out of the question for a prospective European EMU because its central budget is not expected to exceed 3 % of GDP. This compares with federal expenditures that range from around 10 to 30 % of GDP. The size of the Community budget would clearly be too small to provide for an adequate *masse de manoeuvre* for an effective macro-fiscal policy. As a result, in an EMU an appropriate aggregate fiscal policy could not be determined without impinging on the autonomy of national budgetary positions, whether for purely domestic reasons or for the purpose of international policy coordination.

Argument 2: Undue appropriation of EMU savings by one country

Description. There is a danger that without coordinated fiscal policies individual member countries might run excessive national deficits and absorb a disproportionate proportion of Community savings. This lack of convergence would impose unwelcome costs on other countries.

---

[1] It is clearly also possible to construct examples with opposite biases, by pointing to crowding-out effects through increases in interest rates in other countries or to the possibility of higher inflation. The precise results will always depend on the specific assumptions made about the objectives of the authorities and the transmission mechanisms involved. The general point, however, remains valid: greater interdependence in principle raises the potential benefits of coordination.

[2] The implicit recognition of the existence of a coordination problem among regional governments has been the basis for traditional arguments that in a federation the stabilization function should be conferred on the federal government — see R. A. Musgrave and P. B. Musgrave (1973), *Public finance in theory and practice,* McGraw-Hill.

Assessment. A similar argument has traditionally been made in support of capital restrictions designed to ensure that domestic savings are invested in the national economy. Obviously, in a Community with a single market where goods, services and capital can move freely, the 'earmarking' of domestic savings for domestic use would not be a meaningful concept. With fully integrated financial markets any government borrowing would be financed voluntarily, though at a price determined in the market. Only if markets persistently underpriced their lending to governments, or if the fiscal authorities could tax other countries' citizens, directly or indirectly, could there be a danger of one country 'unduly exploiting' the savings of the Community.

Since it can be ruled out that even upon completion of EMU individual governments will be able to tax residents outside their borders directly, an inappropriate (i.e. involuntary) use of private non-resident savings could only occur if circumstances forced all, or at least some, citizens of other Community countries to bear some part of the required financing costs.

One way that this could happen would be if a particular government encountered refinancing difficulties. Since a certain part of claims on that government might result from earlier voluntary lending by residents of other Community countries, there could be strong political pressure throughout the Community to bail out the government in financial trouble. Such pressure might be difficult to resist, especially if the country facing refinancing problems was relatively large and if the EMU implied stronger solidarity ties. Through these bail-out arrangements, citizens of other member countries would effectively be taxed and their savings 'exploited' by the national government concerned.

Another possibility might be that excessive borrowing by one country would raise the interest rate level throughout the Community and crowd out investment in countries where the interest rate would otherwise have been lower.[1] Finally, an 'exploitation' of savings might also occur if one country's borrowing either exerted pressure for a more accommodative monetary policy (resulting in a higher rate of inflation throughout the Community) or led to a depreciation of the Community's exchange rate *vis-à-vis* third currencies (entailing terms-of-trade losses for all Community residents).

The strength of these arguments largely depends on whether, without policy coordination and explicit constraints on national budgets, market forces could exert sufficiently strong disciplinary effects on national governments' fiscal behaviour. There is reason to be sceptical about the adequacy of sanctions imposed by the market mechanisms (see Appendix II). Rather than operating directly (through the higher borrowing cost to the government, partly associated with credit risk differentiation),[2] market forces tend to operate indirectly (through political

---

[1] This argument implicitly assumes that markets do not work efficiently in this case in the sense that the private return on such financing flows exceeds the social return because of the displacement of potentially more useful investment spending, i.e. the market 'underprices' such financing from the social viewpoint.

[2] Evidence from Canada and the United States suggests that markets differentiate between the various regions as regards credit risk.

pressures resulting from the perceived costs of the fiscal stance on the economy) (see Appendix II). Their effectiveness could be enhanced, however, by explicit no-bail-out provisions, which would encourage greater prudence on the part of both borrowers and lenders.

The general absence of constraints on the budgetary policies of regional authorities in federal states would seem to suggest that there is little concern about an excessive use of savings by one region at the expense of the others. Nevertheless, the experience of federal states may be of relatively limited guidance in this respect (see Appendix I). Not only have EEC Member States historically shown markedly divergent attitudes towards the merits of fiscal orthodoxy, but the Community is also unique in having a major fiscal imbalance in one of the large regions.

Argument 3: Bias towards lack of fiscal restraint in an EMU

Description. It is sometimes argued that in an EMU constraints on national budgets would be needed to avoid an excessively lax fiscal stance for the Community as a whole. A tendency towards fiscal expansion could lead to pressures on the monetary authorities to adopt a more accommodative monetary policy. If this pressure was not resisted, it would jeopardize control over the price level. If resisted, interest rates would rise, thereby crowding out investment and undermining longer-term growth prospects. In either case, monetary policy would be unduly compromised.

Assessment. This argument, which has never been spelled out in detail, appears to be essentially a variation of Argument 2. There would seem to be at least three theoretical reasons for less fiscal restraint in an economic and monetary union.

The first has to do with the fact that the EMU would rule out changes in intra-union exchange rate parities. To the extent that the threat of a depreciation of the domestic currency as a result of excessive fiscal expansion had acted as a constraint under the EMS arrangements, its disappearance would encourage financial indiscipline.

The second is that, as outlined above, expectations might arise that the union would tend to make assistance from other member governments more likely in the event of debt-servicing problems. Counting on this assistance, a government might feel less constrained and markets might not properly signal the emergence of difficulties through appropriate risk premiums.[1]

A third reason might be that a move to EMU could entail additional demand for government spending. In the poorer regions in particular, claims could emerge for

---

[1] A situation of this kind would seem partly to explain the difficulties in restraining regional government expenditure in Italy. As noted earlier, in Canada and the United States markets differentiate among the various regions in terms of credit risk, suggesting that bailing-out is not perceived as automatic.

comparable levels of government services and, more generally, comparable living standards. Quite apart from political pressures, in a situation of greater capital and labour mobility there would be clear limits to the possibility of raising tax revenue as higher tax rates would lead to a loss in the regional tax base. Similarly, the possible negative output and employment effects associated with the more competitive environment in the EMU and the disappearance of exchange rate adjustments could give rise to demands for specific assistance over and above what is at present allowed for in the calculations of future Community transfers. Resistance to the implied higher tax burden at the Community level would result in a larger deficit.[1]

On the other hand, fears of a bias towards lack of fiscal restraint may be exaggerated. A move to EMU might in fact increase the constraints on fiscal expansion precisely for national governments with a track record of excessively expansionary fiscal policies. For these are the governments that have tended to monetize their deficits and had recourse to direct controls on domestic and international financial transactions with a view to keeping financing costs artificially low (e.g. Italy, Spain, Greece and Portugal). They therefore stand to lose most from the creation of a union.[2] The abolition of restrictions on residents' purchases of foreign assets would reduce the demand for domestic securities. Similarly, with the liberalization of financial services in the Community the battery of domestic controls which directly or indirectly increase the demand for government liabilities and/or reduce their rate of return would need to be largely dismantled.[3] The abolition of these restrictions, whose link to the deficit is sometimes only vaguely perceived, would be equivalent to the elimination of a 'hidden tax'. By pointing to the true costs of the deficit more clearly, it might tend to encourage discipline.

The available evidence from federal systems would not seem to suggest a bias towards lack of fiscal restraint. Over the period examined, in all cases except one there has been no apparent *medium-term* problem of control of regional expenditures and deficits, which have not tended to grow relative to their federal counterparts. Moreover, beyond the provisions defining the areas of responsibility of federal and regional authorities in the expenditure and tax spheres, there are no *federally imposed* constraints on regional government borrowing. A key aspect of all the federal systems considered is the denial (or strict limitation) of access to central bank financing to regional governments in an attempt to subject them to the discipline of the market. It remains unclear, however, what are the factors ultimately accounting for the apparent lack of a bias in the states examined. This

---

[1] The creation of an EMU could also lead to pressures for reductions in the average level of tax rates in the absence of effective tax rate coordination, as countries with higher than average tax rates may face an erosion of their tax base in favour of those with lower than average rates.

[2] The implicit tax levied through controls on domestic financial holdings alone may be quite large. See, for example *OECD Economic Survey, Spain,* 1986.

[3] Otherwise, quite apart from any legal obligations, the domestic financial industry, notably banks, would face serious cost disadvantages in the face of increased competitive pressures. *Ibidem.*

raises doubts about the extent to which their experience can be of guidance for foreseeable conditions within a European EMU (see Appendix I).

Argument 4: Convergence during the transition period to EMU

Description. A certain degree of convergence in the budgetary positions of member countries is a prerequisite for the transition towards a monetary union. Only if fiscal policies are better aligned among Community countries will it be possible to reduce the need for exchange rate realignments and gradually prepare the ground for an irrevocable fixing of exchange rates. The desirability of a financially disciplined and prudent fiscal stance calls for convergence towards the budgetary positions of the more fiscally conservative countries.

Assessment. The need for convergence (and hence, implicitly, for some form of fiscal coordination) depends on the degree to which divergent fiscal policies are thought to affect exchange rate relationships. Unfortunately, economic theory and empirical research do not provide unequivocal answers on either the size or, indeed, the direction of the pressure that fiscal shocks can exert on exchange rate parities. They merely suggest that factors such as the impact of fiscal policies on interest rates and on the current account are important, and that neither of these can be determined without knowing whether the monetary authorities will monetize the deficit or not. Thus, for instance, expectations of monetization of an increase in government borrowing can lead to a depreciation of the currency, whereas a non-accommodative monetary stance could cause an appreciation by increasing the interest rate differential in favour of domestic assets.

If economic theory emphasizes that the precise effects of divergent fiscal policies can only be analysed with reference to actual circumstances, it also indicates that changes in fiscal policy will in general have important repercussions in asset markets. This view is confirmed by practical experience within the Community and, perhaps even more clearly, by the discussion of the role of fiscal policy in the context of G-7 efforts to achieve a greater degree of exchange rate stability among the main currencies. Thus, measures to coordinate fiscal policies within the Community and to enhance their compatibility with a view to exchange rate cohesion would greatly facilitate the Community's approach to EMU.

While the importance of such measures is beyond doubt, it is more difficult to define in practice what the appropriate degree of fiscal policy convergence should be. As long as countries differ considerably in the structure and relative size of their budgetary expenditure and revenue, in their sectoral saving/investment propensities and in their central banks' ability to resist pressures for monetization, there would be no economic justification for broadly uniform budgetary positions.

As far as the direction of convergence is concerned, the shift towards fiscal consolidation for domestic purposes in a number of countries suggests that convergence towards the position of the more fiscally conservative countries would be desirable.

III — Conclusions

A review of fiscal arrangements in federal states and of their experience with fiscal coordination suggests that there generally exist few constraints on the budgetary policies of sub-federal governments and that concerns about fiscal coordination have not ranked highly. At the same time, there are at least two major differences between conditions in these countries and in the EEC which call for caution in deriving possible lessons for appropriate fiscal arrangements in the Community.

Firstly, with the possible exception of Canada, there have been no large and persistent differences in the fiscal behaviour of the member states in the various federations. This is in marked contrast to the widely divergent 'propensities to run deficits' prevailing in the EEC. Secondly, the Community budget will, in the foreseeable future, remain a much smaller proportion of total public spending in Europe than the federal budget as a percentage of total public expenditure in other contemporary systems.

Much of the fiscal convergence achieved in federal states is probably the result of tradition and history — factors which in Europe appear to favour divergence. Nor would it be wise to rely principally on the free functioning of financial markets to iron out any excessive differences in fiscal behaviour between member countries. It is unlikely that the interest premium to be paid by a high deficit member country would be very large, since market participants would tend to act on the assumption that the EMU solidarity would prevent the 'bankruptcy' of the deficit country. In addition, to the extent that there was a premium, it is doubtful that it would reduce significantly the deficit country's propensity to borrow. There is, therefore, a serious risk that, in the absence of constraining policy coordination, major fiscal imbalances would persist.

This raises two concerns which differ according to the stage reached in the progress towards a fully-fledged EMU. During the transition period (stage two), the greater part of the burden of trying to respect the stricter intra-Community exchange rate commitments would have to be borne by the monetary policies of individual member countries. This task would be harder to fulfil than under the present ERM arrangements and failure to succeed would have more devastating consequences for the whole integration process than it would today.

If the stage of irrevocably locked exchange rates had been reached (stage three), the emergence, or the persistence, of a significant public sector borrowing requirement in one or more of the member countries would mean that real interest rates would be higher in the other member countries than they would otherwise have been. Private investment in these countries would thus be 'crowded out' by the fiscal policies of the deficit countries. This could lead not only to the emergence of intra-EMU political tension, but also to pressure on the federal monetary authority to relax monetary policy.

The combination of a small Community budget with large, independently determined national budgets leads to the conclusion that, in the absence of fiscal coordination, the global fiscal policy of the EMU would be the accidental outcome of decisions taken by Member States. There would simply be no Community-wide macroeconomic fiscal policy.

As a result, the only global macroeconomic tool available within the EMU would be the common monetary policy implemented by the European central banking system. Even within a closed economy, this would be an unappealing prospect as it would imply the serious danger of an inappropriate fiscal/monetary policy mix and pressures tending to divert monetary policy from the longer-run objective of preserving price stability. But such a situation would appear even less tolerable once the EMU was regarded as part and parcel of the world economy, with a clear obligation to cooperate with the United States and Japan in an attempt to preserve (or restore) an acceptable pattern of external balances and to achieve exchange rate stabilization. To have even the smallest chance of reaching these objectives, all cooperating partners will need flexibility in their policy mixes.

On the basis of these arguments, fiscal policy coordination would appear to be a vital element of a European EMU and of the process towards it. Appropriate arrangements should therefore be put in place which would allow the gradual emergence, and the full operation once the EMU is completed, of a Community-wide fiscal policy. Such arrangements should also aim at avoiding disruptive differences between the public sector borrowing requirements of individual member countries.

Appendix I

The experience of federal states and the EEC

I — Introduction and summary of factual findings

When searching for some empirical evidence to assess the various arguments for coordination, it seems natural, for want of a better alternative, to turn to the experience of federal states. This might provide some, albeit crude, parallels with possible conditions within a European EMU. What follows considers five countries (the United States, the Federal Republic of Germany, Canada, Australia and Switzerland) before looking at the present situation in the Community and assessing the relevance of the comparison.

The key findings that emerge from the factual analysis are the following:

— federal states differ markedly with respect to the degree of autonomy enjoyed by sub-federal governments in the fiscal sphere; it is particularly great in Switzerland, Canada and the United States and much less in Germany and Australia;

— federally-decided limits on the borrowing of regional governments exist only in Australia, though in both Germany and the United States there are restrictions imposed by the states themselves;

— with the exception of Germany, where it is in any case of negligible importance, in no country do regional authorities have access to direct central bank financing;

— except for Australia, over the period examined no country appears to have experienced serious problems with, or been much concerned about, medium-term control over sub-federal budgetary positions;

— concern has at times been expressed, however, about an inappropriate overall fiscal policy stance arising from independent decisions taken at the regional level;

— the size of the federal budget has generally allowed these conflicts to be resolved with a minimum of interference in sub-federal budgetary policies.

From a structural viewpoint the main differences between the EEC and the federal states are the following:

— the much smaller size of the Community (central) budget;

— greater concentration of expenditures and, especially, borrowing needs in a few 'regions';

— greater dispersion of net borrowing and indebtedness in relation to regional variables;

— much smaller inter-regional transfers.

II — Federal states

With respect to the degree of autonomy enjoyed at sub-federal government levels, the federal states in the sample exhibit strong variations. In Switzerland, Canada and the United States decisions are very decentralized. They are much less so in Germany and Australia.

1. *Autonomy with respect to expenditure and revenue*

The spheres of *expenditure* over which federal and sub-federal governments have control are normally specified, to varying degrees, in the constitution, with at least defence and social security tending to be the responsibility of the federal government.[1] Beyond that, there are no statutory limits on the expenditure decisions of sub-federal government authorities (henceforth also referred to as 'regional' governments).

A very rough indication of the degree of expenditure autonomy of regional governments can be derived from a look at the breakdown of total government spending (see Table 1). This indicates that the aggregate *expenditure* of regional authorities is always at least one third of total consolidated government expenditure. In two countries, Canada and Switzerland, it actually exceeds the expenditure of the federal government, even when the latter is measured gross of transfers to the regional governments.

The *revenue* autonomy of regional governments varies widely across the sample (see Table 2). The degree of autonomy is particularly high in Canada, the United States and Switzerland, where some three quarters of total revenue comes from either taxes for which the regional authorities are free to choose the base and/or rate, or from other independent sources. It is very low in Germany, where less than one fifth of total revenue is accounted for in this way. In Australia the states' autonomous revenue amounts to about one third of the total, a proportion closer to the German figure.

Tax sources over which sub-federal governments retain a significant measure of discretion account for about half of their total revenue in Canada, the United States and Switzerland, about one third in Australia and a negligible proportion in Germany. In the latter case, the tax revenue of the *Länder* is practically all in the form of tax-sharing agreements, the proceeds coming from taxes for which both base and rate are uniform throughout the Bund.[2]

---

[1] Switzerland is the only case where sub-federal authorities share a substantial portion of social security responsibilities.

[2] Shared tax arrangements of a broadly similar kind are also sizeable in Australia, where they account for about one third of sub-federal governments' revenue. They exist but are of little significance in Switzerland.

Federal governments contribute to the revenue of regional units through *federal grants*. Together with tax-sharing agreements these are the main redistributive mechanism to compensate for regional variations in the standard of living. As a proportion of sub-federal revenue, grants are highest in Australia (about one third) and lowest in Germany and Switzerland (not exceeding some 15 %).

2. Constraints on borrowing

In none of the countries considered are there any federally-imposed statutory limits on the *borrowing* capacity of regional entities. However, in Australia the Loan Council — an institution *de facto* dominated by the federal government — in effect sets both an aggregate borrowing limit for all government levels and decides on its distribution amongst them.[1] In both Germany and the United States[2] states have included borrowing restrictions in their own constitutions.[3] They are generally defined as (qualified) balanced-budget amendments or ceilings on borrowing (the United States) or as a limitation of borrowing for investment purposes (the United States and Germany). In Canada and Switzerland there are no statutory limits of any kind.

Regional governments do not generally have access to *central bank financing*. The exception to the rule is Germany, where, however, these facilities are of minor significance.[4] Beyond these constraints, central banks do not normally influence the financing choices of the various levels of government, although at least the Bundesbank plays a consultative role through a variety of mechanisms.

Federal restrictions on *foreign currency borrowing* exist only in Australia, where the Loan Council regulates the foreign borrowing of the states. In Germany and Switzerland the sub-federal governments have not turned to international capital markets. Canadian provinces have made the largest use of this option.[5]

3. Size and distribution of expenditure and net borrowing

Tables 3 to 7 provide key indicators of the relative size of the regional fiscal units in the various countries and Tables 8 to 12 of the degree of dispersion relative to regional variables.

---

[1] For a detailed explanation of the history and institutional arrangements of the Loan Council, see R. Mathews, 'The development of commonwealth-state financial arrangements in Australia' (1988), *Yearbook of Australia 1988*, Australian Bureau of Statistics.

[2] In the United States the only exception is Connecticut.

[3] The federal government in Germany, with the consent of a majority of the states represented in the Bundesrat, has some limited power to set temporary limits on borrowing by the *Länder* for conjunctural stabilization purposes. This power was exercised only in 1973.

[4] In Switzerland, the central bank may rediscount paper issued by the *Cantons*.

[5] At the end of the 1983–84 fiscal year, for instance, some CAD 10 billion of the outstanding bonds and debentures of the provinces, or almost one quarter of the total, had been raised in foreign markets. About 60 % of total foreign borrowing had been done in the United States.

The distribution of *expenditure* in relation to *union* variables amongst regions tends to be more concentrated in Canada and Australia than in the other countries, with the United States being the country where it is most diffused. In Canada, for instance, Ontario and Quebec account for one third of total consolidated government spending, or some 15% of GDP. By contrast, in the United States only the top 35 states account for a similar proportion of government spending, or some 13% of GDP.

When expenditure is measured in relation to *regional* output (see Tables 8 to 12), all countries show a significant dispersion, with a range of at least some 10 percentage points. Some countries have regions which are clear outliers.

With the exception of Australia, the aggregate *net borrowing* requirement of the regions tends to be smaller than that of the federal government. In the United States and Switzerland sub-federal levels are in fact in surplus.

The degree of dispersion in borrowing needs in relation to *union* output is highest in Canada (see Tables 3 to 7). For the year considered (1982), the net borrowing requirement of Ontario was around 0.3% of Canadian GDP, while Alberta enjoyed a surplus that was equivalent to some 0.5% of national GDP.[1]

The degree of dispersion in net borrowing measured relative to *regional* variables varies significantly across countries (see Tables 8 to 12). It is relatively limited in Australia and Germany, the more centralized countries and, to a lesser extent, in Switzerland. It is especially high in Canada. In the United States there are some outliers. This general picture is also broadly confirmed by the dispersion in interest payments or outstanding debt stocks, which serve as a proxy for the evolution of borrowing over time. Evidence from Canada[2] and the United States indicates that the capital market differentiates between the credit risk of the various regions.

4. Medium-term control and coordination problems

In no country, with the exception of Australia, does experience seem to suggest serious problems with medium-term control over regional spending and deficits.

Tables 13 and 14 indicate no discernible tendency for either the aggregate net lending or the expenditure of regional authorities to grow over time relative to their federal counterparts. In the United States and Switzerland, as already mentioned, there have tended to be surpluses or very small deficits, either because

---

[1] Because of statistical difficulties only the broad orders of magnitude are relevant.
[2] Judging from their international borrowing, the credit ratings of the provinces range from medium to the highest grade.

of explicit self-imposed constraints (the United States) or because of a historical belief in the merits of fiscal orthodoxy (Switzerland). In both, the close association between spending and revenue autonomy has probably also played a part. In Canada and Germany net borrowing of the regions has, if anything, shown a more restrained performance than its federal counterpart.[1] Expenditure exhibits a broadly similar pattern at the two government levels. By contrast, in Australia there have been protracted periods of relatively fast growth in the expenditure and net borrowing of the states.

Consistent with this broad picture, the only country where there would appear to have been much concern about the coordination issue is Australia. The Loan Council has been the main instrument through which the federal government has attempted to enforce restraint on state governments so as to counteract a tendency for their finances to thwart efforts at fiscal consolidation.[2] This centralization has meant that financial markets have not been encouraged to differentiate between the debts of the various government units, in sharp contrast to the Canadian case. Some concern would also seem to exist in Germany, where tax powers are highly centralized and there are a number of institutional, albeit mainly consultative, arrangements for coordination.[3]

5. Short-term coordination and macro-management

The fact that concerns about medium-term coordination do not appear to have ranked highly does not imply a lack of episodes or periods of tension. Recently, for instance, the Canadian federal authorities have expressed concerns about the rate of growth of spending in Ontario associated with its booming regional economy, while western provinces, damaged by the oil price fall and agricultural difficulties, have been unable to cut expenditure in the face of the recession-induced decline in revenue. This pattern of events has partly hampered fiscal consolidation efforts.[4]

Similarly, in all countries, to the extent that macro-management is attempted at all, it is at the federal rather than at the regional level The size of the federal budget seems to have been generally sufficient to allow a minimum of interference with regional budgetary policies.

---

[1] In Canada this does not seem to have been true in the 1960s, however.

[2] In the late 1970s and early 1980s control by the Loan Council was somewhat relaxed. At the same time, states started borrowing in technical forms not covered by the Council's authority. In 1985 the coverage was broadened. For more details, see R. Mathews, *op. cit.*

[3] One such body is the 'Finanzplanungsrat' which coordinates the budgetary policies of the various government levels. The body is composed of the Federal Minister of Finance (Chairman), the finance ministers of the various *Länder* and representatives of the *Gemeinden*. The Bundesbank regularly participates in the meetings. The institution's recommendations, however, are not binding. For the period 1985-87 they took the form of a generalized indicative limit of 3% on the growth of spending of all government units, i.e. below the projected growth of annual income.

[4] See *OECD Economic Surveys,* Canada, 1988.

III — The situation in the Community

Tables 15 and 16 summarize the existing situation in the EEC. There are essentially four structural features that deserve attention in comparison to federal states:

1. the relatively small size of the Community budget;

2. the generally greater degree of concentration of both expenditures and net borrowing in a few 'regions';

3. the historically greater degree of dispersion of net borrowing in relation to regional variables;

4. the small role of inter-country budgetary transfers.

1. The Community budget

The present size of the Community budget is some 1% of EEC GDP. Even after the creation of a single market, it is apparently not expected to exceed 3%. That is clearly much smaller than the size of federal budgets in the countries examined, regardless of whether transfers are included or netted out, which range from around 10 to 30%.

2. Expenditure and net borrowing concentration

The greater concentration of expenditure and net borrowing in the Community is in large measure a reflection of the relative size of the EEC countries, with the big four accounting for some 80% of total EEC GDP and a number of small ones having negligible weight. Such a configuration makes the EEC markedly different from the United States and Switzerland and more similar to Canada and Australia. The greater concentration is also partly dependent on the small size of the Community budget, which does not substitute for member governments' expenditure in the same way as the central budget does in federations. But with regard to net borrowing, it is particularly affected by the existence of a large and persistent deficit in one of the big four countries, namely Italy. That country's deficit alone, at some 2% of EEC GDP, is equal to over 40% of the aggregate EEC deficit.

3. Dispersion of net borrowing

Measured relative to regional output, it appears that the dispersion of net borrowing is greater in the EEC, with Canada being the country that most closely resembles the Community. This dispersion has clearly persisted over time, as indicated by the figures on outstanding stocks of debt and on interest payments. A broadly similar picture is obtained by relating net borrowing positions to revenues.

4. Budgetary transfers

The relatively small present and prospective role of budgetary transfers in the Community is ultimately a reflection of the lack of political unity, which imposes major constraints on the acceptability of redistributional transfers between member countries. It is partly responsible for some of the differences between the Community and other federations just discussed, notably the relative size of the central budget and, possibly, the regional variations in the size of deficits.

IV — How relevant is the experience of federal states?

The review of fiscal arrangements in federal states and of their experience with fiscal coordination has suggested that with the exception of one country few constraints exist on the budgetary policies of sub-federal governments and concerns about fiscal coordination have not ranked highly. At the same time, a number of considerations call for caution in drawing possible lessons for appropriate fiscal arrangements in the Community.

Firstly, all the federal states examined possess a large central budget relative to GDP which can be used to set the short or long-term macro-fiscal stance for the federation. By contrast, the prospective size and structure of the Community budget would make it highly unsuitable for that purpose. Therefore, any distortion in the aggregate fiscal stance of the Community could not be corrected without impinging on the autonomy to determine national budgetary positions.

Secondly, the EEC appears to have presented historically a significantly greater degree of dispersion in budgetary positions than most federal states, with Canada being the only possible parallel. It is furthermore unique in having a sizeable and persistent imbalance concentrated in one large region (Italy). The experience of the federal states may, therefore, not be particularly illuminating with regard to the tensions that a situation of this kind might generate in an EMU.

Thirdly, none of the federal states examined provides guidance for the problems that could be faced during the transition period towards an EMU or as a result of its establishment.

TABLE 1

The expenditure of federal and regional governments, [1]1987

Country	Federal expenditure Gross[3]	Federal expenditure Net[4]	Federal transfers	Sub-federal expenditure[2]
	% of total consolidated expenditure			
United States	70.8	64.0	7.4	36.0
FR of Germany	63.9	60.6	3.2	39.4
Canada	51.0	41.6	9.4	58.4
Australia	69.1	48.1	21.0	51.9
Switzerland	29.6	n.a.	n.a.	70.4[5]

[1] For the United States, state and local governments; for the Federal Republic of Germany, *Länder* and *Gemeinden;* for Canada, provincial or territorial and local governments including hospital sector (i.e. the PLH sector). For Australia, state and local governments. Budget definitions which include public trading enterprises. For Switzerland, *Cantons* and *Gemeinden*.

[2] Consolidated.

[3] Including transfers to regional authorities.

[4] Excluding transfers to regional authorities.

[5] Not consolidated as data on transfers between *Cantons* and *Gemeinden* were not available.

Sources: Council of Economic Advisers, *Economic Report of the President,* 1988; Bundesministerium der Finanzen, *Finanzberichte;* National sources for Canada; Australian Bureau of Statistics, Government financial estimates and budget papers; and Eidgenössische Finanzverwaltung, *Öffentliche Finanzen der Schweiz*.

TABLE 2

The structure of regional governments' revenue

Item	United States	Germany	Canada	Australia	Switzerland
			%		
Taxes					
Exclusive taxes[1]	18.6	—	—	—	10.0
Competing taxes[2]	30.9	—	29.2	31.8	43.5
Sub-federal surcharges[3]	—	—	24.0	—	—
Shared taxes[4]	—	70.3	—	33.9	5.8
Total	49.5	70.3	53.2	65.7	59.3
Other sources					
Federal grants	22.3	13.5	20.4	30.4	14.8
Non-fiscal income	28.2	16.2	26.4	3.9	25.8
Total revenue	100.0	100.0	100.0	100.0	100.0
Memorandum item:					
Autonomous sources[5]	77.7	16.2	79.6	35.7	79.4

[1] The sub-federal government has the sole right to tax the source of income or transactions concerned and is free to choose both the tax base and the rate.

[2] The sub-federal government is free to choose both the base and the rate, but has no exclusive right to tax the source of income or transaction concerned.

[3] The sub-federal government is free to choose the rate but not the base.

[4] The tax base and rates are uniform throughout the federation and the tax proceeds are distributed according to certain rules among the various sub-federal government levels.

[5] Exclusive taxes, competing taxes, sub-federal surcharges and non-fiscal income. The distribution between autonomous sources of revenue and the rest is obviously a matter of degree. The categories chosen serve only as a crude approximation.

Source: EC, 'The distribution of economic powers in the public finances of federal economic and monetary unions', internal working paper.

TABLE 3

Fiscal indicators of regional governments[1] in the United States, 1985

Region	Expenditure[2]	Net lending[3]	Expenditure[2]	Regional GDP
	% of national GDP/GNP		% of total	% of union GDP
California	1.73	0.13	4.6	12.5
New York	1.50	0.13	4.0	8.5
Texas	0.83	0.07	2.2	7.8
Illinois	0.63	0.06	1.7	5.0
Pennsylvania	0.61	0.08	1.6	4.4
Next 4 states:				
Average	0.55	0.05	1.5	3.9
Range	0.47-0.58	0.04-0.05	1.3-1.5	3.6-4.2
Next 14 states:				
Average	0.27	0.02	0.7	2.0
Range	0.20-0.36	0.00-0.04	0.5-0.9	1.3-2.7
Next 13 states:				
Average	0.15	0.01	0.4	1.0
Range	0.10-0.19	– 0.0-0.04	0.3-0.4	0.6-1.6
Next 15 states:				
Average	0.06	0.00	0.2	0.4
Range	0.03-0.09	– 0.0-0.0	0.1-0.3	0.2-0.6
Total[4]	12.9	1.6	36.9	100.0
Federal Government[4]	22.1[5]	– 4.9	63.1[5]	—

[1] State and local governments, consolidated, fiscal year.
[2] Direct general expenditure.
[3] General revenue minus direct general expenditure.
[4] National accounts basis.
[5] Expenditure net of transfers.

Sources: US Department of Commerce, *Statistical abstract of the USA*, 1988; and *Survey of current business*, May 1988; Council of Economic Advisers, *Economic Report of the President*, 1988; and own estimates.

TABLE 4

Fiscal indicators of regional governments[1] in the Federal Republic of Germany, 1987

Region	Expenditure	Net lending	Expenditure	Regional GDP
	% of national GNP		% of total	% of union GDP
Nordrhein-Westfalen	4.7	− 0.3	9.7	26.2
Bayern	3.0	− 0.1	6.2	18.0
Baden-Württemberg	2.7	− 0.1	5.6	16.1
Niedersachsen	2.0	− 0.2	4.0	9.7
Hessen	1.7	− 0.1	3.5	10.0
Berlin	1.1	− 0.05	2.2	3.8
Rheinland-Pfalz	1.0	− 0.1	2.0	5.4
Schleswig-Holstein	0.7	− 0.1	1.5	3.5
Hamburg	0.6	− 0.1	1.3	4.5
Saarland	0.3	− 0.05	0.6	1.5
Bremen	0.3	− 0.05	0.6	1.4
Total	17.9	− 1.1	37.2	100.0
Federal Government	30.2[2]	− 1.4	62.8[2]	—

[1] *Länder* and *Gemeinden*, consolidated.
[2] Expenditure net of transfers, calculated as general government expenditure, including social security, minus expenditure of regional governments.

Source: Statistisches Bundesamt Wiesbaden, *Finanz und Steuern,* Fachserie 14, Reihe 2.

TABLE 5

Fiscal indicators of regional governments[1] in Canada, 1982

Regions	Expenditure[2]	Net lending[2]	Expenditure[2]	Regional GDP
	% of national GDP		% of total	% of union GDP[3]
Ontario	8.0	− 0.3	18.5	38.4
Quebec	7.1	− 0.1	16.6	22.3
Alberta	3.4	0.5	7.8	13.7
British Columbia	2.8	− 0.1	6.5	11.4
Saskatchewan	1.0	0.02	2.4	4.0
Manitoba	1.0	− 0.04	2.3	3.8
Nova Scotia	0.9	− 0.1	2.0	2.4
New Brunswick	0.5	− 0.04	1.2	1.8
Newfoundland	0.5	− 0.03	1.1	1.4
Prince Edward Island	0.1	0.0	0.3	0.3
Northwest Territories	0.1	0.0	0.2	} 0.4
Yukon	0.0	0.04	0.1	
Total[4]	25.4	− 0.02	59.0	100.0
Federal Government[4]	17.7[5]	− 1.6	41.0[5]	—

[1] Provinces or Territories and local authorities, consolidated, fiscal year.
[2] Estimates based on consolidation of expenditures and revenues of provincial and local authorities measured on an administrative basis. Calendar year for the provinces and fiscal year for the local authorities.
[3] 1984 percentage shares.
[4] These figures are not comparable with those in Table 13 because they are estimates based on an administrative, rather than national accounts, basis. This problem distorts especially the revenue side, reducing the net borrowing requirements. The main item responsible is the inclusion of net revenue from pension schemes.
[5] Expenditure net of transfers.

Sources: Statistics Canada, *Canada Yearbook* 1988 and own estimates.

TABLE 6

Fiscal indicators of regional governments[1] in Australia, 1986-87

Region	Expenditure[2]	Net lending	Expenditure[2]	Regional GDP
	% of national GNP		% of total	% of union GDP
New South Wales	7.3	− 0.7	17.3	34.7
Victoria	5.6	− 0.6	13.3	27.6
Queensland	3.6	− 0.3	8.5	14.9
Western Australia	2.2	− 0.2	5.3	9.3
South Australia	1.9	− 0.1	4.6	8.0
Tasmania	0.6	− 0.1	1.5	2.4
Northern Territory	0.5	− 0.03	1.2	1.1
Total	21.6	− 2.1	51.6	100.0[3]
Federal Government	20.3	− 1.0	48.4	—

[1] States and local governments, consolidated. Budget definitions which include public trading enterprises.

[2] Estimates.

[3] The total adds to 100.0 only if the Australian Capital Territory is included, but the latter has no autonomous budget.

Sources: Department of the Treasury, *Economic Round-up,* November 1988 and own estimates.

TABLE 7

Fiscal indicators of regional governments[1] in Switzerland, 1986

Region	Expenditure	Net lending[3]	Expenditure	Regional income
	% of national GNP		% of total	% of union income
Zürich	4.1	0.03	13.5	21.4
Bern	3.2	− 0.04	10.5	12.6
Vaud	1.9	0.02	6.2	8.3
Genève	1.8	− 0.04	5.9	7.3
St Gallen	1.2	0.01	3.9	5.3
Aargau	1.1	0.04	3.6	6.9
Next 10 *Cantons:*				
Average	0.7	0.02	2.2	3.0
Range	0.5-0.9	0.02-0.05	1.5-3.0	2.0-4.4
Next 10 *Cantons:*				
Average	0.1	0.0	0.5	0.8
Range	0.0-0.3	0.02-0.03	0.1-0.8	0.2-2.1
Total	21.5	0.3	70.3	100.0
Federal Government	9.1	− 0.8	29.7	—

[1] *Cantons* and *Gemeinden,* not consolidated as data on transfers were not available.

Source: Eidgenössische Finanzverwaltung, *Öffentliche Finanzen der Schweiz.*

TABLE 8

Regional dispersion of fiscal indicators[1] in the United States, 1985

Region	Expenditure[2]	Net lending[3]	Debt	Federal transfers received	Net lending
	% of regional GDP				% of revenue[4]
California	13.8	1.0	10.1	2.7	6.9
New York	17.7	1.5	18.6	3.4	7.9
Texas	10.7	0.9	13.8	1.6	7.9
Illinois	12.7	1.2	11.0	2.5	8.4
Pennsylvania	13.9	1.8	14.6	2.9	11.8
Next 4 states:					
Average	14.0	1.1	13.1	2.5	7.4
Range	13.2-15.8	0.8-1.3	9.9-15.9	2.2-3.0	5.8-9.2
Next 14 states:					
Average	13.7	1.0	14.3	2.7	6.7
Range	11.2-16.7	0.1-1.8	8.8-24.9	2.1-3.5	0.9-12.6
Next 13 states:					
Average[5]	15.3	1.5[6]	19.9	2.9	8.0[6]
Range	11.6-23.6	−0.2-8.0	9.5-46.7	1.9-3.9	−1.5-25.4
Next 15 states:					
Average	15.1	1.3[6]	16.6	3.4	7.8
Range	9.9-19.1	−1.1-4.7	8.5-24.3	1.7-4.8	−6.7-22.2
Total[7]	12.9	1.6	14.4	2.7	10.9

[1] State and local governments, consolidated, fiscal year.
[2] Direct general expenditure.
[3] General revenue minus direct general expenditure.
[4] Including federal transfers.
[5] Excluding Alaska, an outlier, the average expenditure, net lending and debt as a percentage of state GDP would be, respectively, 14.6, 1.0 and 16.3 %. Average net lending as a percentage of revenue would be 6.6 %. The ranges would be similar to those of the groups with larger states.
[6] Absolute value.
[7] National accounts basis.

Sources: US Department of Commerce, *Statistical abstract of the USA*, 1988; *Survey of current business*, May 1988; and Council of Economic Advisers, *Economic Report of the President*, 1988.

TABLE 9

Regional dispersion of fiscal indicators[1] in the Federal Republic of Germany, 1987

Region	Expenditure	Net lending	Interest payments	Federal transfers received	Net lending
	% of regional GDP				% of revenue[2]
Nordrhein-Westfalen	17.9	− 1.7	1.7	0.9	− 7.6
Bayern	16.9	− 0.4	0.8	0.9	− 2.7
Baden-Württemberg	16.9	− 0.6	0.9	0.8	− 4.0
Niedersachsen	20.3	− 1.7	1.7	1.6	− 9.4
Hessen	17.1	− 0.8	1.2	0.8	− 5.2
Berlin	28.4	− 0.7	0.8	16.8	− 2.4
Rheinland-Pfalz	18.5	− 1.7	1.7	1.6	− 9.9
Schleswig-Holstein	20.8	− 1.7	1.7	2.0	− 9.0
Hamburg	14.3	− 1.4	1.3	0.8	− 11.2
Saarland	20.6	− 2.7	2.7	1.7	− 14.8
Bremen	20.0	− 2.5	2.9	1.8	− 14.3
Total	18.1	− 1.1	1.3	1.7	− 6.4

[1] *Länder* and *Gemeinden*, consolidated.
[2] Including government transfers.
Source: Statistisches Bundesamt Wiesbaden, *Finanz und Steuern,* Fachserie 14, Reihe 2.

TABLE 10

Regional dispersion of fiscal indicators[1] in Canada, 1982

Region	Expenditure[2]	Net lending[2]	Debt[3]	Federal transfers received	Net lending
	% of regional GDP				% of revenue[4]
Ontario	20.7	− 0.7	19.6	2.1	− 3.3
Quebec	32.0	− 0.3	29.0	5.4	− 1.0
Alberta	24.5	3.9	16.4	4.1	13.8
British Columbia	24.5	− 0.5	16.6	3.2	− 2.2
Saskatchewan	25.6	0.7	35.0	4.3	2.6
Manitoba	26.5	− 1.0	36.4	5.6	− 4.1
Nova Scotia	35.7	− 4.3	43.8	8.8	− 13.6
New Brunswick	29.3	− 2.3	42.5	10.6	− 8.6
Newfoundland	32.5	− 2.0	57.2	12.6	− 6.7
Prince Edward Islands	35.9	0.6	38.8	16.1	1.8
Western Territories	} 34.5	} 2.3	} 7.2	} 26.9	6.9
Yukon					4.9
Total	25.4	− 0.0	23.7	4.1	100.0

[1] Provinces or Territories and local authorities, consolidated, fiscal year.
[2] Defined as in Table 5. Regional GDPs were estimated by using 1984 percentage shares in national GDP.
[3] Debt outstanding at the end of March 1984.
[4] Including federal transfers.

Sources: Statistics Canada, *Canada Yearbook* 1988 and own estimates.

TABLE 11

Regional dispersion of fiscal indicators[1] in Australia, 1986-87

Region	Expenditure[2]	Net lending	Interest payments	Federal transfers received	Net lending[2]
	% of state GDP				% of revenue[3]
New South Wales	20.9	− 2.1	1.9	8.0	− 11.2
Victoria	20.2	− 2.0	2.8	7.5	− 11.0
Queensland	23.8	− 2.1	1.7	9.9	− 9.7
Western Australia	23.7	− 2.0	2.5	9.9	− 9.2
South Australia	24.2	− 1.6	2.8	11.3	− 7.0
Tasmania	26.8	− 2.4	4.1	14.2	− 9.9
Northern Territory	47.3	− 2.5	2.0	35.9	− 5.6
Total	21.6	− 2.1	2.3	8.8	− 10.8

[1] State and local governments, consolidated. Budget definitions which include public trading enterprises.
[2] Estimates.
[3] Including federal transfers.
Sources: Department of the Treasury, *Economic Round-up,* November 1988 and own estimates.

TABLE 12

Regional dispersion of fiscal indicators[1] in Switzerland, 1986

Region	Expenditure	Net lending	Interest payments	Net lending
	% of *Canton* revenue			% of revenue[2]
Zürich	22.7	0.2	1.0	0.8
Bern	29.9	−0.4	1.0	−1.3
Vaud	27.1	0.3	1.0	1.1
Genève	29.3	−0.7	1.5	−2.5
St Gallen	26.5	0.2	0.8	0.9
Aargau	18.7	0.7	0.8	3.4
Next 10 *Cantons:*				
Average	26.3	1.0[3]	1.3	3.6[3]
Range	20.4–32.1	−1.0–2.5	0.8–2.3	−3.3–7.8
Next 10 *Cantons:*				
Average	24.9	1.1[3]	0.9	4.2[3]
Range	14.1–34.8	−2.7–1.8	0.4–1.1	−8.6–11.5
Total	25.3	0.3	1.1	1.3

[1] *Cantons* and *Gemeinden*, not consolidated as data on transfers were not available.
[2] Revenue is overestimated as it is not on a consolidated basis. It includes federal transfers.
[3] Absolute value.
Source: Eidgenössische Finanzverwaltung, *Öffentliche Finanzen der Schweiz.*

TABLE 13

Fiscal indicators of federal and regional[1] governments in the United States, the Federal Republic of Germany and Canada, 1970-87

Country/ government level	1970	1975	1980	1981	1982	1983	1984	1985	1986	1987
					% of GNP/GDP					
United States					Expenditure					
Federal, net[2]	18.1	19.4	19.3	20.1	22.0	22.0	21.2	22.1	21.9	21.5
Federal transfers[3]	2.4	3.4	3.2	2.9	2.7	2.5	2.5	2.5	2.5	2.3
Regional	13.2	14.7	13.3	12.8	13.1	12.9	12.6	12.9	13.3	12.1
					Net lending					
Federal	− 1.2	− 4.3	− 2.2	− 2.1	− 4.6	− 5.2	− 4.5	− 4.9	− 4.8	− 3.4
Regional	0.2	0.3	1.0	1.1	1.1	1.4	1.7	1.6	1.3	1.0
FR of Germany					Expenditure					
Federal, net[2]	23.9	32.0	30.9	32.2	32.9	31.8	31.3	30.9	30.2	30.2
Federal transfers[3]	1.8	2.2	2.0	2.0	1.9	1.8	1.7	1.7	1.6	1.6
Regional	17.6	21.4	21.0	21.2	21.0	20.3	19.7	19.7	19.6	19.6
					Net lending					
Federal	+ 0.1	− 3.4	− 1.9	− 2.5	− 2.4	− 1.9	− 1.6	− 1.2	− 1.2	− 1.4
Regional	− 1.3	− 2.8	− 1.9	− 2.3	− 2.0	− 1.4	− 1.0	− 0.9	− 1.0	− 1.1
Canada					Expenditure					
Federal, net[2]	13.4	16.3	15.7	16.3	18.9	19.0	19.5	19.6	18.7	18.1
Federal transfers[3]	3.8	4.5	4.1	4.0	4.2	4.3	4.5	4.5	4.1	4.1
Regional	21.4	23.1	23.8	24.0	26.4	26.7	25.8	25.9	25.8	25.4
					Net lending					
Federal	+ 0.2	− 1.1	− 3.5	− 2.0	− 5.4	− 6.1	− 6.8	− 6.6	− 4.9	− 4.2
Regional	− 0.8	− 1.4	− 0.3	− 0.3	− 1.5	− 1.5	− 0.5	− 1.0	− 1.2	− 0.7

[1] For the United States, state and local governments; for Germany, *Länder* and *Gemeinden*; for Canada, provincial or territorial and local governments including hospital sector (i.e. the PLH sector).
[2] Excluding transfers to regional governments.
[3] Transfers to regional governments.
Sources: Council of Economic Advisers, *Economic Report of the President*, 1988; Bundesministerium der Finanzen, *Finanzberichte;* and Canadian national sources.

TABLE 14

Fiscal indicators of federal and regional governments in Australia and Switzerland,[1] 1970-87

Country/ government level	1970	1975	1980	1981	1982	1983	1984	1985	1986	1987
	\multicolumn{10}{c}{% of GNP/GDP}									
Australia	\multicolumn{10}{c}{Expenditure}									
Federal, net[2]	18.2	19.3	17.5	18.2	19.9	20.6	21.1	21.0	20.3	18.6
Federal transfers[3]	6.6	9.3	8.6	8.5	9.1	9.3	9.3	8.9	8.7	8.2
Regional	16.7	19.5	20.4	21.1	22.5	22.0	21.6	21.8	21.6	20.1
	\multicolumn{10}{c}{Net lending}									
Federal	− 0.0	− 4.6	− 0.7	− 0.3	− 2.7	− 4.2	− 3.2	− 2.4	− 1.0	0.7
Regional	− 1.1	− 0.1	− 2.0	− 2.7	− 2.9	− 2.2	− 1.8	− 2.0	− 2.1	− 1.3
Switzerland	\multicolumn{10}{c}{Expenditure}									
Federal, gross[4]	8.3	9.5	9.9	9.1	9.4	9.5	9.6	9.5	9.5	9.0
Regional, gross[5]	17.4	22.1	21.7	21.4	21.8	22.0	21.5	21.2	21.5	21.4
	\multicolumn{10}{c}{Net lending}									
Federal	0.2	− 0.9	− 0.6	− 0.1	− 0.2	− 0.4	− 0.2	− 0.3	0.8	0.4
Regional	− 0.8	− 0.8	0.2	− 0.1	− 0.5	− 0.4	− 0.1	0.1	0.3	0.3

[1] For Australia, state and local governments. Budget definitions which include public trading enterprises. For Switzerland, *Cantons* and *Gemeinden*. For Australia, fiscal years starting in the year indicated.

[2] Excluding transfers to regional governments.

[3] Transfers to regional governments.

[4] Including transfers to regional governments as data isolating them were not available.

[5] Non-consolidated between *Cantons* and *Gemeinden*.

Sources: Eidgenössische Finanzverwaltung, *Öffentliche Finanzen der Schweiz;* and ABS, Government financial estimates and budget papers.

TABLE 15

Fiscal indicators of national governments in the EEC, 1988[1]

Country	Expenditure	Net lending	Debt	Expenditure % of total EEC expenditure	Debt % of total EEC debt	National GDP % of EEC GDP
	% of EEC GDP					
FR of Germany	12.4	− 0.5	11.9	25.1	19.3	26.3
France	10.2	− 0.5	8.0	20.7	13.1	19.9
Italy	9.0	− 1.9	17.6	18.3	28.6	18.0
United Kingdom	6.6	− 0.3[2]	8.5	13.3	13.9	15.8
Spain	2.9	− 0.3	3.5	5.8	5.7	6.8
The Netherlands	2.9	− 0.3	4.2	5.8	6.8	4.9
Belgium	1.7	− 0.2	4.2	3.5	6.8	3.3
Denmark	1.4	0.0	1.3	2.7	2.0	2.4
Greece	0.5	− 0.1	0.7	1.0	1.2	1.1
Portugal	0.3	− 0.1	0.7	0.7	1.1	0.8
Ireland	0.3	− 0.1	0.9	0.7	1.5	0.7
Luxembourg	0.1	0.0	0.0	0.2	0.0	0.1
Community	1.2	–	–	2.1	–	–
Total EEC	49.0	− 4.4	61.6	100.0	100.0	100.0

[1] Based on estimates and forecasts made by the Economic Secretariat of the European Communities.
[2] More recent figures for the United Kingdom (OECD Economic Outlook, December 1988) indicate a surplus of 0.3% of own GDP and would therefore change the above estimates. They are not markedly different from the above projections for the other three large countries.

Source: EC, *European Economy*, No 34.

TABLE 16

National dispersion of fiscal indicators in the EEC, 1988[1]

Country	Expenditure	Net lending	Interest payments	Debt	Net lending
	% of national GDP				% of revenue
FR of Germany	47.1	− 2.0	2.9	45.2	− 4.4
France	51.3	− 2.3	2.8	40.3	− 4.7
Italy	50.3	− 10.4	7.9	97.9	− 26.1
United Kingdom	41.7	− 2.0[2]	4.1	54.1	− 5.0
Spain	42.1	− 4.9	3.7	51.6	− 13.2
The Netherlands	58.2	− 6.0	5.9	85.2	− 11.5
Belgium	52.4	− 6.1	11.0	128.4	− 13.2
Denmark	57.3	1.7	7.8	53.3	2.9
Greece	47.3	− 9.8	6.9	67.2	− 26.1
Portugal	41.7	− 7.8	7.2	78.5	− 23.0
Ireland	52.1	− 7.8	10.7	138.0	− 17.6
Luxembourg	51.2	3.1	1.1	14.8	5.7
Total EEC	47.8	− 4.4	4.8	61.6	10.1

[1] Based on estimates and forecasts made by the Economic Secretariat of the European Communities.
[2] More recent figures for the United Kingdom (OECD Economic Outlook, December 1988) indicate a surplus of 0.3% of GDP. They are not markedly different from the above projections for the other three large countries.

Source: EC, *European Economy*, No 34.

Appendix II

Market forces and budgetary discipline

This brief appendix considers in more detail whether there exist market mechanisms which can encourage prudent fiscal behaviour on the part of governments.

For a private firm, the ultimate market threat which penalizes imprudent borrowing is the danger of bankruptcy and liquidation. Market forces signal this risk by incorporating a default premium into the cost of funds and/or by rationing them. In addition, lenders may curtail the decision-making autonomy of the enterprise when a position of financial stress is approached. As in a competitive environment there exist strict limits to the extent to which revenue can be obtained by simply raising prices, the borrowing and expenditure decisions of firms tend to be relatively responsive to market pressures.

Whether similar market pressures can be brought to bear on governments is less clear. One may distinguish here between the situation of a single State and of one which is an EMU member. In a single State, a government may be less responsive in the short run to an increase in the cost of its borrowing resulting from market anticipations of future debt problems because it might feel that higher debt service payments can be met by raising taxes and/or, perhaps, by monetizing the deficit. It is only in the longer run that the costs of such actions become apparent, either in the form of resistance to the implied tax burden or higher inflation.[1] At that point, political pressure may be exerted to cut expenditure. As the experience of a number of countries illustrates, however, the lag with which such pressures tend to emerge is considerable.

When a State is a member of an EMU, at least two contrasting forces would seem to be at work. On the one hand, the exclusion from access to central bank credit may make governments more sensitive to signals coming from the market in the form of higher costs of funds. On the other hand, the closer economic and solidarity ties implied by membership of the union may generate market expectations that the country concerned would ultimately be bailed out by other EMU members. That would mean fewer pressures on fiscal consolidation and less differentiation in the cost of funds. The country would effectively benefit from the credit rating of others. The case of New York City may be taken as an example. It is clear that in that instance market mechanisms were not effective in preventing the financial crisis and that central government assistance was indeed forthcoming.

---

[1] They can also show up, probably earlier, as resistance to any perceived crowding-out effects associated with the fiscal policy stance.

IV — Papers relating to monetary union

The further development of the European Monetary System
Karl Otto Pöhl

Contents

		Page
I —	**Introduction**	131
II —	**The final objective of monetary integration**	132
	A — Economic and monetary integration	132
	1. The characteristics of a monetary union	132
	2. Implications for economic policy	133
	B — Principles of a European monetary order	137
III —	**Models of monetary integration**	138
	A — European Monetary Fund	138
	B — A European parallel currency	139
	C — A European monetary authority on the way to a single currency	146
IV —	**Transitional problems**	148
	A — Legal basis	148
	B — Integration in stages	150
	C — Partial integration versus comprehensive integration	150
	D — Integration under the Treaty of Rome or outside it	152
V —	**Concluding remarks**	153

I — Introduction

The member countries of the European Community have made considerable progress in recent years in their efforts to achieve greater convergence in their economic policies and economic development. Stability of the value of money as the prime objective at the national level and exchange rate stability as the common goal within the European Monetary System (EMS) have been achieved to a higher degree than ever before. The generally favourable economic and monetary situation provides sound prerequisites for achieving the objective of creating a single European market by 1992. This would fulfil essential preconditions for an *economic union*.

With the planned creation of an integrated financial market with free movement of capital, a basic component of a future *monetary union* would also exist. An additional basic element, namely firmly fixed exchange rates, is admittedly not in prospect within the foreseeable future because setbacks in coordinating economic policy can no more be excluded than can disturbances in the financial markets and the real economy, which can make exchange rate adjustments necessary. Corrections in exchange rates will remain a necessary safety valve for the foreseeable future also within the EMS in order to reduce any tensions that may arise without incurring excessive damage to individual economies or the Community as a whole. Even the unification of the markets to form a single European market does not necessarily presuppose the existence of a monetary union or a common currency.

The time may nevertheless have come to develop some concrete ideas about the process of integration which can lead to a monetary union.

A number of recent proposals seek to anticipate the emergence of new conflicts between the common objective of exchange rate stability and national notions of price stability through a quantum leap, by coupling the commitment to achieve a single European market and an integrated financial space with freedom of capital movements by 1992 with the creation of a European central bank. From the German point of view it is essential to ensure, in the discussions about the future design of a European monetary order, that monetary and credit policy is not geared to stability to a lesser extent in an economically united Europe than is the case at present in the Federal Republic of Germany. Apart from this, it should be made clear that monetary integration cannot move ahead of general economic integration, since otherwise the whole process of integration would be burdened with considerable economic and social tensions. Moreover, examples from history demonstrate that new nations did not confer a uniform monetary order on themselves until after the process of unification was concluded. Any durable attempt to fix exchange rates within the Community and finally to replace national currencies by a European currency would be doomed to failure so long as a minimum of policy-shaping and decision-making in the field of economic and fiscal policy does not take place at Community level. Without this prerequisite being met, a common European monetary policy cannot ensure monetary stability on its own. Above all, it cannot paper over the problems in the Community arising from differing economic and fiscal policies.

The following considerations begin with the basic elements of an economic and monetary union (EMU). The thread cannot simply be picked up at the ideas contained in the Werner Report as long ago as 1970, namely to move towards this goal via a multi-stage plan. With the 'snake' and the EMS, experience has been gained and with the progress in economic and monetary policy cooperation facts have been created which suggest the need for a new start. In this context, it must be ensured from the outset that agreement exists between the governments and the Community institutions for which they are responsible with respect to the basic issues of economic policy. Above all, agreement must exist that stability of the value of money is the indispensable prerequisite for the achievement of other goals. Particular importance will therefore attach to the principles on which a European monetary order should be based.

Drawing partially on preliminary work conducted within the Community on the second stage of the EMS, three models of monetary integration are then presented and examined with respect to their compatibility with the demands of a future monetary union. The models that have been selected take ideas into account that play a role in political discussions or could play a role in them at any time. Since it can be assumed that the goal of monetary union cannot be reached in a quantum jump but only as the result of a process of integration encompassing economic and monetary policy, individual conceivable stages of integration with their political implications are taken into consideration. The problems arising from the differing speed of integration on the part of individual countries as well as from the institutional and legal aspects of integration are also discussed.

II — The final objective of monetary integration

A — *Economic and monetary integration*

1. The characteristics of a monetary union

The final objective of monetary union was defined as long ago as 1970 in the Werner Report in a formulation that still applies today: '*A monetary union* implies inside its boundaries the total and irreversible convertibility of currencies, the elimination of margins of fluctuation in exchange rates, the irrevocable fixing of parity rates and the complete liberation of movements of capital.' *The decisive criteria for a monetary union are thus the irrevocable fixing of exchange rates and movements of capital within the single monetary area that are free from restrictions.*

The monetary union is the 'monetary superstructure' of the economic union in which the 'four freedoms' have been realized, namely the free movements of goods, services, labour, and capital. Within the common single market, economic activity is to be based on a free market system of competition. Besides agreement on regulative policy, an economic union demands a far-reaching harmonization of government regulations in order to bring about equal competitive conditions and uniform markets. Although structural and regional differences between the member countries (especially differences in income and productivity) are compatible with an economic union, the structural and regional policy of the Community must take them into account.

In principle, national currencies can be retained in the monetary union. However, the introduction of a uniform monetary symbol would give the union a 'monetary identity', eliminate the residual risk of parity changes among the national currencies and hence assure the continuing existence of a single monetary area. The replacement of national currencies by a common currency would indeed be the 'crowning act' of the process of monetary integration.

Above and beyond the integration effects of a single European market, a monetary union provides a number of additional economic *advantages.* Firstly, the irrevocable fixing of parities means that the exchange rate risk associated with the intra-Community exchange of goods, services and capital is eliminated. This will foster, in particular, the integration of the financial markets and the strengthening of competition. Secondly, there will be a saving in transaction costs since market participants will be increasingly willing to accept partner currencies or the common currency without taking recourse to hedging operations and to hold them as a means of payment or investment in the place of national currencies. Thirdly, the creation of a monetary area with a greater weight internationally entails advantages in transactions with third countries since the international acceptance of the Community currencies will grow, the Community will become less susceptible to external shocks and it will be able to represent its monetary policy interests more effectively at the international level. The introduction of a common currency would allow full advantage to be drawn from these benefits.

2. Implications for economic policy

Within the monetary union, economic policy must be directed towards eliminating causes of tension that could jeopardize its cohesion and towards preventing new tensions from arising. The irrevocable fixing of parity rates is possible only on the basis of exchange rates at which differences in rates of price increase, balance of payments positions and in the field of public finances have been eliminated to a large extent. With fixed exchange rates, insufficient convergence in these three fields would give rise to adjustment constraints in the real economy that would endanger the cohesion of the monetary union or would ultimately bring about adjustments in parities forcefully. The harmonization of rates of inflation at the lowest possible level is necessary since any shifts that may arise in terms of price competitiveness can no longer be offset by realignments. Countries with an above-average rate of inflation would suffer competitive losses; conversely, tendencies towards excess demand would be triggered in countries with cost advantages.

When parity relationships are irrevocably fixed, the external positions of the partner countries must be compatible with each other since competitive weaknesses of one partner would burden the aggregate balance of payments position of the monetary union *vis-à-vis* the rest of the world. Even if the current account position of the monetary union were in balance as a whole it would not be possible for a single country within the Community to rely on capital inflows and the corresponding growth of indebtedness indefinitely. Finally, there would have to be a large degree of convergence in the field of public finance. Considerable, or even unlimited, recourse by a Member State (or the central authority) to central bank credit would make monetary control throughout the monetary area difficult, if not impossible, and — no matter how they are financed — excessive national budget deficits would burden the overall current account position of the monetary union.

Securing convergence within the monetary union — with the retention of national currencies initially — will imply losses in independence in terms of national economic policy, i.e. a shift of responsibilities from the national to the Community level. This applies both to fiscal, economic, social and wages policy as well as — to a particularly marked extent — to *monetary policy:* ideally, within the monetary union national currencies are 'perfect substitutes', i.e. market participants are indifferent as regards the various existing currencies. The irrevocable fixing of parity rates under conditions of complete freedom of capital movements implies that national interest rate levels must converge (apart from minor differences arising from market imperfections). It will thus no longer be possible to conduct an independent national monetary policy that is geared to a national standard.

The basic stance of monetary policy must be laid down by a coordinating body at Community level. National central banks will then only be executive organs for the Community's monetary policy. To the extent that they are able to achieve the operational objectives laid down by the Community, the harmonization of their instruments will not be necessary initially. This will in any case be possible only within limits in the preliminary stages since there are wide differences in existing structures of national money, credit and capital markets that will not disappear immediately even after the complete liberalization of capital movements. However, owing to differing national transmission mechanisms of monetary policy as well as structural differences in the demand for money, it will be possible to achieve a uniform policy for monetary growth that is geared to a monetary target for the Community only gradually. Thus, as far as its practical application is concerned, national differences will persist. The creation of a uniform European money market which the central authority responsible for monetary policy can manage with instruments of its own will, however, be necessary at the latest when a common currency is introduced.

Monetary policy coordination needs to be complemented by the *transfer of responsibility for monetary relationships with the rest of the world to the Community level* since the exchange rates of the partner currencies must develop uniformly. Exchange rate policy *vis-à-vis* third countries must therefore be laid down at the Community level, interventions on the foreign exchange market be decided jointly (with intervention operations perhaps being centralized at a national central bank or a common fund for reasons of expediency) and monetary reserves be pooled. In the field of international monetary policy the Community would act as a single entity. Instead of individual countries, it would then also need to be a member of the IMF.

Whereas the national States would necessarily lose their monetary policy independence in a monetary union, they can quite easily retain certain reponsibilities in the field of *fiscal and economic policy,* as is the case in every federation of States. However, in order to exclude any doubts about the cohesion of the monetary union from the outset and at the same time avoid an overburdening of monetary policy, it must be ensured that there is sufficient conformity of action in *fiscal and economic policy* within the Community. This is because any lack of convergence that could give rise to expectations of parity changes would need to be 'bridged' through interventions and interest rate measures on the national money markets in order to ensure the continuing existence of the monetary or exchange rate union. Over time it will thus be necessary to allow for the necessary transfer of economic and fiscal policy responsibilities from national authorities to Community organs.

In order to optimize economic policy as a whole the overall economic objectives for the monetary area should be laid down at Community level. Broad agreement would also need to be reached on the policy mix, i.e. the combination of fiscal and monetary policy appropriate for achieving the overall economic objectives. This would also provide a basic guideline for each country's fiscal policy. Moreover, together with the creation of the single European market, a far-reaching — but not necessarily complete — harmonization of indirect taxes would be necessary in order to avoid competitive distortions. Although, given the existing low degree of mobility of income-earners, direct taxes do not need to be harmonized to the same extent, with unchanged shares of expenditure by the public sector in GNP, the harmonization of indirect taxes will also create a need to adjust direct taxes as well as the overall burden of levies.

In the light of existing structural imbalances within the Community, when parity rates are irrevocably fixed it will be necessary to put in place a system of 'fiscal compensation' through a Community organ in favour of the structurally weak member countries. Transfer payments would compensate the weaker members for the burdens of adjustment associated with the definitive renouncement of devaluations as a means of maintaining their competitiveness. Thus, within the monetary union, balance-of-payments policy is replaced by regional policy, with the latter helping to finance interregional differences in current account imbalances through transfer payments. The differences in the level of economic development of individual member countries of the Community suggest that *extremely large funds* would be needed to finance the necessary fiscal compensation. Only through a very effective regional policy could these differences perhaps be reduced to an extent that would be compatible with the existence of a monetary union.

Incomes policy must also take the fixing of parity rates within the monetary union into account. Divergences in regional developments (such as differing rates of increase in productivity or shifts in demand, for instance) require a correspondingly differentiated development of wages in so far as they are not offset by fiscal adjustment within the Community. Although regional imbalances can be offset through the mobility of the factors of production, this kind of adjustment would be associated with a shifting of capital and finally also of labour out of the less competitive regions that would be undesirable in terms of regional policy (and which, owing to the far lesser degree of mobility of labour, would not occur without friction). Thus, given diverging developments in competitiveness, renouncing exchange rate adjustments will require a *differentiated wages policy,* which would also need to cover ancillary wage costs. In branches of industry that manufacture their products under widely similar conditions a harmonization of nominal wage developments is to be expected within the monetary union in the absence of which diverging rates of inflation could arise. For this reason, even before the inception of the monetary union the basic willingness of both sides of industry to pursue a wages and incomes policy geared to the operating conditions of such a union must exist, especially bearing in mind that an increasing orientation of wage demands towards the highest level in the Community is to be expected within the monetary union. However, given the independent right to conclude collective wage agreements that is appropriate in an economic union based on the rules of free competition, the scope for economic policy to directly affect the development of wages and salaries is very restricted. *Everything will therefore ultimately depend on a credible and rigorously pursued monetary policy that limits the scope for passing on cost increases and hence prevents excessive increases in nominal wages from occurring.*

The economic policy implications of a monetary union can be summed up as follows: *A monetary union presupposes considerable shifts in the responsibility for economic policy to a central authority and hence a far-reaching reshaping of the Community in political and institutional terms in the direction of a broader union.* Although *complete political union is not absolutely necessary for* the establishment of *a monetary union,* the *loss of national sovereignty in economic and monetary policy* associated with it is *so serious that* it would probably be *bearable only in the context of extremely close and irrevocable political integration. At all events, within a monetary union, monetary policy can only be conducted at a Community level. A substantial transfer of authority will also be necessary in the field of fiscal policy.*

B — Principles of a European monetary order

Eschewing technical institutional and monetary details, the following section outlines the decisive principles that absolutely must be taken into account when setting up a European central bank system. (For the sake of simplification, the point of departure is the final stage of monetary integration, namely the transition to a common European currency. However, the following criteria must also be fulfilled already at the stage when the monetary union is created, i.e. the irrevocable fixing of the parity rates of national currencies.) The following principles appear to be indispensable:

1. The mandate of the central bank must be to maintain *stability of the value of money* as the prime objective of European monetary policy. While fulfilling this task, the central bank has to support general economic policy as laid down at Community level. Domestic stability of the value of money must take precedence over exchange rate stability. This does not exclude the possibility that depreciation *vis-à-vis* third currencies and the associated import of inflation be counteracted by appropriate monetary policy measures. In the event of the establishment of an international monetary system with limited exchange rate flexibility *vis-à-vis* third currencies, the central bank would need to be given at least the right to participate in discussions on parity changes.

2. The overriding commitment to maintaining the stability of the value of money must be safeguarded through the central bank's *independence* of instructions from national governments and Community authorities. This simultaneously requires the personal independence of the members of the respective organs, assured by their being appointed to office for a period of at least eight to 10 years without the possibility of their being removed from office for political reasons.

3. All the member countries would need to be represented in the monetary policy *decision-making body,* with voting power being weighted in the light of the economic importance of the member countries.

4. A *federal structure* of the central bank system — according to the pattern of the Federal Reserve System, for instance — would correspond best to the existing state of national sovereignty and would additionally strengthen the independence of the central bank. (Before the final stage involving the introduction of a uniform currency, only a federally structured central bank system is conceivable in any case.)

5. The *financing of public sector deficits* by the central bank (apart from occasional cash advances) makes effective monetary control impossible over the long term. For a European central bank to be able to fulfil its mandate to ensure monetary stability, strict limitations must be imposed on its granting credit to public

authorities of all kinds (including Community authorities). This also applies to indirect government financing through the granting of credit to any central banks of the member countries that continue to exist.

6. The European central bank must be equipped with the *monetary policy instruments* to enable it to manage the money supply effectively without recourse to quantitative controls (or other forms of direct intervention in the workings of the financial markets). Interest rate and liquidity policy instruments must be available both for the general management and for the fine-tuning of the European money market.

7. The European central bank should be given the right to take part in the establishment of general regulations in the field of *banking supervision*. Moreover, owing to its expertise, deriving in particular from its business relations with credit institutions, the central bank should be closely involved in day-to-day banking supervisory activities.

III — Models of monetary integration

A — *European Monetary Fund*

The further development of the European Monetary Cooperation Fund (EMCF) to form a European Monetary Fund (EMF) as a kind of 'Regional IMF' probably comes closest to the concept the architects of the EMS had in mind, seeing that in accordance with the Resolution of the European Council of 5 December 1978 the final system was to be characterized by 'the creation of the European Monetary Fund as well as the full utilization of the ECU as a reserve asset and a means of settlement.' In addition, the 'existing credit mechanisms' would be consolidated 'into a single fund'. Moreover, in conjunction with the conclusions relating to monetary policy reached at the meeting of the European Council in Bremen on 6 and 7 July 1978, besides US dollars and gold, 'member currencies in an amount of a comparable order of magnitude' were to be brought into the Fund. In the discussions in the years 1981-82 about the entry of the EMS into the final stage it was assumed that this could also involve a final transfer of reserves.

A regional Reserve Fund with functions similar to those of the IMF would put this institution in a position to become involved in the process of balance-of-payments adjustment and financing on the part of its members. In this way, it could help to avoid recourse being taken to measures that disturb or delay the process of integration in the event of balance of payments difficulties. In the opinion of the proponents of such a Fund solution, the use of such balance-of-payments assistance as well as the resources made available by the Fund for the specific purpose of financing interventions could at the same time also help to stabilize exchange rate relationships within the EMS. If, in the course of monetary integration, it should come about that national external payments balances cease to exist and there is only a Community external payments balance instead, then the Fund would have to support the process of adjustment and financing of the balance of payments with its resources.

In the case of a Fund along the lines of a 'Regional IMF' whose policy would be primarily directed towards safeguarding the external balance of the Community member countries as well as exchange rate stability, the question arises as to the extent to which such a policy would also foster convergence within the Community on the basis of price stability. This possibility only exists in the case of conditional balance-of-payments credits being granted, i.e. when the consequences of insufficient convergence have already become evident. At stages prior to this, especially when providing resources for intervention purposes without any conditions attached, it could not impose any convergence constraints in the direction of non-inflationary growth in the Community. The danger that within the EMS the orientation towards domestic stability would be pushed into the background in favour of external stability is obvious. Since the general thrust and coordination of economic, fiscal and monetary policy would play a role in this model of a Fund only at the margin (when conditional credits are granted) the stability-oriented monetary policy of the hard currency countries could be undermined. Moreover, mixing central bank functions together with areas of government responsibility within a single Fund bars the way to a European central bank with a decision-making body that is independent of governments, and is thus to be rejected.

B — *A European parallel currency*

1. As an alternative to the gradual development towards a European monetary union — on the basis of greater economic policy convergence, closer coordination of monetary policy and diminishing recourse to exchange rate realignments — the concept of a parallel currency has been under discussion since the mid-1970s. *According to this concept, the driving force behind the process of integration should be the market, not initiatives taken by national governments or Community authorities.*

Alongside national currencies, an additional Community currency would be put into circulation which can fulfil all the functions of money (a means of payment, a unit of account, and a store of value) as far as possible. The parallel currency would be designed in such a way that — without being given preferential treatment — it would be able not only to maintain its position alongside the national currencies but also to gradually crowd out the individual national currencies in line with the generally accepted pace of integration. With the growing importance of the parallel currency, the national central banks would increasingly lose their scope for autonomous monetary policy action in favour of a Community central banking institution since a growing proportion of the money in circulation in each country would no longer be under national control. Thus, there would be a *de facto* loss of independence in the sphere of national monetary policy without the need for any explicit shift in responsibilities to the Community level. This process would end with the abolition of the national currencies through a special sovereign act and the introduction of a single European currency.

Compared with the well-known difficulties of progressively restricting national responsibility for economic policy through political acts, the idea of a parallel currency may appear to be quite 'elegant' at first sight. It would meet with the desire to undertake politically effective and symbolic steps (such as introducing a European currency, including the issuing of banknotes and coins, and setting up a European central bank) without a major need to relinquish sovereignty rights at the outset. However, on closer inspection it becomes evident that *this approach also requires an immediate and far-reaching need for changes in institutional terms* if the 'currency competition' that is set in motion is to proceed in a way that is acceptable for all the member countries. In this context, a large number of open and very complex questions arise. Agreement can be expressed with a recent study on the European Monetary System, which states that 'the full logical implications of this approach were never drawn up at the official level.'[1]

2. Currency competition between the national currencies and a parallel currency can arise only if the latter is placed on an equal footing with all national currencies with respect to their relevant functions. Besides the envisaged complete liberalization of capital movements, i.e. the free use of each national currency and a parallel currency in external transactions, there would have to be equality of status for each national currency within the domestic economy as well. In order to ensure a sufficient degree of acceptance of the parallel currency as a means of payment its utilization would have to be permissible for domestic transactions as well; however, its full recognition as legal tender would not appear to be necessary. A harmonization of exchange rate regulations would be required beforehand in order for an undesirable uneven distribution of the parallel currency not to come about from the start.

3. The economic effects of the introduction of a parallel currency depend on the concrete aspects of its design. On the basis of the existing European monetary unit, the ECU, a large number of parallel currency concepts with in part widely differing implications can be conceived of depending in each case on the criteria that are decisive — an independent status for the ECU as opposed to a basket definition, exchange rate regulations and the role to be played by central banks. As points of reference, two 'interim solutions' of practical relevance constituting, on the one hand, the issuing of ECUs at the national level and, on the other hand, their being issued at the Community level are presented below: in the first case,

---

[1] Gros, Daniel and Thygesen, Niels. *The EMS: Achievements, current issues and directions for the future,* Brussels, 1988.

the ECU is defined, as at present, as a *basket of currencies* with a fixed, but adjustable exchange rate (See Type 1); in the second case, the ECU is an *independently defined unit* which would be put into circulation as an additional currency with a fixed, but adjustable exchange rate (Type 2).

By contrast, the 'present state' (a basket ECU with a fixed, but adjustable exchange rate[1] without the systematic involvement of central banks in the private creation of ECUs) as well as the 'final state' of a *de facto* monetary union (basket ECU or independently defined ECU with an absolutely fixed exchange rate) are not analysed in detail.[2] As far as the 'present state' is concerned, on the basis of experience the purely private circulation of ECUs (which is only possible on the basis of a basket ECU) is of limited significance and such a restricted role of the ECU will not contribute towards monetary integration. Section II already dealt extensively with the final state. In the case of immutably fixed exchange rates *vis-à-vis* the national currencies, the ECU would not be a parallel currency but a dual currency; monetary union would then not be an objective still to be attained by means of the parallel currency but would already exist. The difference between an independently defined ECU and a basket ECU would be meaningless in the final state so that this case does not need to be discussed any further.

4. As already mentioned above, the parallel currency approach seeks to approach the final state of monetary union over the longer term through currencies competing with each other and with the ECU.[3] In order for the parallel currency to have a chance in this competition among currencies it must be attractive from the point of view of individual economic agents as an investment currency (i.e. the net yield from the development of interest rates and exchange rates must be able to compete with the net yield obtainable on assets invested in a national currency) and should not be inferior to the national currency as a transaction currency (i.e. the transaction costs and the exchange rate risk involved in cash management must be as low as possible). To the extent that a crowding out of the national currency occurs, this process must operate in the right direction, i.e. 'good money' must not be replaced by 'bad money' (Gresham's Law) if price stability is to be maintained. How competition between the individual currencies actually develops and what monetary policy implications can be associated with it depends crucially on the way the parallel currency is designed in each case.

---

[1] Ignoring the special role of the lira, sterling and the drachma.
[2] The independently defined ECU with a *flexible* exchange rate (Type 3) propagated in scientific circles is also not examined because, although it is a model with theoretical advantages, it cannot be considered a realistic alternative.
[3] It apears doubtful whether all member countries would be prepared to engage in unrestricted competition among currencies with all its consequences, including large-scale crowding out of the national currency! It can probably be realistically assumed that national monetary authorities do not want to risk their currencies being crowded out of circulation in the domestic economy and will therefore keep the extent to which the parallel currency spreads under control by restricting its use in one way or the other.

(a) The basket ECU as a parallel currency (Type 1)

As things stand today, the use of the basket ECU as a parallel currency while retaining fixed, but adjustable exchange rates *vis-à-vis* the individual national currencies appears to be the most obvious approach. The decisive step towards the introduction of such a parallel currency would consist in making it possible for ECUs to be created by the national central banks (in accordance with uniform directives) or by a Community monetary authority. The basket ECU would then be created not only — as is currently the case — by the private bundling together of the individual components but also through the granting of credit or intervention operations by the central banks or a Community monetary authority.

Under the conditions described above, (apart from third currencies) 12 national EC currencies and the basket ECU as an investment and external transaction currency together with two domestic transaction and accounting units would in this case be available to the citizens of the EC. With fixed, but adjustable exchange rates, the use of the basket ECU would depend on the risk and yield preferences of investors; although the basket ECU would be suitable as a diversification instrument, being the weighted average of the national currencies it cannot be superior to all other individual currencies or mixtures of currencies. With freedom of capital movements and persistent divergences within the EMS it is quite possible that for a number of reasons the German mark will be generally preferred as an investment currency and will crowd out both the ECU and other national currencies. Although with an increasing degree of convergence between the EC currencies the German mark will lose some of its relatively greater attractiveness for non-residents, the diversification motive for ECU-denominated investments will lose importance at the same time. Investments denominated in other Community currencies would tend to be less profitable in the eyes of investors in each country so that in both cases little argues in favour of investments denominated in ECU.

The ability of the ECU as a transaction currency to crowd out national currencies within the domestic economy cannot be judged in much more positive terms either. Especially in the case of foreseeable divergences, the exchange rate risk involved would impair the use of the ECU for day-to-day transactions, for example through the constant need to determine exchange rates, irritating conversion rates and greater difficulty in agreeing prices between domestic contractual partners who would have to take possible exchange rate risks into account if the contract is denominated in ECU. Even in the event of greater convergence, habits, the acquired 'memory of prices' in national currency and similar factors tend to argue against the spread of the ECU. Thus, on balance, the best that can be expected is that the ECU would be increasingly used in intra-Community trade as a 'compromise currency', whereby, however, the crucial factor would probably not least be the negotiating position of the business partners concerned.

As a weighted average of national currencies, a basket ECU can therefore not exert any durable and especially any symmetrical pressure in the direction of crowding out national currencies and hence cannot be seen as an additional instrument for bringing about integration either. Precisely with respect to the fact that the attractiveness of a basket ECU is not assured as far as individual economic agents are concerned, it can be assumed that the EC central banks would be obliged to stabilize the exchange rate of such an ECU through unlimited purchases in order to foster the use of the ECU.[1] Should ECUs circulate on a relatively large scale, such an intervention obligation would have important consequences for monetary policy; in the final analysis, it would be tantamount to undertaking unlimited purchases of partner currencies without settlement and bringing about the integration of the circulation of official and private ECUs. If the market wanted to exchange ECUs for national currency then this would depress the exchange rate of the ECU against the currency in question. Through purchases to support the ECU the desired national currency will then be made available. As a result, ECU holdings would accumulate with the central banks whose currencies are in stronger demand than the currencies of its partners (or ECU) whereas the central banks responsible for issuing the currencies that are less in demand would have to issue ECUs by purchasing their own currency. On the assumption that divergences exist within the EMS, a *de facto* asymmetrical crowding out of the national currencies concerned within Europe would come about. The national stability policy of the hard currency countries would be undermined. National price objectives would necessarily have to be sacrificed to the average rate of inflation in Europe. For these reasons, such a concept alone requires management of the money supply at the European level in order to ensure an equal rate of money creation (ECU plus national currency). Only in this way would it be possible to avoid a 'dual coverage' of GDP in Europe through the circulation of ECUs and national currencies.

Moreover, redesigning the existing ECU to form a parallel currency would make it difficult to statistically record the national money supply if ECU banknotes were to be issued.[2] Although it would be known how many ECU banknotes had been issued all in all, it would not be known how many of them are actually held in the Federal Republic of Germany or any other country. In addition, there would be exchange rate-induced fluctuations in the national money supply expressed in terms of national currency. Finally, account would also need to be taken of the general possibility that already exists today of shifting funds into offshore centres; this might possibly play an even greater role for holdings of ECUs than is the case with respect to national currencies. These reservations apply in equal measure to the independently defined ECU that is discussed below.

---

[1] If, as is assumed, all the basket currencies are part of a system of fixed, but adjustable exchange rates, then intervention points for the basket ECU *vis-à-vis* each individual national currency can be derived from their bilateral intervention points.

[2] In case an ECU parallel currency were introduced, ECU banknotes would probably be issued even if the ECU were not to be declared legal tender.

(b) An independently defined ECU as a parallel currency (Type 2)

In the case of an independently defined ECU with a fixed, but adjustable exchange rate *vis-à-vis* the Community currencies, the development of the value of the parallel currency would be divorced from the development of the components forming the basket as it exists today but would depend on the frequency and extent of future realignments within the EMS. In principle, two possibilities exist as far as the exchange rate regulations governing an independently defined ECU are concerned:

On the one hand, the ECU can be made 'superior' to all EMS currencies by laying down the parities and intervention points of the national currencies *vis-à-vis* the ECU as the focal point of the system. Their bilateral central rates would then be derived from the ECU parity of each national currency with the consequence that the bilateral margin of fluctuation between two national currencies would be twice as large as it is *vis-à-vis* the ECU (for example, a band of ± 1⅛% *vis-à-vis* the ECU would result in a bilateral band of ±2¼%). Thus, as a regional pivotal currency in the Community, the ECU would play a similar role in formal terms as the US dollar did in the former Bretton Woods System (without, however, having its own currency area as a base).

On the other hand, the independently defined ECU could be placed on the same footing as the national currencies; in this case, it would be treated as the currency of a 13th member country and would correspondingly have the same margin of fluctuation as the national currencies (whereby it could nevertheless be the focal point of the parity grid for computational purposes). Although the first variant would be of greater symbolic importance in the field of European politics and would foster the acceptance of the ECU as a parallel currency owing to its narrower margin of fluctuation, in principle both variants raise the same problems to a large extent.

As far as the ability of the ECU to crowd out other currencies is concerned, its being defined as an independent entity could potentially have both advantages and disadvantages because the new ECU could develop a priori more strongly than the strongest Community currency but could also develop more weakly than the weakest Community currency. In the absence of additional assumptions, such as equipping the parallel currency with a 'value guarantee' (whereby, of course, only its use as an investment instrument but not as a borrowing instrument would be fostered) or assuring its usability worldwide, the ability of an independently defined ECU to crowd out other currencies as an investment instrument cannot be assessed conclusively. Ultimately, the decisive factor for the development of its value would be the extent to which ECUs are created by a Community authority (or by the national central banks of the Community member countries in accordance with uniform Community directives) in relation to the monetary demand for ECUs, which in turn would depend on the degree of acceptance of the ECU inside and outside the Community.

As is the case with a national currency, independently defined ECUs would be put into circulation through credits granted by the issuing authority to banks or public sector entities as well as through purchases of partner currencies or third currencies via interventions on the foreign exchange markets. In the final analysis, the governing factor in this process would need to be the monetary demand for ECUs which results from the use of the ECU as a currency in cash transactions, settlement operations and other payment transactions as well as for investment purposes in competition with each individual national currency.

It is, of course, difficult to assess according to which criteria such a monetary demand for ECUs would emerge. This would not least depend on how great the risk of a change in the value of ECU cash holdings is assessed to be in relation to holdings in national currency. Holding ECUs for transaction purposes would probably be a more attractive proposition in countries with a weak currency than in countries whose currencies tend to appreciate *vis-à-vis* the ECU. Economic agents in countries with a strong currency will at best hold ECUs for transaction purposes to the extent that they have to conclude and also settle contracts denominated in ECUs in intra-Community trade and payment transactions for competitive reasons. The wide use of the ECU as a currency by residents as an investment and reserve currency both inside and outside the Community would presuppose wide and deep markets as well as the willingness of bodies inside (and outside) the Community that enjoy confidence to incur debt in the ECU as currency in a form and on conditions that appear advantageous to investors. However, a sufficient degree of acceptance on the part of investors — both inside and outside the Community — is to be expected only if the creation of the ECU as an independent currency is carefully limited by the central bank(s) responsible for this task.

The granting of an excessive amount of ECU credits to the national or Community fiscal authorities (for example, for transfer payments within the Community) in particular could lead to an oversupply of ECUs and ultimately to a deterioration in the value of the ECU *vis-à-vis* national currencies in the Community. This would not only impair the competitive position of the ECU in relation to the national currencies; owing to the obligations of the national central banks to intervene against the ECU, excess ECUs would also need to be taken out of the market by the central banks against national currency, which would make it difficult — if not impossible — for the countries concerned to conduct a monetary policy geared to stability. These risks to monetary policy would need to be assessed all the more carefully the more strongly the creation of ECUs were to be subject to political influences and the less flexible the exchange rate of the ECU were to be.

5. In the final analysis, a parallel currency strategy presupposes that the process whereby other currencies are crowded out through the free play of market forces actually does work. The requisite symmetrical substitution of all Community currencies by the parallel currency would come about only if the parallel currency

- were given the same domestic status as every other Community currency;

- could compete even with the strongest Community currency, taking interest rate and exchange rate developments into account;

- involved minimum costs as a transaction currency, which would practically be the case only if it were pegged to the national currencies sufficiently firmly.

However, this more or less amounts to a definition of the final stage to which the parallel currency is supposed to lead.

The interim solutions comprising

- a basket ECU, or

- an independently defined ECU with fixed, but adjustable exchange rates

do not provide sufficient assurance that the process of integration would be free of tensions. On the contrary, they would involve the risk that national monetary policy would no longer be able to fulfil its mandate to ensure stability owing to larger-scale central bank interventions. In weighing up the costs and benefits of a parallel currency strategy it also needs to be taken into account that for day-to-day payment operations (cash transactions, settlement operations by machine, cashless payment transactions) a parallel currency would be entirely impractical. Ultimately, this leads to the *conclusion that little would be gained politically by introducing a parallel currency but that much would be placed at risk in terms of stability policy.*

C — A European monetary authority on the way to a single currency

If the concept of a 'regional IMF' that was behind the original plans to create the EMS appears to be obsolete in the meantime and a European parallel currency is not an approach towards monetary union that deserves support, then it appears appropriate to prepare the prerequisites for introducing a single European currency at a later date by gradually harmonizing the national currencies in qualitative terms. Such a development could be brought about by extending the role of the EC Committee of Governors. In this context, it is not absolutely necessary for it to become the management body of an EC monetary authority equipped with operational tools immediately; it could also exercise the function of a central decision-making body within a Community central bank system comprising the Committee and the national central banks involved.

The Committee of Governors is particularly suitable for an extension of its functions because (in contrast, for example, to the Administrative Council of the EMCF) it is *de jure* free from instructions. However, taking part in this Committee does not automatically annul the *de facto* dependence on instructions of individual Governors that exists under national law. It would therefore be desirable if this dependence could be gradually eliminated as the functions of the

Committee are further extended and be replaced by increasing independence. As in the case of all other models, its mandate (maintaining the stability of money) and its status (freedom from instructions) should be assured at the outset.

Since the process of integration is to be seen as an evolutionary process, before decision-making responsibilities are transferred to supranational institutions, the question should be examined as to whether additional possibilities to extend coordination exist and in which direction they lie. Above all, further steps appear conceivable and would also be useful where the present forms of cooperation are based mainly on an *ex post* exchange of information (policy *vis-à-vis* third currencies, changes in the field of supervision, laying down the interim objectives of monetary policy, etc.). They could gradually be developed into an *ex ante* exchange of information, such as is already occasionally practised on an informal basis.

In principle, the activity of the Committee of Governors (the title of which could be changed in the course of this process to 'European Central Bank Council', for instance, in order to emphasize its importance) would be directed towards coordinating national objectives, individual decisions and the employment of monetary instruments. *Based on current procedures, the degree of coordination could be gradually increased in the direction of obligatory advance consultations to the level of a kind of right to issue general directives.*

In this way, the scope for national monetary policy action would be gradually reduced. It would, for example, encompass the pursuit of intermediate objectives adopted in the process of coordination or set later on as part of the power to issue directives. The scope for action would remain greatest in choosing appropriate instruments for achieving the objectives, but here again the Committee would gain increasing influence over the course of time with the aim of gradually harmonizing the criteria on which the employment of certain instruments is based, extending to the creation of as uniform a set of instruments as possible.

As a kind of natural continuation of the tasks already undertaken by the Committee at present with respect to the exchange rates of the Community currencies in relation to each other and *vis-à-vis* third currencies, it would have to coordinate the intervention policy of the EC central banks with respect to the internal and external relationships of the Community, with a sufficient degree of exchange rate flexibility *vis-à-vis* third currencies being assured. In this context, account would need to be taken of the differing weights of the currencies within the EMS as well as their international role. Exchange rate policy *vis-à-vis* the rest of the world would have to take into consideration the fact that the third countries concerned (the United States and Japan) play a major part in determining the various exchange rate relationships. At a later stage, the Committee could assume the responsibility for influencing exchange rates that is still a national preserve, so that in the event of any foreign exchange market interventions, the national central banks would progressively operate in the framework of 'their administering a mandate'. The responsibility for determining central rates could also be transferred from the member governments to the Committee. In this way, there would be a greater scope for relevant decisions to be asserted regardless of political expediency.

A Committee of Governors with scope to influence exchange rate policy and monetary policy in the member countries could make an effective contribution to convergence that would foster integration. The objective behind the basic thrust of its policy would need to be to influence monetary policy in each member country in such a way that a symmetrical development is brought about on the basis of as great a degree of price stability as possible. The success of such an undertaking is indivisibly associated with comparable progress in terms of integration being achieved in fiscal policy and other areas relevant to economic policy.

IV — Transitional problems

A — *Legal basis*

Competence in the field of economic and monetary policy has not yet been transferred to the European Community. The Member States continue to be responsible for these spheres of policy; however, they do have the commitment to coordinate their policies (Sections 2, 104, 105 and 145 of the Treaty of Rome) in order to achieve their common objectives, to maintain a high level of employment and stability of the price level, to ensure equilibrium in the overall balance of payments and to maintain confidence in their currencies (Section 104 of the Treaty of Rome). A certain restriction for the member countries through Community law is to be seen in the fact that they should consider their exchange rate policies as a matter of common interest (Section 107 of the Treaty of Rome).

Restrictions that go further result from the rules governing the EMS. Leaving aside two Council Directives relating to the EMCF and the ECU, they are based on multilaterally agreed acts of self-restriction on the part of the central banks concerned and hence are not part of the legislation of the Community proper. In accordance with a regulation in respect of the Treaty (Section 102(a) of the Treaty of Rome) introduced together with the Single European Act of 1986, institutional changes in the field of economic and monetary policy undertaken in the course of further developments require the conclusion of a new Treaty under international law in accordance with Section 236 of the Treaty of Rome. How far an international Treaty is necessary in individual cases depends on the scope each central bank has in extending economic policy cooperation under its basis in law. This probably differs from country to country since the central banks in the individual member countries have a differing status in law.

(No definitive catalogue can be drawn up for Germany indicating what acts of legislation would be required in each case for measures that are designed to further develop the EMS. In abstract terms, the following guidelines can be set forth:

1. In the Federal Republic of Germany, under Section 24 of the Basic Law the transfer of sovereign rights to international institutions requires an Act of Parliament. This requirement of constitutional law is to be interpreted strictly (Federal Constitutional Law 58, p. 1 ff., and especially p. 35).

2. The Deutsche Bundesbank is able to participate in closer monetary policy cooperation through greater cooperation among central banks only within certain limits. A limit would be reached if the Bundesbank were to accept decisions by an external body — such as the Committee of Governors — with respect to monetary policy measures which it is its duty to decide upon autonomously. In doing so, it would relinquish the exercise of the authority it has under the Bundesbank Act. German public and administrative law assumes that a body that has been entrusted with tasks and responsibilities exercises these responsibilities directly; delegating them to another body is only possible if it is empowered to do so by law. It is also not permissible for such a body to link the decisions entrusted to it to the agreement of other bodies. In contrast, mutual agreements and concertations are and remain possible.

3. The Deutsche Bundesbank is not able to establish a joint institution together with other central banks and grant it powers in the field of monetary policy either; for this, owing to the lack of the necessary authorization, it does not have the power of organization required under public law.

4. Finally, on the basis of existing law, the Deutsche Bundesbank cannot transfer parts or all of its monetary reserves permanently and irrevocably to a common fund; such a transfer would go beyond the scope of the 'operations' the Bank is empowered to conduct.)

Before national responsibilities are transferred to the Community sufficient clarity should exist as to the distribution of responsibilities at the Community level. The point behind this is to ensure that the principles of a European monetary order as described above have been put into effect at least in basic terms at every stage of integration. With respect to the position of the Community monetary authorities this means that no rights of any kind to issue instructions are granted to the political level and that an influence on national central banks does not accrue to the national political authorities to which they do not have a right under national law. This would speak in favour of making the Committee of EC Central Bank Governors, which is free from political instructions both at the national and the Community level, the starting point for further development in institutional terms. The members of this Committee would need to enjoy personal independence from the bodies that appoint them, which admittedly also presupposes corresponding independence in their functions at the national level. In contrast, the EMCF, which is tied to directives issued by the EC Council of Ministers and hence is subject to political instructions, is not suitable as a monetary authority for the Community.

B — *Integration in stages*

Whether responsibilities in the field of monetary policy can be transferred to the Community level in several steps or in a single act of law depends on the concept on which the integration process is based. *In principle, preference should be given to a global concept of integration with a clearly formulated final objective, as described above, with the individual steps being geared to this objective.* A process of integration determined only by pragmatic considerations would not offer any guarantee that the final objective will actually be attained. It would be in accordance with this global concept of integration if the necessary authorization were not to be restricted to individual steps in the process of integration but were to relate to the stage-by-stage plan as a whole, or at least to its major components. The member countries applied this procedure successfully in bringing about the customs union in the first decade of the Community's existence. However, experience with the plan of 1970 to achieve economic and monetary union in stages argues against setting a rigid timetable for the process of integration. *Rather, institutional changes, which also include extensions in the spheres of competence of existing Community institutions, should be made dependent on qualitative progress towards convergence in the field of economic and monetary policy.* The member countries would, of course, need to agree on a common procedure to determine whether the prerequisites have been fulfilled for the next stage towards economic and monetary union to be put into effect.

From a legal point of view, the establishment of an economic and monetary union in the Community does not depend on the existence of a political union. Rather, it is an accepted fact that the member countries of the Community can separate certain tasks from the multitude of responsibilities they have and transfer them to a supranational institution. They nevertheless continue to exist as States. They continue to pursue their own policies in major fields and have the necessary executive power to do so (territorial and individual sovereignty). To this extent, the jointly created supranational entity — in this case, the European Community — exists as an 'association for the specific purpose of integrating certain functions'.

As was already stated in the Werner Report of 1970, a lasting economic and monetary union requires the transfer of far-reaching responsibilities of national authorities to the Community plane above and beyond the direct field of monetary policy. An 'association for the specific purpose of integrating certain functions' would therefore probably only be able to survive if it is supported by a far-reaching reshaping of the Community in political and institutional terms in the direction of a more comprehensive union. To this extent, progress towards economic, monetary and general political union is mutually interdependent and thus sets the framework in which progress in institutional terms appears possible.

C — *Partial integration versus comprehensive integration*

Important political considerations can also plead against integration by stages where individual groups of countries move towards integration at varying speeds.

Endeavours should therefore be made to include all the Community member countries in the process of monetary integration. So long as considerable differentials exist within the Community in terms of prosperity and productivity that are not offset to a large extent and in good time through corresponding transfers of resources in the context of fiscal compensation within the union, movements in the factors of production between the various regions can occur as internal market conditions are brought about. The more developed regions will be given impulses to growth at the expense of the periphery. To the extent that they do not prefer to allow themselves to be guided by general political considerations, this risk will probably deter a number of member countries of the Community from joining a monetary union. In contrast, a core group of countries, such as those comprising the members of the present EMS exchange rate system, appear to be quite strong enough in economic terms to agree to closer and closer ties with corresponding consequences in the field of economic policy.

The concept of integration by stages was practised under the 'snake' system and is practised *de facto* within the EMS. Since monetary policy coordination largely took place in these systems up to now on a cooperative basis the coexistence of differing rights and obligations in various countries did not impair cooperation. If, however, substantial progress towards integration is tied to major institutional bonds individual countries, by exercising their veto, could bring about a situation where such progress is made only on the basis of the lowest common denominator. The countries capable of integrating could escape this situation by agreeing on more rapid steps towards integration among themselves. In this case, the *countries at the lower level of integration would no longer be able to participate in the monetary policy decision-making bodies of the Community on an equal basis as is the case at the present level of cooperation by means of a gentlemen's agreement. Only the countries prepared to subject themselves to its standards could have a claim to participate fully in the monetary union.*

Integration by stages would be tantamount to dividing the Community into two parts which would not remain restricted to the monetary sphere as integration progressed but would also lead to the individual member countries of the Community having different rights and obligations. Although such a system of differing rights and obligations in individual spheres would not be considered to be incompatible with the Treaty of Rome, independent bodies of the monetary union would need to be created alongside the organs of the Community in order to meet the demands of the final objective. In the light of the present state of development of the European Community, this division between the level of cooperation and the level of integration would not only raise serious problems of a practical nature but the unification of Europe would gain a new quality through the partial integration of a number of core member countries as compared with the approach to integration adopted in the past. New hurdles would be raised for the countries on the periphery that would be increasingly difficult to take. The proponents of faster integration of the core member countries see this primarily as a transitional problem; they argue that, with the system being open to a corresponding extent, the countries initially excluded from this process could catch up with the train of integration later on when the economic prerequisites to do so have been created. However, the danger must not be dismissed that ultimately the differences between the member countries in economic terms will become cemented with the division of Europe into two parts in the field of monetary policy and in the related institutions. Although the pull of an incipient monetary union would be strong for the countries on the periphery, the high barriers of access to it might possibly frustrate their joining it in the long run. If the unification of Europe as a whole is also being striven for, then two-speed integration in the monetary sphere would tend to be an obstacle.

D — Integration under the Treaty of Rome or outside it

The stage-by-stage plan together with the description of the individual steps up to the final stage could be decided upon in a single package and extend the Treaty of Rome by the dimension comprising economic and monetary union. This 'package solution' would have the advantage that it would be the subject of forming a political opinion in all the member countries only once and that it would not be necessary to negotiate the union several times over in 'small coin' before the national legislative bodies, apart from the imponderables of the procedure as arose with the ratification of the Single European Act.

Through a 'package solution' of this nature, not only would the objectives be laid down in contractual form but the requisite responsibilities of the Community would also be established. As a result, the issuing of 'Regulations in unforeseen circumstances' under Section 235 of the Treaty of Rome would no longer be necessary. Disagreements would be excluded on the issue, for instance, as to when 'institutional changes' occur (see Section 102(a)) or whether a measure in the field of monetary policy is still accessible to — extensive — interpretation under Section 235.

If, in the context of such an extended Treaty, a decision-making body decides to conclude one stage of integration and initiates the next step in monetary policy cooperation, then the question arises as to which body should be granted this responsibility. Several solutions to this question are conceivable. The Treaty already entrusts the Council with the authority to take decisions on such determinations in other cases (see, for example, the determination of the Council with respect to the transitional period; Section 8 of the Treaty of Rome). In principle, the Commission could also be entrusted with making such a determination. As regards the technical expertise involved, however, the Committee of Central Bank Governors could also be considered for this task. A mixed body is conceivable as well.

However, if it is assumed that not all the member countries enter the integrational stage in the field of monetary policy at the same time, it will hardly be possible to grant these member countries the right to participate in its design. The countries engaged in the process of integration will not want to expose themselves to the risk of being partly governed by outsiders and expect that only those countries take part which expose themselves to the same risk. For this reason, it could prove necessary to lay down the corresponding rules among the active participants outside the Treaty of Rome initially. Basically speaking this route was taken with the inception of the EMS. It would avoid the 'systematics' of the Treaty of Rome and make monetary integration within the framework of the Committee of Governors possible, which corresponds to the basic features of a European monetary order described above. At a later stage, ways would need to be discussed on how to harmonize the new set of rules with the Treaty of Rome.

The objection could be raised against bringing about monetary integration outside the Treaty of Rome that this approach would not correspond to the final objective of creating an economic and monetary union within the Community. Under Section 102(a), it could be argued, member countries have undertaken a mandatory commitment to adopt the procedure laid down in Section 236 of the Treaty of Rome when they enter the institutional stage. They would have to refrain from all measures that could jeopardize the achievement of the objectives laid down in the Treaty of Rome (Section 5, Subsection 2). The Commission will also have a considerable interest in incorporating the monetary policy institutions in the Treaty of Rome.

If the route prescribed under Section 236 of the Treaty of Rome is taken then the entry into force of changes in the Treaty is made dependent on their being ratified by all the member countries. An individual member country would then be in a position to prevent the institutionalization of cooperation, or at least to delay it considerably.

V — Concluding remarks

Since the inception of the EMS considerable progress has been made in the Community in the field of monetary policy cooperation. In conjunction with the latest measures to establish an integrated financial area and the planned establishment of the single European market, the perspective of an economic and monetary union now appears in a favourable light again. Economic and monetary union would mark the end of a development which, despite all the considerable progress that has been made, will still take some time to achieve. Not all the member countries of the Community participate in the exchange rate mechanism of the EMS, and not all the participating countries subject themselves to the same conditions. The economic prerequisites for a monetary union that is characterized by immutably fixed exchange rates between the participating countries will probably not exist for the foreseeable future. Even among the members who form the nucleus of the exchange rate system, tensions must repeatedly be expected for the foreseeable future owing to differing economic policy preferences and constraints as well as the resultant divergences in their economic development, which will make realignments in the central rates of their currencies necessary. Even within a common single market these problems will not simply disappear, especially seeing that this market will trigger additional structural adjustment constraints, the extent of which cannot as yet be fully assessed. For this reason, too, it will not be possible to do fully without occasional realignments in central rates for the foreseeable future. This indicates the necessity for further progress in the direction of greater convergence in a large number of macroeconomic as well as structural fields.

The existing EC Committee of Central Bank Governors offers itself as the basic unit in organizational terms of an EC monetary authority which does not threaten to run counter to the demands of the final stage at the outset. Competence in the field of monetary policy could be increasingly transferred to it over the course of time. In the initial stage it would direct its activities towards coordinating national monetary policy objectives, individual decisions and the employment of monetary policy instruments. Parallel to this, it would ensure an increasingly greater degree of harmonization of the exchange rate policies of the member countries. Working from this basis, its responsibilities could gradually be extended in the direction of obligatory advance consultations and go as far as having the right to issue directives on questions of monetary and exchange rate policy. A major factor in coordinating monetary policy at the Community level is the centralized process of shaping policy, which could be undertaken by the national central banks as the constituent parts of a European central bank system. In organizational terms, the Committee of Governors could be supported by its own enlarged secretariat.

Developing its own activities in the money and foreign exchange markets on the part of an EC monetary authority equipped with technical resources and staff as well as monetary policy instruments would not appear to be necessary until the national currencies have been abolished and a single European currency has been introduced. The step-by-step transition from a national to a Community monetary policy should take place on a legal basis that does not relate to individual steps in the process of integration but to this process as a whole. As far as possible, all the member countries of the Community should embark jointly on the path towards economic and monetary union in order not to handicap the integration of Europe as a whole at a later date.

If only a few Community member countries were to spur forward this would have serious economic and political consequences. Ultimately, the danger would exist of Western Europe being permanently divided into two parts if the barriers to access to the smaller system were to become too high. However, to the extent that separate action in Europe were politically desired, the door would have to be left open for the countries excluded in the initial stages to join later. *But these countries could not be granted any right to participate in the affairs of the monetary union.* Besides institutional arrangements of this nature, however, it is of outstanding importance for the success of monetary integration for the gradual transfer of monetary policy to the Community level to be accompanied by sufficient progress in the integration of economic and fiscal policy. Isolated steps in the monetary field would overburden monetary policy in political terms and jeopardize the credibility of the process of unification in the longer run.

A European central banking system —
Some analytical and operational considerations

Niels Thygesen[1]

The author is indebted to colleagues in the Delors' Committee and particularly Governor C. Ciampi, to the two rapporteurs and to Dr Daniel Gros for discussions on some of the ideas in the note; he retains sole responsibility for the analysis and the views expressed.

Introduction

The purpose of the present note is to review briefly some analytical and operational issues which arise at an advanced stage of monetary integration. These issues are relevant to the present rather tightly managed EMS which has developed gradually since 1983, and their resolution could be experimented with in the decentralized and pre-institutional first stage. They are essential in any effort to clarify how monetary policy might be designed and operated in the second stage if a 'gradual transfer of decision-making power from national authorities to a Community institution' has to take place (paragraph 57, *Report on economic and monetary union in the European Community,* hereinafter referred to as 'the Report'). This note accepts that it may not be possible at the present juncture to propose a detailed blueprint for accomplishing such a transition in stage two, but the considerations in the following sections are kept in sufficiently general terms to incorporate a range of analytical and operational approaches. The note is also relevant to the collective management through the proposed European System of Central Banks (ESCB) in stage three prior to the introduction of a common currency.

The note contains three sections. The first asks how the ultimate objective(s) of monetary and other macroeconomic policies might be formulated to give concreteness to the general description in the Report. The second discusses to what extent intermediate objectives might be helpful in underpinning the attainment of the ultimate objectives. Finally, the third section looks at the possible instruments by which the ESCB and the participating national central banks might discharge and divide their responsibility for monetary policy.

---
[1] Professor of Economics, University of Copenhagen.

TABLE

Ultimate and intermediate objectives of monetary and other macroeconomic policies and the instruments of monetary policy

	Collective	National/relative
Ultimate objectives	Maintain approximate medium-term stability of producer prices in the internal market	Keep growth in nominal private final demand close to targeted path in each country
	Maintain sustainable current account position for area *vis-à-vis* rest of the world	
Intermediate objectives	Keep growth of monetary aggregate for area as a whole within targeted interval	Keep growth in domestic credit (DCE) within targeted interval in each country
		Keep stable exchange rates *vis-à-vis* other currencies within the area
Instruments available	General (and differentiated) reserve requirements against national DCEs	Intervention rates and policy in intra-area currency band
	Lending rates of ESCB	Interest-rate differentials within area
	Intervention policy *vis-à-vis* third currencies	(Small) parity realignments

Throughout the paper reference will be made to the Table which lists ultimate and intermediate objectives and the main policy instruments.

All three subjects raised in this note obviously require further analytical work, study of empirical regularities and assessment of practical feasibility. They are treated here in a highly preliminary way, though with some confidence that the issues will have to be addressed in order to properly prepare for the second and third stages outlined in the Report.

Ultimate objectives

As regards the ultimate objectives of policies in an economic and monetary union the Report states (paragraph 16) that 'these policies should be geared to price stability, balanced growth, converging standards of living, high employment and external equilibrium'.

It is difficult to assess, in the absence of additional precision on the relative weight to be given to these wide-ranging objectives, how procedures may be developed for monitoring whether policies are appropriate. The present note assumes that the prime contribution of monetary policy to the attainment of ultimate policy objectives will be made if the ESCB is committed to the objective of price stability, while supporting — subject to this proviso — the general economic policy set at the Community level by the competent bodies. This is the formulation chosen in paragraph 32 of the Report which describes the mandate for the ESCB.

Implicitly this division of responsibilities implies that all the remaining objectives would, in principle, be the concern of the non-monetary authorities at the national and Community levels. Since exchange-market interventions in third currencies would also be carried out 'in accordance with guidelines established by the ESCB Council' (paragraph 57 on stage two) and subsequently 'on the sole responsibility of the ESCB Council in accordance with Community exchange rate policy' (paragraph 60 on stage three) it is, however, necessary to recall that such interventions would provide not only an additional instrument for influencing price trends in the Community, but also the objective of external equilibrium. The ESCB Council would accordingly be faced with the problem of designing guidelines for interventions which take into account both its prime objective of price stability and the need to contain the build-up of unsustainable external disequilibria, most appropriately defined as large collective current account imbalances *vis-à-vis* the rest of the world. The Report does not say explicitly that internal price stability always has to take precedence over the external value of EC currencies in terms of third currencies, but it clearly envisages no significant degree of commitment to stabilize the latter. Though it may well be in this area that the issue of designing an appropriate mix of monetary and non-monetary policies will find the clearest expression, the attainment of some degree of external equilibrium would impinge primarily on the budgetary authorities.

In view of this interpretation, the judgment on the performance of monetary policy and the fulfilment by the ESCB of its mandate would hinge on an interpretation of the objective of price stability. That objective would have to be expressible in collective terms for the Community, but it could also usefully be linked to national indicators of a nominal nature in order to monitor the compatibility of policies. There appear to be two main contenders for the role of collective objective.

The first is to use medium-term stability of *average producer prices in the internal market* for goods as an indicator. The increasing competition and specialization resulting from the completion of the internal market will tend to make prices for internationally traded goods more homogeneous, removing gradually the scope for price discrimination between national markets. A weighted average of national producer price indices for the participating countries, expressed in a common unit, for example ECUs, would provide an increasing reliable indicator of a common price trend. There is evidence from earlier periods of stable exchange rates, notably the gold standard, that close convergence in producer prices is observable in an exchange-rate regime of the tightness envisaged, see, for example, McKinnon and Ohno (1988).

While such an index would give expression in a meaningful way to a common price performance in the Community, it might be desirable to focus particularly on the domestic (i.e. internal to the EC) sources of inflation in producer prices for which ESCB monetary policy would be most directly accountable. A deflator of value added in manufacturing industry calculated as a weighted average for the internal market would leave out of account the inflationary (or disinflationary) shocks such as terms-of-trade changes resulting from swings in the prices of energy or of other intermediate imports or of raw materials. Such external shocks generate fluctuations in the inflation rate which may in practice have to be at least in part accommodated by variations in the collective money supply. An ultimate objective expressed in terms of stability in the average of national value-added deflators would not be radically different from the course followed in the Community in the 1980s; the second oil-price shock led to a temporary acceleration of producer prices in Europe, even in the Federal Republic of Germany, while the 1985-86 decline in import prices for raw materials, energy and other intermediate inputs (as well as in the dollar) temporarily pushed the rate of change of producer prices below zero in the low-inflation EMS countries.

In short, by aiming to keep the rate of inflation measured by an average of value-added deflators within a narrow band close to zero, say between 0 and 2 %, or to keep the average increase in producer prices within a slightly wider band, similarly centred around a minimal rate of inflation, the ESCB could give specific content to the notion of a stability-oriented monetary policy and simplify the monitoring of its policies.

The other main contender is a broadly-based index such as *a Community-wide consumer price index,* widely perceived to reflect the cost of inflation to the economy. In an area as large and diverse as the Community national price trends measured by consumer prices may, however, diverge substantially between countries even over the medium term, because the weight of non-traded goods and services in this index is substantial and price trends for these goods are less directly constrained by the process of market integration. It might be confusing to public opinion to announce a collective price objective around which substantial variation in national performances persisted.

A collective price objective formulated in terms of an essentially common indicator, such as average producer prices, may be sufficient for guiding the aggregate thrust of monetary policy. However, for the purpose of linking up with monetary instruments or with national macroeconomic objectives which will continue to have great importance throughout stage two and into stage three, the collective objective could be supplemented by criteria of national performance, consistent with the common inflation objective. One possible way of doing so, broadly in line with trends in national policy-making in a number of industrial countries in the 1980s would be to set targets for *the rate of increase of some measure of nominal income for each participating country.*

To be more specific, objectives for the rate of increase in private final demand (private consumption, business fixed investment and residential construction) might be thought of as the national income measure most relevant in the context of monetary policy. For each participating country, the national and Community authorities would make a judgment on the unavoidable rate of inflation in private final demand prices expressed in the national currency and a rate of increase of real demand judged feasible in the light of trend capacity growth and the initial situation. The national inflation rates thus calculated would typically in their average be a bit above the collective objective for producer prices in the Community, because the broader price indices for final demand would comprise non-traded goods and services for which productivity increases are typically slower than for the sectors producing internationally traded goods in the EC market. National inflation rates in terms of final demand prices might also diverge slightly year by year, as the differentials in productivity between sectors are unlikely to be uniform across countries. Gradually goods market integration would tend to impose approximate parallelism on national price levels in this broader sense, as the range of traded goods expands and factor mobility increases.

Various forms of nominal income targeting have appeared in national policy-making in the 1980s when the confidence in monetary aggregates as intermediate targets was weakening, while a turn to objectives for the growth of real output was perceived as unrealizable and potentially inflationary. Maintaining a suitable measure of nominal income close to a steady growth path provides a framework for monitoring national economic policies and for coordinating them internationally, as is recognized in some of the main proposals for improving global policy coordination and reforming the international monetary system, see, for example, Williamson and Miller (1987) and Taylor (1989).

In the present context, nominal income targeting would provide a linkage to potential intermediate objectives at the national level and through them to decisions relating to a money supply process which will remain, at least through stage two, largely national in execution if not in design. Such a framework would be suitable for the coordination of monetary and fiscal policies in the Community in so far as it would facilitate the identification of policy conflicts. The latter would arise if the execution by the ESCB of its mandate for assuring price were to be eroded by the sum total of national fiscal policies implying a growth rate in nominal final demand in one or more countries inconsistent with the objective for average inflation. In this way the framework would pinpoint requirements for fiscal coordination in an analytically more satisfactory way than by simply looking at the size of budget imbalances relative to GNP, or to national savings, as a basis for imposing 'binding rules' on such imbalances. By monitoring both the national component of ESCB monetary policy and fiscal policy in terms of the same nominal income targets, the risk of open conflicts is reduced.

Intermediate objectives

In principle, it would be possible to gear monetary instruments directly to ultimate objectives. If the Community-wide index of producer prices were to accelerate — and information on prices could be available with a time-lag of one to two months — such an observed development would provide an indication that average interest rates in the Community should be raised to contain money creation. If the growth rate of nominal demand in a particular country were to run well ahead of the agreed national target that would — after a somewhat longer information lag — trigger a country-specific response by the tightening of one or more monetary instruments in the country concerned. Symmetric responses could be envisaged if a deceleration of average inflation or a shortfall of nominal demand became observable. Simple feedback rules of this type could provide a stabilizing framework within which both average and nationally differentiated departures from targets were dampened.

But further attention to the way changes in monetary instruments influence the ultimate objectives of average inflation and the rate of growth of nominal demand in the participating countries through monetary and/or credit aggregates is advisable for at least two reasons. First, formulating policy with respect to one or more appropriately chosen aggregate(s) will improve the understanding of monetary policy and enhance its credibility; it will become easier to monitor the actions of the ESCB than in the situation where policy performance is assessed only on the basis of the ultimate objectives over which monetary policy has, within any given shorter time horizon, only a limited influence. Second, if reserve requirements are to be applied as one of the main instruments of the ESCB, they have to be seen to work in a broadly similar way in the participating countries by relating to a monetary or credit aggregate which exerts some longer-run influence on the ultimate objectives.

A possible procedure would consist in setting a collective target for total annual money creation in the participating countries, consistent with the objective for average inflation. Abstracting temporarily from net interventions in third currencies by the participants, total additions to the broad money stock (M2 or M3) would be matched by the sum of domestic counterparts to money creation in each country, since purchases of other participating currencies by one participating central bank are offset by sales elsewhere within the system. There would, in principle, be no sterilization of interventions in partner currencies. The task of controlling total money creation would then consist in applying instruments which influence, through incentives or obligations, the readiness of each central bank to keep domestic credit expansion (DCE) close to a targeted, and collectively agreed, rate for the country in question. Setting the latter through a collective decision-making process in the ESCB would constitute the core of the *ex ante* coordination effort. The process would assist in making mutually consistent the national objectives for the growth of nominal demand from which the national DCEs are derived. Deviations between actual and targeted DCE would in turn give some early information on deviations between actual and targeted growth in nominal demand. A procedure of this nature has been outlined in some detail by Russo and Tullio (1988).

It can not be claimed with confidence that (1) national DCEs can be closely controlled or that (2) they are tightly linked to nominal demand over shorter periods of time, two desirable characteristics of intermediate monetary objectives, as analysed meticulously by Bryant (1980). A recent OECD study shows a fairly weak quarter-to-quarter relationship between DCE (and different monetary aggregates) and changes in nominal demand for the four largest EC economies. On the other hand, a clear tendency for both to decelerate has been observable in Germany, France and Italy (but not in the UK) since the early 1980s (see graph).

Despite the evidently high degree of slack in the relationship of DCE and nominal demand, using the former as intermediate objective may be justified by two considerations: (1) it provides the most direct linkage to total money creation in the area; and (2) it is an extension, in the direction of symmetry, of the present informal practice in the EMS in which most countries, with the significant exception of Germany, look to rates of domestic credit expansion relative to others in the EMS as the consistent underpinning for the main intermediate objective of maintaining stable exchange rates in the EMS. For the Federal Republic of Germany the shift from the present intermediate objective (target for

GRAPH

**Domestic credit expansion
and growth rates in nominal and real private final demand**

- REAL PRIVATE DEMAND
- NOMINAL PRIVATE DEMAND
- DOMESTIC CREDIT

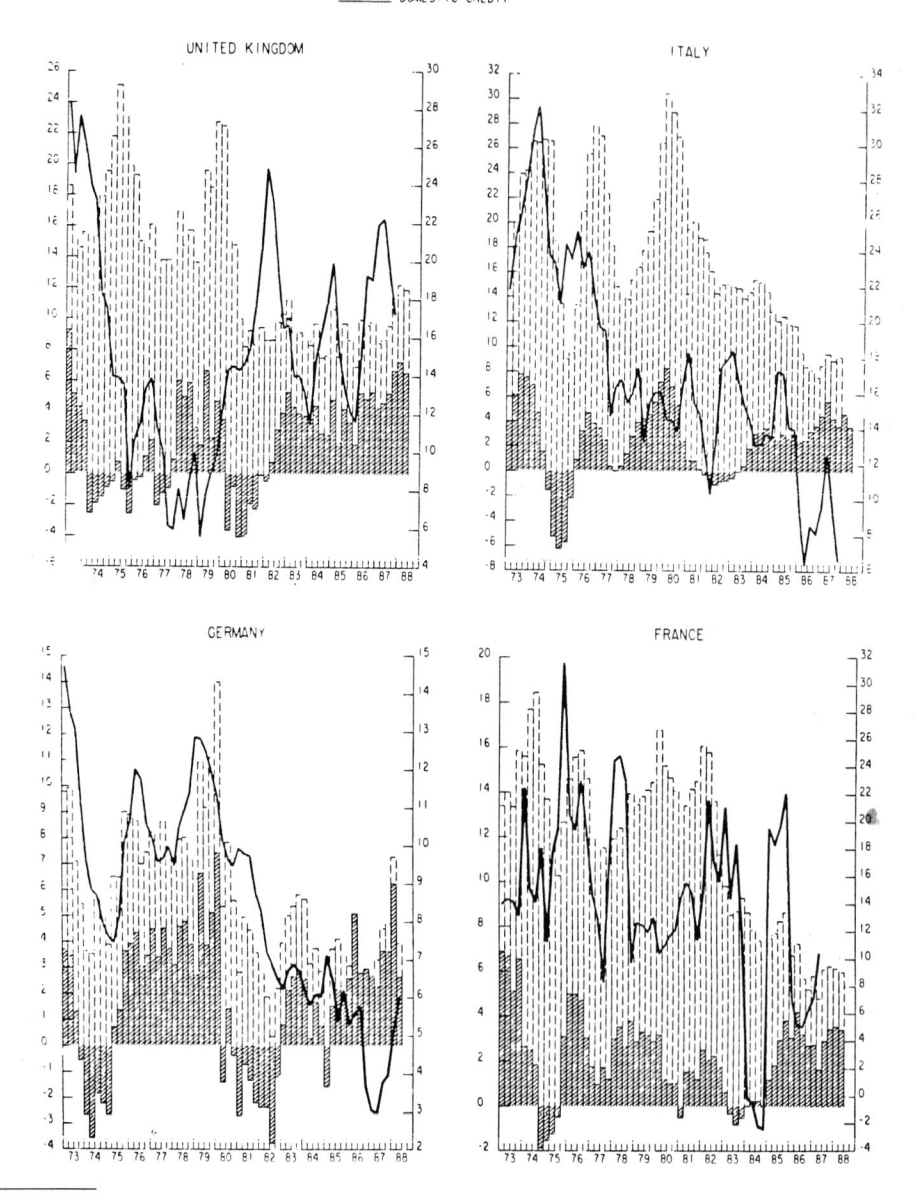

Source: OECD.

broad money, M3) to a DCE-target, with in principle no provision for sterilization, should be acceptable, provided overall money creation in the area were seen to be more directly subjected to stability-oriented, collectively agreed decisions and efficient instruments for implementing them, as is proposed in the main Report through the establishment of the ESCB with a mandate to pursue price stability.

Total money creation would depart from the sum of national DCEs to the extent that non-sterilized interventions *vis-à-vis* third currencies were undertaken by the ESCB directly or by one of the participating central banks. There is no presumption that such interventions would be sterilized; efforts to stem what was considered excessive depreciation of the area's currencies *vis-à-vis* the dollar through sales of dollars might well require some overall tightening of monetary conditions and higher average interest rates for the Community as a whole, and vice versa in the case of purchases of dollars to stem overly rapid appreciation of the participating currencies. The degree of sterilization would be matter for discretionary decisions arrived at collectively through the ESCB Council. The latter would also, in consultation with the participating central banks, take a view on which currency or currencies to use in dollar interventions. One important criterion in reaching such decisions would be to maximize the cohesiveness of the currencies within the system as that finds expression in the exchange markets. Guidance would be found also in the degree of correspondence in each country between a central bank's DCE objective and the observed growth in credit including potential effects of sterilization operations linked to interventions in third currencies which the ESCB may assign to that particular central bank.

For the individual central bank, the main short-term intermediate objective would continue to be the maintenance of stable exchange rates *vis-à-vis* other participating currencies. Some *ex ante* coordination of DCE objectives should make that taksk easier on average; but in practice, the DCE objective may, in particular situations, have to be overridden to maintain exchange-rate stability.

Instruments available

Even prior to the attribution of any particular instrument to the ESCB, the collective formulation of ultimate and intermediate monetary objectives would in itself constitute a major step towards *ex ante* coordination desirable in stage one. Nothing would prevent the EMS central banks from keeping their present exchange of information on their respective formulation of domestic monetary policy, or from giving the reports prepared by a special group of experts for the Committee of Central Bank Governors a more deliberately common analytical framework along the lines above. Similarly, the reports prepared by another expert group on exchange-market interventions could begin to be used in a more forward-looking way to formulate intervention strategies rather than to review the past record. Closer coordination could begin to replicate the effects of a more advanced stage, even while the policy analysis and recommendations emerging from it remain strictly advisory, as is the case for stage one.

Yet it is unlikely that anything resembling closely a common monetary policy could be conducted merely through discussions, but without vesting in the ESCB genuine decision-making power with respect to at least some significant instruments of monetary policy. Indeed, that is the rationale of suggesting the set-up of the ESCB for stage two before the irrevocable locking of parities which makes a common monetary policy a simple necessity. But there are difficulties in determining how monetary authority might be shared between a centre — the ESCB Council and Board — and the participating national central banks. The efficiency of operations requires that there should never be any doubt in the financial markets, among national policy-makers or elsewhere as to which body has the responsibility for taking particular decisions. Monetary authority is less easily divisible than budgetary authority where elements of decentralization and even of competitive behaviour between different levels of government, or within the same level, may be observed in national States.

Four types of policy decisions have to be considered as being at the core of any design of a workable allocation of responsibilities within an ESCB in stage two:

(1) adjustment of short-term interest differentials;

(2) intervention policy *vis-à-vis* third currencies;

(3) changes in reserve requirements; and

(4) changes in intra-area parities (realignments).

Reference is again made to Graph 1 above.

The adjustment of relative short-term interest rates is the central instrument in managing the present EMS, and a high degree of coordination and occasionally *de facto* joint, or at least bilateral, decisions have been observed. As the paper by Governor Godeaux explains, participants have developed, particularly since the so-called Basle-Nyborg agreement of September 1987, a flexible set of instruments for containing incipient exchange-market tensions: intramarginal intervention, wider use of the fluctuation band, and changes in short-term interest rate differentials. This combination has proved fairly robust in most periods of tension since September 1987. But a risk remains that the experience of earlier periods of tension will be repeated; then public criticism and mutual recrimination between Ministers for Finance occasionally intensified tensions and made monetary management very difficult. The main examples of such episodes are December 1986 to January 1987, November 1987 and — to a minor extent — April 1989.

The participation of additional currencies in the EMS in the course of stage one, notably sterling, which has traditionally been managed with considerable involvement on the part of the UK Treasury and even of the Prime Minister, will make it urgent to strengthen procedures for genuine coordination further and to make the transition to a more joint form of management in stage two at an early stage.

While decision-making in this sensitive area would still remain in national hands in stage two, the launching of the ESCB at the beginning of stage two would in itself imply that national governments would be less likely than in the past to involve themselves directly in the management of exchange crises. in the course of stage one the Committee of Central Bank Governors will already have begun to perform more efficiently the role of a multilateral arbitrator that has been missing occasionally in the past. A common analytical framework developed around the intermediate targets will give more explicit guidance as to who should adjust to whom. If the proposal to develop a joint operational facility for exchange and money market operations, as outlined in Professor Lamfalussy's paper, is pursued that would in itself bring participating central banks into more continuous contact also with respect to their transactions in their domestic financial markets and facilitate coordinated action on interest rates.

The gradual and partial upgrading of decision-making on relative interest rate adjustment from the purely national level to a Community body, in the first stage the Committee of Governors, from the second stage the ESCB Council, will not in itself assure that the average level of interest rates in the participating countries is appropriate, though it should tend to make such an outcome more likely than the present system with its occasional inefficiencies of interest-rate escalations and tensions. To get a firmer grip on the average level of rates, the attribution to the ESCB of an instrument which permits a collective influence on domestic sources of money creation would be necessary. Such an instrument is described briefly below in the form of the ability for the ESCB to impose compulsory reserve requirements on domestic money creation and to develop gradually a market for a European reserve base with its own lending rate.

A second instrument for which some degree of joint management could be envisaged is *foreign exchange interventions in third currencies*. There are two economic arguments for such an attribution: (1) the medium-term need to contribute to the containment of major misalignments, and (2) the smoothing of short-term volatility *vis-à-vis* third currencies.

The former argument can hardly be assessed without making a judgment on the feasibility of a more managed global exchange rate system and the degree of commitment by other major monetary authorities, notably in the United States, to support, through interventions and domestic monetary adjustments, any understanding reached on the appropriate level of the main bilateral exchange rates. Given the experience of the period since 1977 and the major present current-account imbalances, projected to persist well into the 1990s, it would be hazardous to assume that an emerging joint dollar policy of the EMS countries would be anything more than *ad hoc* guidelines for managing a collective appreciation of the EMS currencies as smoothly as possible. Calculations with large macroeconometric models suggest that the appreciation may have to be at least in the order of 20% in real terms on average for the EMS currencies from the levels prevailing in mid-1989, if the European countries are to assume a reasonable share of the adjustment of the US current deficit to a sustainable low level, see Cline (1989). This will put the cohesion of the EMS currencies to a severe test, but it will also provide a unique opportunity, as was the case in 1985–87, for reconciling low inflation in Europe with a relatively expansionary monetary policy in the Community, hence contributing to an improved and satisfactory price performance in the crucial transition period from the present more decentralized operation towards economic and monetary union.

As regards the task of smoothing short-term volatility, it must be noted that tensions among EMS currencies have often in the past decade been triggered by financial disturbances from third currencies, notably movements in the dollar, The currencies participating in the EMS were seen by the markets as being sensitive in different degrees to such disturbances. These perceived differences had their origins in varying degrees of controls on capital movements and in expectations of the likelihood of divergent policy reactions to the external financial disturbances. For example, a depreciation of the dollar was normally expected to strengthen the German mark relative to most other EMS currencies, both because the German mark had a far larger domestic financial base and the most liberal regime for capital flows and because non-German authorities in the EMS were seen as more prone than the Bundesbank to try to avoid the contractionary effects of the appreciation of their currencies. The tensions to which these – real or perceived – differences in structure and/or behaviour gave rise were occasionally mitigated by an EMS realignment. Conversely, in periods of an appreciating dollar, outflows from Europe were observed to be particularly strong from the German mark area, reflecting primarily the closer substitutability between the US dollar and the German mark than that prevailing for other EMS currencies, but presumably also a decreasing probability of a realignment within the system. In recent years the liberalization of capital movements in France and Italy and in some smaller EMS countries, the deepening of continental European financial markets and the improved cohesion of the EMS economies have all contributed to a weakening of the earlier negative correlation between movements in the US dollar (in effective exchange rate terms) and movements in non-German mark currencies in the EMS *vis-à-vis* the mark, as shown, for example, by Giavazzi and Giovannini (1989). But the tendency for dollar movements to affect the EMS currencies differentially may be expected to persist in moderate form into stage two. The task remains in that case to avoid that such tensions, if they are unwarranted by more fundamental economic divergence within the EMS, persist and force realignments.

While this could in principle be achieved through joint guidelines for essentially decentralized interventions by the participating national central banks, a visible capacity to intervene jointly in third currencies, and to do so in ways that further the cohesion of the EMS, is potentially important. Without a presence in the major exchange markets the ESCB would lack the capacity to check the impact of external financial disturbances on EMS stability at source. Hence 'a certain amount of reserve pooling' (Report, paragraph 57) as well as ample working balances in EMS currencies would be desirable in stage two.

It is impossible to determine *a priori* what percentage of external official reserves would have to be pooled in order to create a credibility effect in the financial markets for an emerging joint intervention policy. Leaving the percentage low, say 10 to 20 %, would run the risk of simply complicating existing cooperative procedures without making a qualitative difference, though even with limited pooling some beneficial effects could be expected simply from the learning experience of coordinating interventions through the same trading floor rather than by concertations over the telephone. Governor de Larosière describes these gains relative to the present EMS in his paper.

Joint interventions in third currencies by means of pooling of part of exchange reserves did not win general favour in the Report as a proposal for the first stage; too much emphasis might be put on external considerations relative to the correction of imbalances within the Community (paragraph 54). This argument would not apply to an ESCB capacity to intervene in stage two along with the attribution of other monetary instruments with more direct domestic implications for the participants as proposed here.

A third instrument, specifically assigned to the ESCB would be the ability to impose *variable reserve requirements on domestic money creation*.

Whereas the two first instruments (and the fourth to be discussed below) are directed primarily at relative adjustments within the EMS, changes in required reserve ratios affect the overall thrust of monetary policy. International monetary agreements, including the Bretton Woods system and the EMS, have typically been more explicit on relative than on aggregate adjustment in the participating countries. The EMS procedures for relative adjustment may leave something to be desired, as explained above and they may leave too much discretion to national monetary authorities to remove ambiguities and tensions. Yet more attention has been given to these procedures than to discussion of whether monetary policy has an appropriate aggregate thrust.

The Bretton Woods system and the early EMS did not have to face up to this issue directly, because both systems were protected by a mixture of capital controls for the short term and some scope for changing the exchange rate in the longer term. The post-1983 EMS has had more difficulty in avoiding the issue. In the absence of some aggregate monetary target for the whole system, an implicit monetary rule has emerged: monetary policy in all participating countries has tended to be determined, via the ambition to hold more rigidly fixed nominal exchange rates, mainly by that of its largest and least-inflationary participant. The practice in the EMS that reserves used for intervention in defending a weak currency have to be reconstituted within the span of a few months is that convergence – provided that exchange rates do remain fixed – will be towards the low inflation in the Federal Republic of Germany and not towards some average as would be the case if intervention credits provided a more permanent safety net. In that case efforts at sterilization would have become more widespread in the weaker currency countries, and aggregate money creation could have drifted upwards.

By using the degree of freedom for aggregate monetary policy by implicitly attaching policies to the domestic monetary target in Germany the EMS has succeeded since 1983 to an unexpected degree in becoming 'a zone of monetary stability' in the double sense of promoting both exchange rate *and* price stability. The challenge for stage two and stage three is to design intermediate objectives and monetary instruments so as to make likely an extension of these desirable features within the more collectively managed system marked by the transition to the ESCB.

A major reason why the past system would in any case have to be revised is that the hegemonial role of the largest country already shows signs of weakening and must be expected to be eroded further during stage one, as additional currencies join the EMS and short-term capital transactions are fully liberalized. This process affects the size of potential flows in the new member countries, in those countries that undertake additional liberalization, notably France and Italy, and in Germany. The ability of the Bundesbank to keep a preferred domestic monetary target as close to a desired path as has typically been the case for the past 15 years must be expected to weaken further. Financial integration increases the risk of policy errors and hence the incentive for all participants to modify the present paradigm. Another factor working in the same direction is the increasing ease, as the credibility of fixed exchange rates becomes more well founded, with which all non-German participants can attract inflows of capital by maintaining short-term rates only moderately above those in Germany. The improved substitutability between participating currencies inexorably pushes the thinking of all monetary authorities in the direction of more attention to aggregate money creation in the area and to the formulation of intermediate objectives for domestic money creation consistent with an aggregate target and to designing procedures whereby the latter can be kept roughly on their agreed course.

Governor Ciampi's paper spells out in some detail how an ability for the ESCB to impose variable reserve requirements on the domestic money creation for which each national central bank is primarily responsible could be set up in stage two, and the present note associates itself fully with the basic idea of that paper and the analysis of the various technical options available. The essential feature is that the ESCB should be empowered to impose — uniform or differentiated — reserve requirements on either the increase in the monetary liabilites of each national central bank or on the credit extended by the member banks to their respective domestic sectors. This requirement would be met only by holding reserves with the ESCB; and the supply of reserves would be entirely controlled by the latter through allocations of a reserve asset (official ECUs) to each central bank corresponding to the demand for reserves which would arise, if agreed targets for money creation or DCE were observed. Alternatively, the supply of reserves would be created by open market purchases of the ESCB. Both cost and availability considerations would provide central banks with an incentive to stay close to declared objectives. The ESCB would have to be given some discretion in extending or withdrawing reserves to provide marginal accommodation. The new system could replace the present method of creating official ECUs through temporary swaps of one fifth of gold and dollar reserves as well as the credits extended through the very short-term facility of the European Monetary Cooperation Fund.

The system would create a monetary control mechanism analogous to that through which national central banks, who use reserve requirements, influence money and credit creation through their banking systems. It would introduce a certain hierarchy in the relationship between the ESCB and its constituent national central banks, while leaving some freedom for each national central bank in designing its domestic instruments.

The reserve requirements could also be applied directly to DCE in the total national banking system, i.e. on the domestic sources of broad money creation. The advantage of this method would be to assign the collective monetary instrument more directly to a natural intermediate objective — DCE — underpinning fixed exchange rates, but it might introduce more slack in the control mechanism, as it would no longer apply to items that appear on the balance sheet of the central banks for which the latter could be regarded as more directly responsible.

In the variants of an operational framework for an integrated monetary policy described in Governor Ciampi's paper and in the previous paragraph, the ESCB would not have any direct contact with commercial banks or with financial markets in general. Its sphere of operation would be confined to transactions with the second tier of the three-tier system, the national central banks. This would be unduly confining from the time during stage three when a common currency is introduced. To manage a common currency the ESCB would need to have direct transactions with commercial banks, as does any national central bank at present. To prepare for this during the earlier part of stage three, possibly already in stage two, it may be useful to explore in what ways the ESCB could be put into a position to have some direct influence on liquidity conditions without always relying on its ability through guidelines and incentives to exert its influence indirectly via the national central banks. In any case, since legislation enabling the ESCB to deal directly with financial markets in the final stage of economic and monetary union would also be part of a comprehensive Treaty revision, attention to the nature of such contracts is not premature.

One way to give the ESCB such influence would be to allow it to make open market operations in national markets. The ESCB might, for example, use the securities it has acquired from the national central banks for such open market transactions. One could impose, initially, limits on the total amount of purchases and sales which can be made within any given period. This would be especially important at the start, when the ESCB would be mainly purchasing securities, since its initial stock would be small. These limits could be raised over time, allowing in stage three the operations of the ESCB to become more important than those of the national central banks in their respective markets.

A different and complementary approach, more directly in extension of the reserve requirement system applied to national central banks, would be to introduce a uniform European reserve requirement on commercial bank deposits, or on increases thereof. A small fraction of such deposits would be held with the ESCB and denominated in ECU. A federal funds market, in which the ESCB as the only issuer would have strict control of the total supply, could then develop in which commercial banks would trade among themselves the reserve balances they need to satisfy the European reserve requirement. The approach would imply that the ESCB be given direct influence on a market which reflects system-wide liquidity conditions.

The approach could be implemented by giving the ESCB the authority to set, within limits set in its statutes, a compulsory reserve requirement on all deposits of Community residents with Community commercial banks. To give banks initial access to deposits with the ESCB, the latter could initially buy the appropriate amount of securities in the market; hence the system could be regarded as complementary to the idea outlined above to permit the ESCB to undertake limited open market transactions in initial periods. The securities purchased could be denominated either in ECU or in national currencies, provided, if introduced in stage two, the proportions of the latter correspond to the weights in the ECU basket. Once the initial amount of reserves has been created and absorbed into required reserves, the ESCB could engage in additional marginal accommodation by supplying federal funds through modest discretionary open-market operations. A tightening of the federal funds market would come about if required reserves were to run ahead of this process of supplying them; and a rise in the federal funds rate would induce banks to slow down the underlying deposit creation. The approach is compatible with the usual range of operating procedures for a central bank from interest rate to reserves targeting.

Different operating procedures would presumably be appropriate as the ESCB extends its authority from stage two to stage three and to the ultimate management of a single currency, but the basic mechanism would not have to be modified. In effect, the ESCB could, from its beginning, act in some respects as a true central bank, reinforcing its more indirect and orchestrating functions inherent in the way that the earlier proposals constrain it to being a bank for the central banks only.

Suggesting some form of reserve requirements as the major instrument for an emerging joint policy to influence the domestic sources of money creation — as a complement to the control over the external sources which a joint exchange rate and intervention policy *vis-à-vis* third currencies would provide — is bound to raise critical questions on the approach. Although reserve requirements have historically been the prime method by which central banks have achieved monetary control in most countries, reliance on that instrument may appear to be limited in the Community today (see, for example, the survey of Kneeshaw and Van den Bergh, 1989). In most industrial countries the banking system has become indebted to the central bank to an extent that makes it dependent on the terms on which marginal accommodation of reserve needs is provided. The mechanisms suggested illustrate ways in which an analogous influence may be brought to bear through a reserve requirement system on the relationship between the ESCB and the participating central banks (the three-tier system) and gradually extended to financial markets in general. A direct contact between the central institution and the financial market would provide a smooth passage to the final stage when the ESCB is to manage a common currency.

The three instruments proposed so far — collective guidance of relative interest-rate adjustments, joint interventions in third currencies with a definitively pooled part of foreign exchange reserves and imposition of variable reserve requirements on domestic money creation — are all major examples of shifts towards the European level of decision-making authority in well-specified areas of the kind that could be considered for stage two and extended into stage three as long as there is no single currency issued by the ESCB beyond the restricted circuit for the management of the reserves market referred to above.

It remains to consider how the one decision in the EMS which is today subject to *de facto* joint decision-making, namely realignments of central rates, could be handled in stage two. Would there be a case for vesting authority over this instrument with the ESCB as part of monetary management rather than leaving it as in the present EMS with the Ecofin Council? There are arguments for and against such a transfer.

A major purpose of setting up elements of a collective monetary authority — the ESCB — *before* the irrevocable lacking of parities which marks the transition to the third and final stage of economic and monetary union is to constrain realignments and eliminate the need for them. A more specific objective would be to assure that the occasional and rare recourse to them will be made in sufficiently small steps to preserve continuity of market exchange rates around realignments. This has been an important feature in the containment of speculative pressures in the recent EMS experience. If financial market participants would interpret a transfer of authority for making the residual small realignments to the participating central banks as part of the ESCB's task as a signal of an intended tightening of the EMS in the transition to full economic and monetary union, such a transfer could prove stabilizing and hence desirable.

Putting the question in this way, however, suggests the counter-argument, namely that governments might not succeed in conveying such a signal. They might instead feel relief at not having, as in the present EMS, to bear the political burden of visibly initiating a realignment – and without a new, more hidden, discipline inherent in membership of a union with irrevocably fixed exchange rates. The Council of the ESCB might be faced with *fait accompli* situations in which only a realignment would ease tensions and with national policy-makers blaming either private speculators or the central bankers themselves for the outcome. This would imply a deterioration relative to the recent performance of the EMS.

On balance, these arguments suggest that the decisive considerations in assigning the authority to undertake realignments are how close participants have come to meeting the prerequisites for full union. It would be dangerous, if feasible, to shift the responsibility for deciding on realignments to the ESCB in stage two, if any major divergence of economic performance has persisted into that stage. But it would be desirable to shift that responsibility, if the need for realignments were generally accepted as residual only, and if adequate monetary instruments for underpinning fixed rates had been assigned to the ESCB along the lines proposed above. A tentative conclusion is that the authority to decide on realignments could become part of the mandate of the ESCB in stage two, but that this is less of a priority than the attribution of the other, day-to-day, instruments of an increasing collective monetary policy.

References

Bryant, Ralph C. *Money and monetary policy in interdependent nations,* Brookings Institution, Washington DC, 1980.

Cline, William R. *United States external adjustment and the world economy,* Institute for International Economics, Washington DC, 1989.

Frenkel, Jeffrey. 'A modest proposal for international nominal targeting' *NBER Working Paper* No 2849, National Bureau of Economic Research, Cambridge, Massachusetts, 1989.

Giavazzi, Francesco and Giovannini, Albato. *Limiting exchange-rate flexibility: The EMS,* MIT Press, 1989.

Kneeshaw, John T. and Van den Bergh, Paul. 'Changes in central bank money market operating procedures in the 1980s', *BIS Economic Papers* No 23, Bank for International Settlements, Basle, 1989.

McKinnon, Ronald and Ohno, Kenichi. 'Purchasing power parity as a monetary standard', *unpublished,* Memorandum No 276, Center for Research in Economic Growth, Stanford University, 1988.

Russo, Massimo and Tullio, Giuseppe. 'Monetary policy coordination within the European Monetary System: Is there a rule?' Giavazzi, Francesco, Micossi, Stefano and Miller, Marcus H. *The EMS,* Chapter II, Cambridge University Press, Cambridge, 1988.

Williamson, John and Miller, Marcus H. 'Targets and indicators: A blueprint for the international coordination of economic policy', *Policy analyses in international economics* No 22, Institute for International Economics, Washington DC, 1987.

First stages towards the creation of a European Reserve Bank

The creation of a European Reserve Fund

J. de Larosière

Obviously, the economic and monetary construction of Europe will not be achieved in a single stage, although much has been secured already. This construction calls for a pragmatic approach, centred around the gradual fulfilment of the final objective ultimately chosen.

The purpose of this note is to sketch out some ideas on the nature and pace of possible initial steps that could lead ultimately to economic and monetary union.

To pass through the different phases, monetary authorities will need a clear vision:

— not only of the medium-term direction in which they should be channelling their initiatives in the monetary sphere;

— but also of the daily implementation of the policies they are responsible for framing and coordinating.

With a view to giving more practical and more visible form to their cooperation on exchange rate and interest rate management, the gradual construction of a permanent body for joint action and deliberation would be a highly significant step forward. There would be three advantages to this:

— it would demonstrate politically, and to the markets, the governments' determination to progress more actively towards economic and monetary union;

— it would rapidly create effective means, on the eve of the opening of the single European market and in a spirit of cooperation with the other currency zones, to ensure with more efficiency the smooth functioning of the markets;

— it would enhance the efficiency of central banks' monetary management at both domestic and European levels.

The European Reserve Fund (ERF) would be built up progressively. Its powers would depend on progress towards the construction of Europe and on the responsibilities that the Member States would be prepared to devolve upon it. Its immediate creation — as a first step towards a European Reserve Bank — would establish a nucleus around which more ambitious functions could gradually be assembled, the final stage being the realization of an economic and monetary union.

I — The spirit of the proposal to create a European Reserve Fund

The proposal is inspired by four guiding ideas.

1. *Initiating a training ground process*

The creation of a European Reserve Fund aims at promoting joint deliberation and a common approach with regard to monetary issues in a framework which would allow permanent information exchanges, regular comparison between analyses and a closer knowledge of short-term economic developments and of the policies implemented in individual countries.

The target is to initiate a training ground process allowing individual member countries to improve not only the coordination of their monetary policies but also the management of the increasingly growing interaction between exchange rate and monetary policies.

2. *Strengthening the impact of intervention policies in the foreign exchange markets as designed within the Group of Seven*

The aim of intervention, that the European Reserve Fund would undertake, will be to underline as far as possible and considered useful the central banks' will to act on a coordinated basis within the EC framework.

In its implementation, intervention by the European Reserve Fund would, in a first phase, strengthen the impact of operations agreed in common by central banks, without necessarily increasing their volume. Such intervention would thus have no additional effect, either directly or indirectly, on the domestic monetary policies of Member States. Indeed, it could be agreed that the ERF's intervention should only take place after unanimous agreement has been reached between member central banks.

3. *Creating a permanent 'think-tank' on monetary analysis*

In order to continue to play its strategic role in the construction of Europe, monetary policy must have the support of a common 'think-tank' on monetary developments. In this area, the current framework of cooperation may be further improved, not as a substitute for national decision-taking, but in order to harmonize, in a first phase, concepts, analyses and instruments available for monetary policy.

Obviously, decisions are not to be reached at the level of the experts in charge of such surveillance. Policy choices in this area will still be made by individual central banks, but, prior and parallel to these decisions, analyses and recommendations will be made in common. This phase is therefore of major significance in order to promote a consistent analysis of monetary developments and to reaffirm *vis-à-vis* the markets the highest priority given to the common objective of price stability.

4. *Increasing the role of the Committee of Governors*

With such a goal in mind, the role of the Committee of Governors will have to be strengthened. However, in order to ensure that the Governors do not limit themselves to exchanging views, but can enter into discussions which might result in recommendations, the regular advice of their experts will have to be made available to them, not only on specifically monetary issues, but also, as is already the case each month for the foreign exchange market, on any matter influencing monetary policy implementation, including short-term economic developments.

It is thus in this spirit that my proposal calls for the creation of an institutional embryo, i.e. the European Reserve Fund, which has the advantage of gathering within a permanent framework monetary and foreign exchange policy experts from participating central banks in order to make available to the Governors regular and global assessments of monetary developments. This is a major aspect of the proposal, as it is indeed necessary, from the initial phase of the process, to create between central banks a common framework for deliberation which goes beyond the continuation or even a deepening of cooperation between central banks.

II — Functions and structure of the European Reserve Fund

The Fund could be built up on the following basis:

A. It would be given certain functions in the foreign exchange and the monetary sphere;

B. its organization would foreshadow the structure of a European Reserve Bank;

C. it would have to fulfil certain legal and institutional conditions.

A — *The functions of the ERF*

In an international monetary system in which the main reserve currencies are floating, markets are worldwide and capital moves freely, close cooperation is required among central banks responsible for keeping their currency within fluctuation margins. Central banks would significantly enhance the impact of their foreign exchange interventions if, under certain circumstances, they were to decide not only to consult among themselves, but also to act through the agency of a common body. Operations conducted through the ERF would have the advantage of reinforcing the effect of central bank action while permanently focusing attention on visible progress towards the construction of a European monetary union.

The ERF's functions would include:

1. intervening in the foreign exchange market;

2. ultimately taking over the powers of the EMCF;

3. progressively setting up a body to exercise surveillance over monetary and interest rate trends;

4. preparing for the harmonization of national money markets with a view to the institution, in successive stages, of a European Reserve Bank.

1. Intervention in the foreign exchange market

(a) *Areas of intervention*

In the first place, this would concern interventions in third currencies which would be agreed in common by members, thus preventing any operation from hindering the domestic policy followed by any given country.

The role of the ERF would be to intervene directly in the markets, thus embodying the cohesion of the monetary authorities in pursuing a common policy towards third currencies. It is here that the role of the ERF would be most directly perceptible and would illustrate the tripolar structure of the international monetary system: the United States, Japan and Europe. This role would of course be exercised in line with the broad thrust of the Group of Seven policy.

Secondly, the ERF could intervene in Community currencies — with the agreement of the central banks concerned — either intra-marginally or at the limits, in order to supplement individual action by central banks when strains appear in the system and require visible affirmation of solidarity.

Obviously, in a first phase the ERF's role with regard to intervention would be a complementary one, while there would continue to be concerted intervention by the different central banks. But the ERF would have the advantage of ensuring close coordination between the individual actions of the central banks and the overall policy of participants in the Fund.

In a second phase — to be agreed upon unanimously — the shareholding central banks could decide to hand over to the ERF the power to undertake certain operations on its own initiative in compliance with the guidelines set by the Governors on the Board of Directors.

(b) *Means of intervention*

In order to play the role assigned to it in the foreign exchange markets, the ERF would require sufficient currency reserves to enable it to assert *vis-à-vis* the markets its capacity for intervening. These reserves would consist of:

— an initial endowment, which would be independent of current contributions in gold and dollars to the EMCF and would represent, for example, initially 10% of the gold holdings and 10% of the foreign currency holdings of each of the central banks participating in the European exchange rate mechanism. The foreign currency component would be paid in dollars; there would be an additional contribution by participants in their national currency, based on a formula to be defined. This endowment would be made on a permanent basis (and not in the form of renewable swaps as is the case with the EMCF);

— additional resources in the form of swap lines with the Federal Reserve Bank and, possibly, with the Bank of Japan.

As a counterpart to their permanent contributions, central banks would receive shares. The question arises whether the contributions of individual central banks should be periodically readjusted.

There are two possible approaches:

— on the one hand, as is the case with the EMCF, a fixed percentage ratio could be maintained between the amount of reserves held by the shareholding central banks and their contributions to the ERF. Such a solution, which calls in question the permanent nature of the initial contributions, would be rather complex in practice;

— on the other hand, it could be decided not to establish an automatic link between the volume of the ERF's assets and the amount of reserves held by its shareholders. The permanent nature of the contributions would be confirmed by the decision to forgo any periodical readjustment; moreover, the relatively low level set in the proposal for shareholders' initial contributions should prevent any central bank from pointing to a decrease in its reserves as grounds for reducing its contribution to the ERF and strengthening its own means of intervention.

(c) *Management of reserves*

The ERF would manage these reserves itself, thereby further reinforcing — including in the view of the markets — the degree of cooperation between central banks.

2. Subsequent taking over of the powers of the EMCF

In working towards greater exchange rate policy coordination among the members of the EMS, and for reasons of simplicity, the body responsible for carrying out interventions probably ought not to remain permanently separate from the one responsible within the Community for managing the holdings of official ECUs and the Community credit mechanisms.

Consequently, it would be appropriate to give immediate acknowledgement to the intention that the ERF should ultimately assume the powers of the EMCF once all the EEC's central banks have joined the European Reserve Fund.

3. Monetary surveillance

Alongside the creation of a foreign exchange department, the ERF would set up a monetary policy department responsible for:

— analysing in particular interest rate trends, monetary aggregates and domestic demand;

— thereby underpinning from both a conceptual and a Community point of view the concerted management of exchange rates and the coordination of monetary policies among the different participating central banks.

This phase could go hand in hand with the creation of a monetary policy coordination committee, which would define common surveillance instruments, propose harmonized objectives, and progressively graduate from *ex post* analysis to an *ex ante* approach to monetary policy adjustment.

In a second phase, one could envisage vesting in the ERF powers to act in support of central banks' actions in their respective money markets, by undertaking swap operations for limited amounts, with commercial banks. Such supporting action would in any case be marginal, but pending more structured action (see paragraph 4 below) it could be a first step towards operational functions in the monetary field.

4. Harmonization of national money markets

A third phase would begin once harmonization of the fundamentals of monetary and exchange rate policies was practically completed and coordination of domestic demand adjustment (in fiscal terms notably) an accomplished fact. It would then be possible to work constructively towards harmonizing the instruments and policies of intervention in national money markets.

Throughout these different stages, the ERF would be responsible for preparing the way for the advent of a common currency. In this regard, effective progress in the development of the ECU — without prejudging its future definition and issuing process — should be secured alongside the process leading to the ultimate phase of economic and monetary union.

B — *Organizational arrangements*

The structure of the European Reserve Fund should clearly reflect the conditions prevailing at the time of its creation, in other words it should be sufficiently:

— flexible, so as to adapt to changes in its powers and to the gradual adhesion of all the members of the EC to its operational function;

— ambitious, so as to foreshadow the broad outlines of a future European Reserve Bank.

Its officials should also be assured of the continuity they need in order to operate effectively.

The organization of the ERF would be based on a collegiate and consensus principle, guaranteeing that its operations are coherent with those that the central bank will continue to perform individually, which implies in particular active participation in all concertation procedures.

These few principles are not intended to give an exhaustive definition of the ERF's operational basis, which should be the subject of appropriate discussions.

1. Eligibility

All the EC central banks would be eligible to join the ERF. However, membership would be subject to:

— the pooling of a portion of their reserves;

— participation in the exchange rate mechanism, the reason being that the EMS implies specific constraints on monetary policy and foreign exchange interventions, both of which require a common approach of the central banks concerned.

2. Management

Foreshadowing the future organization of a European Reserve Bank the management of the ERF would consist of:

(a) A Board of Directors, which would comprise, ex officio, the Governors of each central bank participating in the ERF. The Chairmanship would rotate, every two years for example, among each of its members. The Board of Directors would decide on the organization and administration of the ERF, would approve the accounts and decide on the appropriation of results.

The ERF's operating income would derive from the investment of exchange reserves. The ERF's income statement would take the operating costs of the Fund into account and the net income — possibly after allowing for provisions — would be allocated among shareholders in proportion to their contributions.

(b) An Executive Committee; owing to the specific nature of its powers and to the role that it would eventually play directly in the markets, the ERF would have a permanent Executive Committee whose members would be selected by the Committee of Governors on the basis of competence.

This Executive Committee would be small in size, consisting of three or four members who would have direct responsibility for the different departments of the ERF.

(c) Two committees would be given the task of supervising the foreign exchange and monetary policy spheres. These organs, inspired by the US Federal Open Market Committee, would report regularly to the Committee of Governors and, in the framework of a more active 'monitoring', would recommend appropriate action.

The members of these two committees (a Foreign Exchange Committee and a Monetary Policy Committee) would be appointed by the Committee of Governors from among its own members and those of the Executive Committee of the ERF, with the possibility of co-opting one or two outside personalities. Their term of office should be long enough to ensure continuity of action (five years' minimum).

3. Internal organization

Initially, the ERF would comprise a Foreign Exchange and Reserves Management Department and a Monetary Policy Department, which would both require a permanent staff.

Subsequently, its structure would be modified in order to incorporate the powers of the EMCF or other functions, when decided by the monetary authorities.

4. Location

The question of where to locate the ERF is obviously a difficult one and should be treated as a political matter. Before reaching a decision, it might be worth considering entrusting the management of the ERF to each of its members in turn. However, this kind of organization would diminish the public impact of the Fund and would encounter very serious operational obstacles.

Another solution, initially, could be to locate the ERF temporarily in Basle, where the Secretariat of the Committee of Governors and the EMCF are already located.

C — *Legal requirements for the creation of a European Reserve Fund*

It appears, at first sight, as if the legal foundation of the institution of a European Reserve Fund would have to be the provisions of Article 102a of the EEC's founding Treaty, which were introduced by the Single European Act in July 1987. This is because the creation of a new organization with monetary purposes — and its corollary, the abolition of the European Monetary Cooperation Fund (EMCF) — may be regarded as 'institutional modifications' and therefore require, according to the aforementioned Article 102a, the Treaty review procedure provided for under Article 236.

The procedure in question would entail, in addition to consultation with the European Parliament and the Commission:

— the calling of a conference of representatives of the Governments of Member States, whose decisions are taken 'by common agreement';

— ratification of the proposed amendments by all Member States 'in keeping with their respective constitutional rules'. In principle, this provision implies — although there is no explicit mention of this point in Article 236 — approval of the aforementioned amendments by the national Parliaments.[1]

Presumably it would be desirable to secure Parliamentary ratification of a document that would lay the legal foundations for carrying the process of monetary integration through to its conclusion. In other words, the document should provide not only for the initial steps sketched out in this note, but also for the subsequent stages leading to economic and monetary union and to a European Reserve Bank. It would be made clear that each stage would require the prior consent of the Member States.

One of the important questions that would have to be dealt with would concern the relationships between the European Reserve Bank and the political authorities in charge of setting exchange parities and framing the main lines of the economic policy of the Community. In this respect, it would seem that the role of the Council of Ministers would have to be decisive.

---

[1] The Article 236 procedure was used in 1986 for the adoption of the Single European Act.

The ECU as a parallel currency

W. F. Duisenberg

Any discussion on promoting the ECU as a parallel currency requires answers to two obvious questions: what do we mean by it and what does one expect to achieve with it? There are various possible definitions of the ECU as a parallel currency but they all have one characteristic feature in common: the development of the ECU as a parallel currency would imply its increased use in international transactions, both within and outside the European Communities, while national currencies would — at least for the foreseeable future — retain their functions and their central rates could continue to be adjusted. A parallel currency therefore implies the absence of a monetary union, which can be defined as an area with either a single currency or with national currencies with margins eliminated, full convertibility and central rates irreversibly locked.

Some technical features

At present two separate ECUs exist:

- the official ECU, created according to fixed rules by converting international reserves and held exclusively by central banks;
- the private ECU, assets denominated in ECUs and held primarily by the market.

The development of the ECU as a parallel currency widely used in international transactions refers, of course, to ECUs held by the private sector. At first the use of the ECU by the private sector has shown a remarkable development, but recently the increase in its use has not continued at its initial pace. However, if the market were to feel the need, a resumption of its initial growth rate could occur without changing either the separation of the two ECUs or the basket definition of the ECU.

Proponents of the further development of the private ECU are reluctant to await market developments and they feel the need for a more active stance on the part of the authorities. They see two major distinct avenues along which official measures can be taken to promote its use, which I shall call the market-oriented approach and the institutional approach.

In the market-oriented approach the techniques of the ECU are left unchanged, but the private ECU market is stimulated by actions like those taken by the UK authorities. These actions are taken with a view to facilitate the functioning of the private ECU market and to contribute to its depth and its overall liquidity. A greater use of the private ECU by governments, especially in the sphere of the Community budget, could also be seen as a possible element in this market-oriented approach.

If such an approach indeed would lead to an increase in the use of the ECU by the private sector, this could possibly have implications for monetary policies in the Member States. For example, this would be the case if the share of the private ECU in official reserves of EC central banks were to rise substantially. To this end it has already been agreed that the Dalgaard Group will closely monitor the development of the private ECU, and will call for consultations if problems of a monetary character were to arise. A further step could be taken by the inclusion by Member States of liquid assets denominated in ECUs held by residents in their domestic monetary aggregates. In that case, of course, liquid assets denominated in all Community currencies should be included also in this extended M aggregate.

In general, it would seem that the market-oriented approach would ensure that a further increase in the use of the ECU would indicate market appetite for the ECU. Therefore, this avenue would seem to be less problematic than the situation in which the authorities would provide the market with private ECUs which at times may not be absorbed by the market without consequences for the exchange rates, and, by implication, the monetary policies of the Member States.

The second avenue, the institutional approach, is advocated by those who feel that the use of the private ECU can only be stimulated by giving that task to a European institution. More precisely, official involvement in the private ECU would be increased by charging the European Monetary Cooperation Fund (EMCF) with responsibility for the ECU. Thus the suggestion has been made to give the Fund a responsibility for the exchange rate relationship between the ECU and third currencies. Another suggestion is to abolish, in addition, the basket definition, introducing an 'abstract' ECU.

Charging the Fund with responsibility for the exchange rate *vis-à-vis* third currencies would mean that, for instance, the decision at what level and for what amounts to support a weak dollar — at present taken by the central bank of the strongest EMS currency — would be transferred to the Fund. The Fund would of course have to be permanently provided with both third currencies and with either Community currencies or the possibility to sell newly created ECUs to be able to discharge its interventions.

The effect on member countries would depend on the ECU's definition. Among the many possibilities for such a definition three major variants can be distinguished:

— if the basket definition were maintained any intervention would affect exchange and monetary policies of all member countries, strong and weak;

— if the basket definition were abolished and an 'abstract' ECU were introduced, the maintenance of stable exchange rates between member currencies and the ECU would require the introduction of ECU intervention obligations for each member currency.[1] In that case dollar purchases by the Fund against ECUs would lead to ECU purchases against national currency by the strongest members. The difference compared to the present situation, where the stronger members buy dollars directly, would be that the decision to intervene is taken by the Fund and no longer by the countries concerned. This implies that exchange and domestic monetary policies of mainly the strongest member countries would be affected by actions beyond their control. The size of the dollar purchases by the Fund and thus of the monetary consequences for the latter countries would increase if the EMCF would be enabled to create ECUs by granting credit;

— if an 'abstract' ECU through its definition were to become a near-perfect substitute for the strongest ERM currency, its creation by the EMCF would have monetary consequences for all Community countries. The need for the monitoring of an extended M aggregate, referred to earlier, would increase.

In all three variants official policy aiming at increasing the ECU's private role, promoting its development into a parallel currency, would imply an increase in the European Monetary Cooperation Fund's functions. These functions would be external, but they would by implication not only comprise interventions but also the creation of central bank money. Therefore they would tend to decrease the scope for national central banks' internal policy. It is therefore necessary to consider what its purpose would be and whether all would agree with it.

Arguments for a parallel currency

Various motives, explicit or implicit, can be identified on the part of proponents of the ECU as a parallel currency. These motives can also lead to different forms of the ECU as a parallel currency.

— It is believed that the increased use of the ECU in international transactions will enable it to compete with the dollar to an extent that would be impossible for

---

[1] To be able to comply with their intervention obligations in ECUs the central banks would require ECU reserves that can be used directly for intervention. One way of providing them with such reserves would be through abolition of the separation between official and private ECUs.

any national currency in Europe and that this in time would help Europe to reduce its sensitivity for dollar fluctuations.

— The ECU as a parallel currency is expected to contribute to the development of a decision-making procedure in the EMS which would be considered more 'European' than the present one.

— Some hope that if the ECU is widely used for international transactions it may in time develop into a common currency in a way that is less painful than the process foreseen in the Council Resolution of 1971, which requires a high degree of economic convergence and surrender of sovereignty.

— It is suggested, *inter alia* from the industry side, that a wider use of the private ECU would diminish transaction costs for intra-Community trade on the assumption that the exchange risk would diminish also.

Reducing Europe's dependence on a strongly fluctuating dollar would probably be welcomed by most of us. The obvious way to achieve it would be genuine European economic and financial integration. Further convergence would enable European currencies to form a solid bloc, diminishing the adverse effects of dollar fluctuations on any single member country. However, the development of the ECU as a parallel currency would by itself not diminish the exchange rate risks, neither outside nor inside the EMS. There is no inherent disciplinary capacity of the private ECU which would bring about price and exchange stability. This can be brought about only by firm national policies directed towards domestic price stability. If these policies succeed in wiping out expectations of EMS realignments, then a true independence of the dollar will be achieved, all the more so if they were accompanied by the complete liberalization of capital movements.

Increasing the European Fund's role in managing the ECU and notably charging it with interventions would transfer decisions from national central banks to the Fund, limiting national central banks' domestic monetary control. It is precisely for that reason that this could never take place in isolation but only in the context of wider economic and monetary integration, while tasks and autonomy of the European Fund would have to be agreed upon and guaranteed in the Treaty.

How far could a parallel currency provide a road towards a common currency less painful than the one agreed in 1971 requiring convergence and loss of sovereignty? In fact it would not. At best it would imply an unnecessary detour towards a common currency. But it could equally turn out to become a permanent feature not facilitating further integration in any way. In so far as it would weaken discipline in member countries experiencing more inflation than others and balance-of-payments deficits, it might be rather the reverse.

It is a valid point that a decrease in the transaction costs for European industry would be desirable. Presently there are in most countries no major obstacles for

European industry to use the ECU as the transaction currency or the currency of denomination. It is up to industry to judge whether there is a need to use this possibility. However, it is not the greater use of the ECU which will determine the exchange risk, but the level of convergence, as discussed above. A measurable decrease in transaction costs can only be achieved by the near-elimination of realignments.

Conclusions

Three conclusions can be drawn from the foregoing.

First. Economic and monetary union requires economic convergence and the acceptance of the loss of sovereignty implicit in the abolition of the exchange rate as an adjustment instrument. The development of the ECU into an international currency used in parallel to national currencies cannot enable us to avoid this requirement nor can it facilitate its realization.

Second. While we can agree that no obstacle should be put to the increased market use of the ECU, the future developments should be closely monitored and the implications of an increased use for internal monetary policies should be signalled at an early stage.

Third. New responsibilities for the European Monetary Cooperation Fund involving market intervention in ECUs imply a shift in decision-making and restrict national central banks' scope for control of domestic money supply. Such new responsibilities therefore would not be consistent with the present institutional framework but would constitute an institutional change in the Single European Act.

The working of the EMS: A personal assessment

J. Godeaux

Introduction

The existence of an extensive body of background material relating to the functioning and performance of the EMS, including academic research as well as reviews conducted by official committees, makes it possible for this paper to limit itself to what I consider to be the main elements of an assessment. I have aimed at a balanced judgment; however, the views here expressed, while hopefully acceptable to many fellow Governors, are mine only.

Before dealing with the actual performance of the System, a brief overview of the EMS features and developments will be presented. Section I will therefore address five topics, covering the technical functioning of the System while at the same time pointing towards the challenges ahead in these domains. Section II will then discuss the performance of the System under a number of aspects. No attempt to draw overall conclusions was made as these would involve policy preferences and personal judgments.

A final remark is that the terms EMS and ERM (exchange rate mechanism) are used intermittently in this paper as one and the same thing, unless specified otherwise.

I — Assessment of the technical functioning of the EMS

In the present section the basic characteristics of the EMS will be recalled, namely an exchange rate mechanism, based on a regime of fixed, though adjustable exchange rates, supplemented by credit facilities and destined to involve the participation of all the Community Member States, giving Europe a distinct place on the international monetary scene. In particular, attention will be paid as to how these features have evolved over time since the inception of the EMS and what may be the challenges ahead.

1. *Exchange rate management: The issue of realignments*

When looking back on 10 years of EMS experience, one cannot but conclude that the scepticism and concerns voiced initially as to the durability of the System were unfounded. Expectations that it would develop into a regime of unduly frequent 'crawling-peg' type of exchange rate adjustments have not materialized. Neither has the system generated an excessive rigidity of exchange rates yielding misalignments of real exchange rates.

In the annex to the conclusions of the Presidency of the European Council in Bremen, it was stated that in terms of exchange rate management the EMS would be at least as strict as the 'Snake'. With the benefit of hindsight one can discern a number of definite improvements in comparison with the 'Snake' concerning the issue of realignments.

Firstly, changes in central rates have become truly multilateral decisions. Secondly, their frequency as well as their magnitude have been markedly reduced after the initial learning period, i.e. 1979 to 1983.

Thirdly, as a result, adjustments in market exchange rates have been smaller, making speculative capital movements less rewarding. Fourthly, realignments have been accompanied most of the time by domestic policy adjustments, granting credibility to the newly established central rates. And, finally, the merits of exchange rate stability and discipline have been better recognized.

None the less, some problems remain. The timing of realignments and their magnitude are still influenced by comments and debates of a 'political' nature. Moreover, the policy option of small and infrequent realignments geared to combat speculative capital movements in a technical way may give the impression that exchange rate changes are simply an adjunct to monetary policies. Their capacity to contribute to the correction of fundamental economic divergences has been less clearly put in evidence. Realignments should not simply be a periodic adjustment to inflation rate differentials. These differentials should not be fully corrected so as to retain an element of exchange rate constraint.

2. *Exchange rate management within the band*

Over the years, views regarding the management of currencies within their fluctuation margins in the EMS band have shifted rather markedly. At the outset, flexible use of the band width was regarded as a cushion which could absorb or dampen some external shocks without necessitating immediate exchange rate interventions or monetary and other economic policy measures. Only if and when a currency was out of line with the average of all other participants should this entail a presumption of action by the authorities concerned. To ascertain that this rule would apply symmetrically in the case of both weak and strong currency positions, a divergence indicator was constructed.

Experience showed that this strategy entailed some disadvantages: the ECU did not prove very helpful for the operation of the divergence indicator and delaying intervention until it became obligatory, i.e. at the margins, at times resulted in a market perception that the authorities were no longer committed to defend the existing parity grid, fuelling speculative pressure and necessitating more intervention than initially warranted.

This led the authorities to believe that a strategy of keeping their exchange rates well within the band and limiting movements against key currencies of the EMS to a minimum would be more rewarding both in terms of influencing market sentiment and in terms of domestic monetary stability. This new strategy did entail an increased recourse to intra-marginal interventions relative to marginal ones as well as a more timely use of interest rate policy, especially for weaker currency countries.

With the progressive integration of financial markets and with the objective of the abolition of the remaining capital restrictions, in line with the goal of completing the internal market in 1992, the exchange rate mechanism of the EMS might have to face the prospect of increased or new strains calling for some reinforcement of the System. The result was the so-called Basle/Nyborg agreement providing for a more active and flexible use of all the instruments available to central banks for meeting short-term exchange rate pressures and for better coordination of such action among the ERM participants.

Thus, a more flexible use of the EMS band width was called for, without returning to the original situation of letting currencies drift to the limits. This in turn justified the provision of very short-term financing of intra-marginal interventions under certain conditions. It also made more cooperation on monetary policy measures imperative. To promote a more effective use of the instruments available, a strengthened monitoring procedure was put in place.

Although it is still somewhat early to assess the working of the Basle/Nyborg agreement, experience gained up to now is encouraging. This does not exclude, however, that further measures be considered, essentially in order to gradually replace the system of *ex post* concertation by one of *ex ante* coordination of monetary policies.

3. *Financing and settlement of interventions*

Contrary to early fears by creditor countries that the EMS would open the door for more inflationary financing, in view of the increase in volume of available credit facilities and the creation of the ECU as a means of settlement, the evidence turns out to be much more balanced. No permanent net ECU positions have developed, VSTF arrangements have never been abused and the STMS facility has even remained unused. Instead, Member States have preferred market related balance of payments financing and the use of foreign currency reserves to settle interventions.

The shift in intervention strategy referred to earlier has contributed to the German mark becoming the prominent intervention currency to the detriment of the US dollar. This evolution carried with it both advantages and disadvantages. The former consisted of opening up the possibility of intra-marginal interventions against the traditionally strongest currency without influencing the German monetary base (so-called asymmetrically sterilized interventions). The latter pertained to the fact that only one EMS currency, namely the strongest one, was being sought after to this end by the weaker-currency central banks.

The role of the ECU has thus remained limited, far from attaining a position at the centre of the System as originally envisaged. Notwithstanding its remarkable development as a financial instrument, the effective impact of the private ECU use on the operation of the EMS is still marginal.

4. *Coordination of exchange rate policies* vis-à-vis *third currencies*

It is undeniable that the greater degree of convergence in monetary performance and policies of the EMS countries since 1983 under the leadership of the Bundesbank (see also Section II) has reduced the EMS exposure to outside shocks in general, US dollar instability in particular. As long as convergence remains incomplete though — preventing EMS currencies from becoming close substitutes — the international environment will remain a potential source of instability for the exchange rate mechanism.

With the German mark as the nominal anchor in the EMS, the policy choice of the ERM participants to accept whatever exchange rate target (or absence of target) the German monetary authorities had chosen for the German mark was understandable. As such the German mark came to serve equally as the linchpin between the EMS and the international monetary system.

The EMS has failed to become a representative homogeneous monetary entity on the international level. This was demonstrated for instance by the fact that the Plaza and Louvre agreements have incorporated more than one EMS member on an individual basis, while for their implementation a coordinated intervention approach by all EMS members was solicited. It has to be said though, that the EMS has come to receive greater recognition over the years as a specific part of the international monetary system.

5. *Non- or incomplete participation in the exchange rate mechanism*

The fact that the EMS in its wider sense encompasses all EEC currencies whereas only seven out of 12 fully participate in the exchange rate mechanism has so far caused no major difficulties for the working of the System, perhaps even saved it from encountering more frequent tensions. However, ERM participation of sterling might have facilitated exchange rate management for specific countries such as Ireland. Besides, apart from generating greater instability for the ECU, the prolonged non-participation of the UK has sustained doubts about the merits and the potential development of the System, especially in those circles where natural scepticism was already prevailing.

II — Assessment of the EMS performance

To be able to assess the performance of the EMS, it is necessary to bear in mind its objectives. For this it suffices to recall the following passage in the conclusions of the Presidency of the European Council in Brussels in December 1978: 'The purpose of the EMS is to establish a greater measure of monetary stability in the Community. It should be seen as a fundamental component of a more comprehensive strategy aimed at lasting growth with stability, a progressive return to full employment, the harmonization of living standards and the lessening of regional disparities in the Community. The System will facilitate the convergence of economic development and give fresh impetus to the process of European Union'.

In the following subsections the attainment of the abovementioned goals will be assessed under three headings: the EMS as a zone of monetary stability, as a determining factor of economic performance and convergence, and as an instrument of increased (monetary) cooperation.

1. *The EMS as a zone of monetary stability*

Monetary stability comprises an internal as well as an external aspect: low inflation and exchange rate stability. Although no priority between these two was established at the outset, it gradually became accepted that monetary policies should be geared to make national inflation rates converge on price stability and that this in turn would lay the foundations for lasting exchange rate stability.

Nevertheless, even in the absence of convergence on price stability, the EMS has already made a definite contribution to the realization of the objective of exchange rate stability. Indeed, as numerous studies using different methodologies have shown, the variability of exchange rates of ERM participants — whether in nominal or in real terms — decreased markedly not only in comparison with the 'Snake' period but also over time, when comparing the first half of the 10 years of EMS experience with the second half. Moreover, the EMS results compare favourably with those of non-ERM participants inside and outside Europe.

More important still is that this outcome did not result from capital controls or interest rates acting as shock absorbers. In effect, capital controls have gradually been diminishing while the observation of interest rate variability before and after the EMS does not show a clear tendency towards rising instability.

Concerning internal monetary stability, the same three types of comparison as presented above can be made. Compared with the 'Snake' the EMS did not lay the ground for looser monetary policies but rather provided a framework in which anti-inflationary policies could be pursued more effectively. Of course, one cannot brush aside the favourable external monetary environment in assessing the relative merits of the EMS. It is, however, extremely difficult to quantify this effect in isolation.

As to the question whether the EMS provided a better framework than other national experiences, where one has also witnessed a remarkable deceleration of inflation, the debate has so far been inconclusive. What should be borne in mind in this respect is that these other countries in bringing down their inflation rates frequently resorted to an increase in the short-term variability of exchange rates or even accepted the occurrence of misalignments, elements which are incompatible with the overall monetary stability objective of the EMS.

Last but not least, the more recent evidence and projections on monetary and credit policies and performances is indicating a clear trend towards convergence of money growth and inflation performance among the ERM participants at low levels as compared with the other Community members. This seems to imply that the EMS is finally paying off in terms of credibility with regard to its anti-inflationary stance.

One should warn, however, against too relaxed an attitude in these matters. Internal monetary convergence on price stability is not fully achieved yet, with the measure of dispersion in inflation still having to reach the low level attained in the 1960s on average. Monetary and exchange rate policies should therefore proceed along the lines followed in the past to preserve the acquired stability firmly.

Thus, exchange rate realignments will remain unavoidable for the time being, which raises the difficult issues of their timing and their being accompanied by the necessary adjustment measures so as not to rekindle the vicious circle which nearly made the System collapse in 1981-83.

2. *The EMS as a determining factor of economic performance and convergence*

Three issues will be addressed in this subsection: firstly, a sketchy description of the degree of convergence in economic performances and policies in the EMS; secondly, the question whether the causes for the less satisfactory results can be attributed to the System proper; and, thirdly, what will be their consequences for the working of the EMS. It is obvious that these are complex and even controversial matters which the present paper can only describe in a general way.

2.1. Economic performances and convergence

It can be said that the prime goal of the EMS is the creation of a sound basis for internal and external stability as a precondition for the achievement of the broader economic objectives set out by the European Council in December 1978. To attain this goal, a fair degree of convergence in economic performances must be achieved, especially in the field of costs and prices.

If differences in economic variables such as real GDP growth, current-account and fiscal balances must no longer endanger exchange rate stability, a reasonable degree of convergence needs to be achieved in these areas too. One cannot deny that results obtained so far have fallen short of what was desirable or necessary.

Real GDP growth may have been converging slightly, but at a low level instead of at the higher figure arrived at elsewhere in Europe. Recent developments of growth performances have shown more encouraging signs. It remains to be seen though, if this does announce a reversal of the long-term trend of sluggish growth in the EMS. Current-account imbalances have not disappeared, with shrinking deficits for some Member States only being replaced by increasing surpluses for others. Fiscal disequilibria have remained large with public-debt levels consequently still on the rise in a number of countries.

2.2. Is the EMS to blame?

The question has to be asked whether the situation as described above was caused by the EMS. Or, phrased otherwise, would the situation have evolved more favourably without the existence of the System? Complete answers are not available. Statistical analysis cannot provide decisive evidence on all counts if only because several standards of reference may be put forward to assess the performance of the EMS.

In a broader time perspective one must not overlook the fact that at the start of the 1980s the current-account and/or fiscal balances of most of the ERM participants were not very satisfactory, quite often being worse off than in other non-EMS countries in Europe. The adjustments imposed on some EMS members led them to policy measures conducive to dampening domestic demand, leading in turn to slower growth in the EMS compared with growth performances outside.

The necessary adjustments could surely not have been delayed in the absence of the EMS. On the contrary, the existence of the EMS provided the weaker currency members with a credible commitment to strengthen their public finances in a non-inflationary way. Their willingness to resist inflationary pressures arising out of the devaluations of their currencies in order to improve their current account situations, however, gave rise to realignments that most of the time did not totally wipe out differences in their real exchange-rate movements *vis-à-vis* the German mark in particular. As mentioned above, this limit placed on realignments has the merit of maintaining some 'foreign exchange constraint' in the weaker economies.

But one may ask whether the tendency to a relative undervaluation of the German mark might not have enhanced German competitiveness and added external stimulus to Germany's growth rate. This would have alleviated the need for Germany to give further stimulus to domestic demand.

It appears extremely difficult, if not impossible, to identify the relative importance of the various factors that account for the persistent divergences in the area of fiscal-policy and current-account developments. With regard to the latter which are increasingly mentioned as a possible threat to EMS stability, the analytical work done so far does not offer a satisfactory explanation of the persistent divergences by referring to the relative cyclical positions and cost/price developments only. It seems that other more structural factors need to be taken into consideration equally.

2.3. Consequences for the EMS

Irrespective of the causes of disappointing growth performances, current-account disequilibria and fiscal-policy divergences, the persistence of these phenomena will clearly have an unfavourable impact on the functioning of the System.

As yet two major consequences can be perceived. The first one is a credibility problem in so far as references to a possible deflationary bias of the System and to the risk of a build-up of fundamental balance-of-payments disequilibria do cast some doubt on the intrinsic stability of the System and on its potential development. Secondly, it is undeniable that fiscal-policy and current-account divergences imply the persistence of interest-rate differentials which themselves could delay or complicate the progression of convergence.

The System has to defend itself against the objection that it is a low-growth area. It has also to defend itself against the objection that it is an 'asymmetrical' system. To avoid misunderstanding, the whole question of asymmetry deserves deeper analysis and research.

3. *The EMS as an instrument of increased monetary cooperation*

The EMS monetary cooperation has now reached a content that largely outweighs the degree of cooperation achieved in most other areas of Community policy. A lot of the credit for this achievement is due to the flexibility of the System. Pragmatic arrangements were often preferred to strict or explicit rules. This pragmatism has permitted the evolutionary change as evidenced in the ECU package of July 1985 and most visibly in the Basle/Nyborg agreement of September 1987.

It may be recalled that the 'flexible cooperation approach' was at the outset conceived as a transitory arrangement only. According to the Brussels Resolution, an institutional phase had to be reached not later than two years after the inception of the System. However, in December 1980, the European Council decided to postpone *sine die* such a step. Frankly speaking, there is not much hope that this institutional step will be taken in the near future nor much insistence that it should be.

One can therefore say that in the perennial debate on 'rules versus discretion', the participants in the System have laid great weight on discretion.

I am quite sure that this pragmatic approach is still capable of bringing further progress. Yet one cannot avoid the fact that, in order to cope with the challenges ahead, namely, preserving monetary and exchange rate stability in an environment of free capital movement while contributing to the completion of the internal market, one should except a continuous move towards collective decision-making on even the most vital parts of national monetary policy. Although the present strategy of voluntary policy coordination undoubtedly still leaves room for ample improvement, the question arises how long such a stance can continue meeting the increasing requirements of joint monetary policy-making and can remain a satisfactory answer to the expectations of market operators, of public opinion and of the political sphere.

We therefore have to ask ourselves whether a new Basle/Nyborg package can be put together and made public or what institutional step can be taken despite our obvious preference for the pragmatic approach. To paraphrase the English expression about justice, 'not only must progress be made, it must be *seen* to be made'.

The ECU banking market[1]

A. Lamfalussy

After strong growth in the earlier years of this decade, the expansion of the reporting banks' ECU-denominated assets and liabilities slowed down markedly in 1986, and the share of ECU assets in banks' total non-dollar Euro-currency assets has since then remained stable at around 9%, although there have been renewed signs of dynamism and vitality more recently.

In mid-1988 the reporting banks' ECU assets amounted to ECU 95 billion. The bulk of this was booked with banks in Belgium/Luxembourg, France, the United Kingdom and Italy, with very little business elsewhere.

The ECU market is first and foremost an interbank market, with direct business with non-banks being relatively less important than in most other sectors of the Euro-market. For example, in mid-1988 interbank positions accounted for 77 and 89% respectively of the reporting banks' ECU assets and liabilities. Apart from supporting their ECU business with non-bank customers and their role as intermediaries in the ECU bond market, the banks use the ECU for arbitrage, funding and hedging operations. There is an active exchange market in ECUs, with spot and forward contracts and an efficient private clearing system with an estimated daily volume of ECU 15 billion.

The reporting banks' outstanding credits to non-bank entities amounted to ECU 22 billion in mid-1988, whereas deposit liabilities to non-banks totalled barely ECU 7 billion, or only 4% of overall non-dollar Euro-currency deposits. Given this very pronounced net creditor position, it would appear that the growth of the ECU market has been driven above all by borrowing demand. By far the most important borrowers were non-bank entities in Italy and France, where use of the ECU has been officially encouraged through its partial exemption from foreign exchange restrictions and by public-sector borrowings in ECUs. In mid-1988 residents of these two countries accounted for over one-half of total ECU credits.

---

[1] The author acknowledges the valuable assistance of Helmut Mayer in the preparation and drafting of this paper.

In more general terms, ECU borrowing may be attractive to entities from countries where domestic currency interest rates are higher than ECU rates, and at times when there seems to be relatively little danger of a depreciation of the domestic currency *vis-à-vis* the ECU. This helps to explain the buoyancy of the demand for ECU credits in the period up to 1985, when the strength of the German mark within the EMS exchange rate band was mitigated by the unusually firm dollar. ECU borrowing may also be attractive for international firms with operations in several EC member countries and for firms (such as Saint-Gobain) which have begun to use the ECU for their published accounts. Finally, ECU borrowing may to some extent be related to the role of the ECU as a unit of account in commercial transactions. Around 1 % of France's and Italy's international trade is reported to have been invoiced in ECUs.

The relatively small amount of ECU-denominated non-bank deposits suggests that its attractiveness as a near-money substitute and store of liquidity is quite limited. In fact, since end-1985 ECU deposits have not, on balance, shown any growth at all. Moreover, the supply of ECU deposits is geographically highly concentrated, with nearly 45 % of the total amount coming from residents of the Benelux countries. One important reason why non-bank ECU deposits grew much less than ECU credits was that, in contrast to ECU borrowing, depositing in ECUs was restrained by foreign exchange controls (e.g. in Italy and France) or other legal restrictions (Germany). However, these regulatory obstacles have now largely been removed, or are in the process of being removed.

On the positive side, a possible argument in favour of the ECU as a deposit outlet is its high interest level and its relative exchange rate stability due to its basket characteristics which should make it attractive as an alternative to the dollar in times of dollar weakness. As on the borrowing side, the ECU denomination should be attractive as a hedging intrument for firms with operations in several EC member countries and for firms that keep their accounts or conduct business in ECUs. Moreover, in some countries the ECU is also used to some extent for payment purposes, for example via current accounts or in the form of travellers' cheques.

Finally, it should be noted that there has been a fairly steady growth of the private ECU for official reserve purposes, although, at ECU 2.1 billion, the identified amount of crossborder official ECU deposits in mid-1988 was still quite modest. In addition, there are about ECU 34 billion of ECU bonds outstanding in the international issue market. A substantial proportion of this paper is undoubtedly in the portfolios of non-bank holders.

One factor that may affect the demand for ECU assets, and possibly also ECU borrowing, is the forthcoming five-yearly review of the composition of the ECU basket in September 1989. Particularly if the Spanish peseta and the Portuguese escudo were to be included in the basket, this would tend to reduce the weight of the German mark and the Dutch guilder in favour of currencies which bear higher interest yields and which tend to be more depreciation-prone in the eyes of the market. While the rules for changing the ECU weights require that on the day of adjustment the ECU's exchange rate shall not be affected, this provision obviously cannot safeguard the spot (discounted) value of longer-term ECU assets, unless the change in the basket weights has been fully anticipated by the market. This, however, will primarily affect the demand for ECU bonds. The demand for private ECU deposits, which are mainly short term, could only be affected shortly before the basket adjustment, and possibly afterwards if the market felt that the higher interest yield was no adequate compensation for the higher exchange risk involved. It should, moreover, be noted that the combined weight of the peseta and the escudo in the ECU basket would be unlikely to exceed 7 %.

To sum up, following the vigorous growth in the first half of this decade, the expansion of banks' ECU business has fallen back in line with the overall development of the non-dollar sector of the Euro-currency market. Whilst by no means negligible in absolute amounts, the bank's ECU operations with non-banks are still very small in relation to total Euro-currency business. In particular, ECU deposits have, on balance, shown no growth in recent years, despite the removal of a number of regulatory constraints. The ECUs used by the banks for lending purposes have, therefore, had to be created largely through the 'bundling' or forward covering of the constituent currencies. Moreover, the geographical distribution of non-bank ECU borrowers and depositors remains highly skewed and some special incentives for ECU-denominated borrowing have fallen away as a result of the scrapping of exchange controls.

Despite a recent pick-up of its rate of growth, the ECU market does not at present appear very likely to take over from the other sectors of the Euro-currency market and develop spontaneously into a major parallel currency in the EEC member countries. For this purpose the geographical spread of borrowers and the non-bank deposit base in particular would have to be much broader. Greater use of the ECU in commercial transactions and also for payment and accounting purposes would undoubtedly help the further development of the market. Enhanced confidence in the stability of the EMS exchange rate structure would probably also be supportive, although this would tend to reduce the differentials between ECU and national currency interest rates. Increased use of the ECU for official borrowing, exemplified by the recent UK issue of Treasury bills, together with the prospects for 1992, should provide some renewed stimulus to the growth of the market. Nevertheless, it seems doubtful whether, without major further official efforts to encourage its use, the ECU will in the foreseeable future play a pivotal role in the growth of the international banking market.

TABLE 1

Development of the ECU banking market[1]

(outstanding amounts in billion ECU)

	end-Dec. 1982	end-Dec. 1983	end-Dec. 1984	end-Dec. 1985	end-Dec. 1986	end-June 1987	end-Dec. 1987	end-June 1988
ECU assets	6.7e	**14.4**	**39.8**	**63.2**	**70.7**	**74.6**	**82.4**	**95.0**
of which: *vis-à-vis* banks	..	9.7	28.6	49.3	54.9	57.8	62.1	73.0
vis-à-vis non-banks	..	4.7	11.2	13.9	15.8	16.8	20.3	22.0
ECU liabilities	5.7e	**12.1**	**31.4**	**57.5**	**61.2**	**64.9**	**69.6**	**82.2**
of which: *vis-à-vis* banks	..	10.4	27.9	49.3	53.9	57.3	60.9	73.2
vis-à-vis non-banks	..	1.4	2.8	7.2	6.2	6.0	6.8	6.9
vis-à-vis monetary authorities	..	0.3	0.7	1.0	1.1	1.6	1.9	2.1
Memorandum items								
ECU assets:								
in billion DM	15.4	32.4	88.7	138.0	146.9	154.5	169.9	197.3
in billion USD	6.5	11.9	28.2	56.1	75.7	84.5	107.4	108.4
(share in non-dollar Euro-market[2])	(1.7)e	(3.1)	(7.3)	(9.1)	(8.7)	(8.5)	(8.6)	(9.2)
ECU Euro-bonds outstanding:								
in billion ECU	3.2	5.6	9.7	18.6	24.8	29.8	31.5	34.1
in billion USD	3.2	4.6	6.9	16.5	26.5	33.8	41.0	38.9
(share in non-dollar international bond market[3])	(2.8)	(..)	(..)	(6.8)	(7.0)	(7.3)	(7.3)	(7.0)

e = Estimates.
[1] External and local positions in ECUs of banks located in Austria, Belgium, Luxembourg, Denmark, Finland, France, Germany, Ireland, Italy, Japan, the Netherlands, Spain, Sweden, Switzerland (as from end-December 1987) and the United Kingdom.
[2] As a percentage of total non-dollar foreign currency assets (expressed in current dollars) of reporting banks.
[3] As a percentage of total non-dollar international issues (expressed in current dollars).

TABLE 2
The structure of the ECU banking market

(outstanding amounts in billion ECU)

	Assets								Liabilities							
	end-Dec. 1983	end-Dec. 1984	end-Dec. 1985	end-Dec. 1986	end-June 1987	end-Dec. 1987	end-June 1988		end-Dec. 1983	end-Dec. 1984	end-Dec. 1985	end-Dec. 1986	end-June 1987	end-Dec. 1987	end-June 1988
Positions vis-à-vis non-banks																
domestic: EC residents	3.3	6.6	6.0	5.9	5.8	8.1	8.5		0.6	1.3	3.6	3.1	2.6	3.0	3.3
non-EC residents	.	0.2	0.1	0.2	0.4	0.4	0.3		.	.	.	.	0.1	0.2	0.1
crossborder: EC	1.0	2.9	4.9	5.7	5.9	6.7	8.0		0.4	0.9	2.1	1.7	1.8	2.0	1.9
other countries	0.1	0.6	1.4	2.3	2.7	2.9	2.5		0.2	0.5	1.1	1.0	1.0	1.2	1.2
unallocated	0.3	0.9	1.5	1.7	2.0	2.2	2.7		0.2	0.1	0.4	0.4	0.5	0.4	0.4
Total non-banks	**4.7**	**11.2**	**13.9**	**15.8**	**16.8**	**20.3**	**22.0**		**1.4**	**2.8**	**7.2**	**6.2**	**6.0**	**6.8**	**6.9**
Positions vis-à-vis banks																
domestic: EC residents	2.8	7.5	12.4	12.6	13.2	12.5	16.8		3.1	7.5	12.0	12.0	12.7	12.4	16.9
non-EC residents	.	.	0.1	.	0.1	0.2	0.3		.	.	0.2	.	0.1	.	0.3
crossborder: EC	6.1	18.4	28.6	29.8	30.2	32.7	37.5		6.8	18.6	29.0	31.4	32.0	33.8	39.2
other countries	0.4	1.4	3.7	6.6	7.0	9.2	10.4		0.5	1.9	5.1	7.3	8.1	10.9	12.8
unallocated	0.4	1.3	4.5	5.9	7.3	7.5	8.0		0.3	0.6	4.0	4.3	6.0	5.7	6.1
Total interbank[1]	**9.7**	**28.6**	**49.3**	**54.9**	**57.8**	**62.1**	**73.0**		**10.7**	**28.6**	**50.3**	**55.0**	**58.9**	**62.8**	**75.3**
Total	**14.4**	**39.8**	**63.2**	**70.7**	**74.6**	**82.4**	**95.0**		**12.1**	**31.4**	**54.5**	**61.2**	**64.9**	**69.6**	**82.2**

[1] Includes positions *vis-à-vis* monetary authorities.

TABLE 3

The role of individual market centres in ECU banking operations

(outstanding amounts at end-June 1988, in billion ECU)

Banks	Belgium	Luxem-bourg	France	FR of Germany	Italy	The Nether-lands	United Kingdom	Other EC countries[1]	Total EEC	Other[2]	Grand total
ECU assets											
vis-à-vis banks	14.0	6.6	17.9	1.5	8.8	2.5	17.5	1.5	70.3	2.7	73.0
domestic	2.7	2.5	5.3	.	1.5	0.2	4.4	0.3	16.9	0.2	17.1
crossborder	11.3	4.1	12.6	1.5	7.3	2.3	13.1	1.2	53.4	2.5	55.9
vis-à-vis non-banks	4.1	2.5	4.9	1.2	2.8	0.8	3.7	0.9	20.9	1.1	22.0
domestic	0.3	0.3	3.0	.	2.8	0.1	1.1	0.9	8.5	0.3	8.8
crossborder	3.8	2.2	1.9	1.2	.	0.7	2.6	.	12.4	0.8	13.2
Total ECU assets	**18.1**	**9.1**	**22.8**	**2.7**	**11.6**	**3.3**	**21.2**	**2.4**	**91.2**	**3.8**	**95.0**
ECU liabilities											
vis-à-vis banks	13.0	6.6	18.5	2.1	11.5	2.1	16.4	2.0	72.2	3.1	75.3
domestic	2.5	2.7	4.9	0.1	1.5	0.1	4.8	0.3	16.9	0.3	17.2
crossborder	10.5	3.9	13.6	2.0	10.0	2.0	11.6	1.7	55.3	2.8	58.1
vis-à-vis non-banks	1.3	2.2	0.6	0.2	0.5	0.7	1.0	0.1	6.6	0.3	6.9
domestic	0.4	1.2	0.3	.	0.2	0.4	0.7	0.1	3.3	0.1	3.4
crossborder	0.9	1.0	0.3	0.2	0.3	0.3	0.3	.	3.3	0.2	3.5
Total ECU liabilities	**14.3**	**8.8**	**19.1**	**2.3**	**12.0**	**2.8**	**17.4**	**2.1**	**78.8**	**3.4**	**82.2**

[1] Denmark, Ireland and Spain.
[2] Austria, Finland, Japan, Sweden and Switzerland.

TABLE 4

Nationality of non-bank borrowers and depositors in the ECU banking market

(outstanding amounts in billion ECU)

	Borrowers								Depositors						
	end-Dec. 1983	end-Dec. 1984	end-Dec. 1985	end-Dec. 1986	end-June 1987	end-Dec. 1987	end-June 1988		end-Dec. 1983	end-Dec. 1984	end-Dec. 1985	end-Dec. 1986	end-June 1987	end-Dec. 1987	end-June 1988
EEC[1]															
Belgium/Luxembourg	0.1	0.2	0.4	0.4	0.4	0.5	0.7		0.6	0.9	1.6	1.8	1.8	2.0	2.0
Denmark	.	.	0.1	0.3	0.4	0.4	0.4		.	.	.	.	.	.	.
France	1.0	2.0	2.4	2.2	2.2	4.2	3.9		0.1	0.2	0.3	0.3	0.3	0.4	0.4
FR of Germany	.	.	.	.	.	.	.		.	0.1	0.6	0.3	0.2	0.3	0.3
Greece	.	0.1	0.1	0.2	0.2	0.2	0.2		.	.	.	.	.	.	.
Ireland	.	0.1	0.3	0.3	0.3	0.4	0.4		.	0.1	0.2	0.2	0.1	0.2	0.1
Italy	2.8	6.1	5.3	5.5	5.0	6.1	7.6		.	.	0.1	0.1	0.1	0.1	0.2
Netherlands	0.2	0.2	0.4	0.3	0.4	0.3	0.5		0.3	0.6	2.0	1.2	1.2	1.0	1.0
Portugal	.	0.1	0.4	0.6	0.5	0.5	0.5		.	.	.	.	.	.	.
Spain	.	0.4	0.8	0.7	0.6	0.7	1.0		.	.	.	.	.	.	.
United Kingdom	0.1	0.3	0.6	1.0	1.5	1.3	1.2		.	0.2	0.8	0.9	0.7	1.0	0.9
Total EEC	**4.3**	**9.5**	**10.9**	**11.6**	**11.7**	**14.8**	**16.5**		**1.0**	**2.2**	**5.7**	**4.8**	**4.4**	**5.0**	**5.2**
Other developed countries	.	0.3	0.6	1.1	1.3	1.4	1.2		.	0.1	0.5	0.4	0.4	0.6	0.6
Rest of the world	0.1	0.4	0.6	1.0	1.3	1.3	1.0		0.1	0.1	0.2	0.3	0.3	0.3	0.3
International institutions	.	0.1	0.3	0.4	0.5	0.6	0.6		0.1	0.3	0.4	0.3	0.4	0.5	0.4
Unallocated	0.3	0.9	1.5	1.7	2.0	2.2	2.7		0.2	0.1	0.4	0.4	0.5	0.4	0.4
Total non-banks	**4.7**	**11.2**	**13.9**	**15.8**	**16.8**	**20.3**	**22.0**		**1.4**	**2.8**	**7.2**	**6.2**	**6.0**	**6.8**	**6.9**

[1] Local and crossborder positions; due to rounding, individual figures may not add up to totals.

The ECU, the common currency and the monetary union

Gunter D. Baer
Tommaso Padoa-Schioppa

I — Issues and options

1. The following terminology may be used to facilitate the discussion of the common currency and the ECU:

A *common currency* describes a currency which is used throughout the Community and is *not* the national currency of either a Member State or a third country. Two types of common currency can be distinguished:

(i) a *parallel currency,* which is a common currency that is created independently of, and in addition to, national currencies. It circulates in parallel with national currencies and competes with them;

(ii) a *single currency* is a common currency that has replaced all existing national currencies as a result of an institutional decision (rather than a market process).

A common currency may, however, also be understood as signifying the use of a *common numeraire* (as in the case of the private ECU today) or a *common reserve instrument* as a means of implementing a common monetary policy.

2. The issue of the currency in a monetary union revolves around two interrelated questions:

(a) What is the need for, and role of, a common currency in the process leading to monetary union?

(b) What should be the future role of the ECU?

3. *A common currency in the process leading to monetary union.* Varying views may be held on this question. One is that no common currency is needed in order to achieve monetary union, because the irrevocable locking of parities, full mobility of capital and the pursuit of a single monetary policy suffice for the creation of such a union, i.e. a single currency area. Alternatively, it may be argued that ultimately the move to *a single currency* is necessary in order to reap the full benefits of monetary union. According to this view, only a single currency can provide a

convenient *numeraire* for the transactions of private economic agents and substantially reduced uncertainties and transaction costs. It can also be pointed out that no monetary union has ever existed without a common currency, and that the credibility of the 'irrevocable locking' would be at risk if many different currencies continued to exist.

4. *The role of the ECU.* Any proposals concerning the role of the ECU obviously depend very much on the views held regarding the need for a common currency. However, it should be borne in mind that the ECU already exists, that it holds a place in private markets, that certain expectations have been raised concerning its future role in the process towards monetary union and that it carries a symbolic value to which political leaders may attach importance. To many observers it seems natural that the ECU's role should grow with progress towards monetary union and that it should become the Community's single currency. Others may consider that it is premature to formalize arrangements for a common currency, and that all that is needed is to promote convergence and monetary stability.

5. There are three options regarding the future role of the ECU, which are not necessarily mutually exclusive.

6. Firstly, the ECU would remain a basket of Community currencies and serve as a *common numeraire*. All possible impediments to its voluntary use in private financial and commercial transactions would be removed, but no particular official action would be taken to promote it; no new institution would be required to manage the ECU, but the monetary effects of its growing use would have to be monitored.

7. Secondly, the official ECU (which could remain a basket) would be used as a *common reserve instrument* in managing a common monetary policy; in this case the ECU would become the reserve money of the European system of central banks. This approach has been suggested in Governor Ciampi's paper. The expanded use of the official ECU in this way wold not require a link between the official and the private ECU, and the latter would evolve in accordance with the first option.

8. Thirdly, as has been suggested by some academic economists, the ECU could be made *a parallel currency*. It would be issued by a central institution and permitted to circulate freely throughout the Community as a means of payment, store of value and unit of account. The ECU would be an additional — 13th — Community currency, it would have to be defined in its own right (so-called abstract ECU) and it would form part of the exchange rate arrangements. Its acceptance and use by private market participants would depend essentially on its quality as money.

II — Propositions relating to the ECU

9. Four possible propositions are stated and examined below:

10. *'A parallel currency approach is neither a useful nor a desirable way of establishing a monetary union'.* Under the parallel currency approach the ECU would be created independently of, and in addition to, national currencies, circulating in parallel with them and competing with them. The idea of its advocates is that the ECU would 'crowd out' national currencies, thus establishing a monetary union in a 'painless' way. The critics of this approach reject it on two grounds. Firstly, it would not contribute to solving in an orderly manner the problem of coordinating national monetary policies; on the contrary, it would add a 13th player to an already difficult coordination exercise. Secondly, it could undermine a monetary policy oriented towards price stability, because it would add a source of money creation that is difficult to link to the needs of economic activity.

Some concrete implications of this proposition are that before the final stage:

(i) the ECU should remain a basket;

(ii) no independent monetary policy would be instituted for the ECU;

(iii) no link would need to be established between the private and the official ECU circuits.

11. *'An "imprimatur" should be given to the ECU as the future single currency of the Community'.* A single currency, while not strictly necessary for the creation of a monetary union, might — for economic as well as psychological and political reasons — be seen as the natural and desirable further development of such a union. However, before the Community could consider adopting a single currency, exchange rates would have to be irrevocably locked (the timing of which might depend much more on the effective coordination of policies than on growing use of the ECU). Once exchange rates are permanently fixed the ECU will become a very close substitute for any national currency.

One concrete implication of this proposition is that:

(i) there should be no discontinuity between the present ECU and the future single currency, i.e. any debt contracted in ECUs before the introduction of the single currency would be payable at face value in ECUs if, at maturity, the transition to the single currency had been made.

12. *'All impediments to the voluntary use of the ECU as a common numeraire and a means of settlement by private economic agents would have to be removed'.* Barring official action discriminating in favour of the ECU (which would result in undesirable financial market distortions) and excluding a link between the official and the private ECU, there are, broadly speaking, two types of measure: direct

encouragement (e.g. increased borrowing in ECUs by public sector entities; larger exchange market interventions in ECUs; some official support for the ECU clearing system) and indirect encouragement (e.g. removal of restrictions on the private use of the ECU by giving it the status of a foreign or national currency in each member country; demonstration effects through increasing operations in official ECUs within the EMS and by enlarging the group of other holders).

Some concrete implications of this proposition are that:

(i) as a *numeraire* the ECU would have equal, but not privileged, status *vis-à-vis* the national currency denomination; therefore

(ii) the ECU would be an additional unit of account wherever national legislation specifies the use of a *numeraire*.

13. *'The official ECU could play a role in the conduct of a common monetary policy in an advanced stage of monetary union'*. Governor Ciampi presented a scheme in which the official ECU would be used as a reserve instrument in managing a common monetary policy in the Community. This scheme represents one, but not necessarily the only, way of giving operational meaning to the concept of a single monetary policy. In considering whether there are other operational schemes for a common monetary policy, it has to be borne in mind that the ECU should not become a parallel currency (i.e. the official ECU must remain an asset used only within the circle of central banks) and that the official ECU already performs a number of functions in central bank operations.

A proposal for stage two under which monetary policy operations would be centralized in a jointly-owned subsidiary[1]

A. Lamfalussy

I — Introduction

1. This note describes an institutional reform that EC central banks could introduce to mark stage two of the transition to European monetary union. The proposal is based on the following premises concerning stage two:

— it is assumed that the new Treaty has been ratified and that the enhanced policy concertation carried out by the Committee of EC Governors during stage one has yielded results;

— in the monetary field, stage two is supposed to go beyond stage one in three important respects: (a) at least the embryo of a federal central banking system should be put in place; (b) while the final word on the conduct of national monetary policies is to remain with the Member States, there should be a visible further strengthening in the extent of policy coordination; and similarly, (c) while it would still be possible to alter intra-Community exchange rates, there should also be visible progress in coordinating intervention policy in the exchange markets;

— progress in these three areas should be such that it prepares the ground for the move to stage three, i.e. the irrevocable locking of exchange rates and the full operation of a federal central banking system.

2. With these premises in mind, three possible approaches to stage two are proposed. The first would be to implement a gradual but formal transfer of decision-making power from the monetary authorities of the member countries to a federal central banking institution. The second approach — outlined in Governor Ciampi's contribution to this collection of papers — would be to set up a formal two-tier system of monetary control based on the requirement that

---

[1] The author acknowledges the valuable assistance of Creon Butler in the preparation and drafting of this paper.

member central banks back their creation of local currency reserves with ECU reserves supplied by a federal central banking institution. Finally, at the core of the third approach set out in this paper is the idea that EC central banks should set up a jointly owned subsidiary, whose facilities they would share in performing certain of their functions — notably the implementation of monetary policy through the domestic money and foreign exchange markets — but which would not require them to give up any substantial degree of individual sovereignty over those functions.

3. The first two approaches implicitly assume that some element of central bank authority or resources would need to be put under collective control as a necessary condition for establishing a new operational institution in stage two. By contrast, the third approach essentially reverses the order of progress so that operations are centralized in a new institution *before* resources are formally pooled or authority is granted to a collective body. Following recent EC terminology, the resulting situation could be characterized as common operational facilities with 'home-country control'.

4. Section II describes the central bank operations that would be centralized in the joint subsidiary, while Sections III and IV examine the likely benefits and costs of the scheme. Sections V and VI consider some more detailed questions of implementation. Section VII contains conclusions and poses some unresolved questions.

II — What functions should be centralized?

5. In principle, several functions of the EC central banks could be performed through shared facilities. However, the largest boost to the monetary union process would come from centralizing the operations through which national monetary policies are implemented. This would cover domestic open market and lending operations, as well as intervention in the foreign exchange markets. It would be achieved by establishing a common operations floor and accounting system within the jointly owned subsidiary which could be known from the outset as the European System of Central Banks (ESCB). Initially, each member central bank would staff its own operations on the common floor rather like a branch, but over time these separate national staffs would be merged into a single unit (see Section V). Although their operations would be performed through common facilities, and hence be completely transparent to their partners, individual member central banks would retain ultimate responsibility for the deployment of their national foreign exchange reserves, and for the supply of domestic bank reserves.

III — Benefits of the scheme

6. By centralizing the implementation of national monetary policies in a single institution, the EC central banks would give a powerful demonstration, both politically and to the markets, of the progress that had already been made in the concertation of national economic policies, and of the seriousness with which they were pursuing the ultimate goal of monetary union.

7. To maximize the reform's impact on market perceptions the member central banks could agree fairly early on in stage two not to reveal the source of instructions for operations by the ESCB. Thereafter the market would find it much harder to exploit differences in emphasis among member central banks. Moreover, the risk of separate actions by member central banks being misinterpreted in the markets would be greatly reduced. At the same time the common use of the ESCB for exchange rate intervention would impose considerable discipline on member central banks to coordinate their actions so as to give consistent signals to the markets. This would apply to all users of the shared facilities, even those which were not full participants in the ERM.

8. The transparency of individual national operations, together with the experience of working closely together, would enhance the level of trust and understanding among the staffs of member central banks, at the operational level and perhaps also at the policy-making level. When combined with the rapid interchange of information on both domestic and foreign operations, this would help to improve coordination on market tactics and might also lead to further advances in policy concertation.

9. Over the longer term the sharing of detailed information on national money market institutions and short-term transmission mechanisms, in conjunction with the 'installation' of all EC control mechanisms on common facilities, would encourage efforts to clarify and converge the domestic operating mechanisms for each currency. This would not only ease the transition to a unified monetary control procedure, but would also help to ensure that the ESCB developed into an institution focused on the objective of price stability within the Community.

10. A less certain benefit of the scheme would be the cost savings that might result from centralizing monetary operations. There could be substantial economies of scale, with the added interim benefit for small countries of being able to develop more sophisticated operating procedures than would be possible on an individual basis.

IV — Implications for national sovereignty

11. The scheme could impinge on national sovereignty in two respects. Firstly, member central banks would no longer be able to disguise the content of their domestic and foreign monetary operations from their EC partners. This loss of privacy is the key to many of the benefits described above, but to the extent that it does represent a sacrifice it provides an opportunity for all member central banks to demonstrate their commitment to the ultimate goal of monetary union. Indeed the inclusion of all important monetary operations in the scheme is essential to ensure that all EC central banks make an equivalent commitment to it, even those without well-developed money market operations.

12. Secondly, there could be a tendency over the long run for national money markets to migrate to the country in which the ESCB operations were located. However, it should be recognized that the development of one dominant financial centre could well be an inevitable long-run consequence of achieving monetary union, even with the adoption of a federal system for policy-making. The US experience illustrates this to the extent that monetary policy implementation is centralized at the Federal Reserve Bank of New York. Indeed the individual reserve banks' open market operations were centralized at the FRBNY before a centralized approach to policy-making was clearly established.

V — Implementation

13. Structuring the ESCB as a jointly owned subsidiary would enable all member central banks to participate despite their heterogeneous legal structures.

14. Initially, each member central bank would staff its own operations on the common floor; thus the ESCB would essentially consist of a collection of 'branches' of the member central banks, albeit sharing the same facilities. If necessary, individual banks could transfer their operations gradually, but they would all have to meet the same deadline for transferring their complete monetary operations to the floor.

15. Full transparency within the ESCB would exist from the outset. This would be essential both to achieve the key benefits of the scheme and to enable rapid progression to the point at which the various branch staffs of the member central banks could be reorganized as a single corporate unit. Direct home-country control over operations could be maintained even after the merging of branches is complete, but it is more likely that the member central banks will be increasingly willing to give discretion to the ESCB staff to manage their respective operations within broad policy guidelines.

16. One look at the global treasury operations of a large commercial bank today should lay to rest any doubts regarding the technical feasibility of the plan. Such operations span multiple currencies and instruments with separate books and lines of responsibility to senior management for individual dealers.

17. A more difficult questic is whether the geographic separation of a member central bank's operating personnel from their counterparts in the domestic private sector would lead to a loss of market 'feel'. This problem may in the long run be alleviated by the relocation of important domestic counterparts to the financial centre hosting the ESCB's operations. But in any case, any loss of domestic information would increasingly be compensated for by the growing relevance of the information on operations in other member countries made available through participation in the joint facilities.

18. At first the ESCB balance sheet could be structured as a collection of accounts owned by the member central banks and their private sector counterparts, mirroring the monetary accounts that at present exist on member central banks' balance sheets. However, as the ESCB increasingly raised its profile, it would be desirable to interpose ESCB-owned accounts in all monetary transactions between the member central banks and private financial institutions, and possibly in transactions with certain official entities as well. One could envisage a situation arising towards the end of stage two in which the entire monetary operations of the individual member central banks were captured in their accounts and in their transactions with the ESCB. At the same time, all the likely private sector participants in a stage three European 'fed funds' market would, by the end of stage two, have well-established direct relationships with the ESCB.

VI — Treatment of non-monetary operations

19. At present the domestic monetary operations of some member central banks may be closely integrated with other financial tasks performed on behalf of the government or private sector. This could pose a problem since it is not the intention of the scheme to transfer the whole of a member central bank's financial activities to the ESCB. However, it should be recognized that the substantial disengagement of the monetary and non-monetary activities of member central banks would be a necessary precondition for achieving a unified monetary control procedure in stage three.

20. It is also possible that member central banks may wish to take advantage of the facilities provided by the ESCB to centralize more operations than would be strictly necessary to capture the implementation of monetary policy. For example, a natural complement to the transfer of monetary operations would be the centralization of member central banks' 'town' clearing systems used to perform the final daily clearing among the major commercial banks in each country. This role for

the ESCB could have important side benefits since it would help to ensure that the progressive integration of European banking systems under the single market programme was closely monitored from the perspective of monetary policy and systemic risk.

21. The long-term management of member central banks' foreign and domestic assets is also closely related to their monetary operations and could easily be centralized at the ESCB using the principle of shared facilities with home-country control. However, some countries may wish to make a distinction between foreign assets with monetary and non-monetary uses, and therefore retain some part of their foreign exchange reserves under the control of national treasuries.

VII — Conclusion

22. The scheme presented here has two distinctive elements. First is the *implicit* constraint that it places on member central banks by requiring them to implement their national monetary policies through shared facilities. By comparison with the various possible *explicit* mechanisms for demonstrating the existing level of monetary policy concertation and encouraging further advances, this approach involves a smaller risk of unintended disruption in national implementation procedures.

23. A second distinctive feature of the proposal is that the new institution would *replace* rather than duplicate facilities that already exist in the member central banks. This would minimize the risk of real or perceived conflicts emerging between the member central banks and the new collectively owned institution. It would also mean that once the merger of the different national operating staffs had been completed, the new institution could fit, with little further adaptation, into the institutional framework that would ultimately be required in stage three.

24. There is much that the scheme presented here does not do. Most importantly, it does not attempt to solve the problem of how a stage three decision-making body will determine the appropriate EC monetary stance to achieve domestic price stability. In addition, it only ensures instantaneous as opposed to *ex ante* policy consultation, and it does not introduce any automatic mechanisms tending to discourage realignments. Finally, it does not do anything directly for the development of the ECU.

25. However, there can be little doubt that, as an institutional demonstration of the Member States' stage one achievements in policy concertation and of their commitment to reach the final goal of monctary union, the plan would have a major impact. Over the longer term the scheme could significantly improve the scope for convergence in monetary procedures and for further policy concertation, provided the political will for such goals existed. At the same time, the

scheme would exert subtle pressures of its own by forcing Member States to present a consistent common front to the markets.

26. The proposal raises some questions regarding institutional arrangements which would require further clarification. For example:

— What would be the legal constraints on individual central banks in delegating their monetary operations to a mutually owned subsidiary while retaining sole ultimate control over those operations?

— What are the key monetary operations of each central bank? Would it be difficult to disentangle these from other financial tasks carried out on behalf of the government or the private sector?

The basic difference between the frameworks for policy decision-making provided by the EMS and EMU

Pierre Jaans

In the European Monetary System (EMS) policy decisions in the monetary, economic, fiscal and budgetary fields are within the unrestricted competence of national authorities. Decisions are taken autonomously, sometimes after consultations with Community bodies, which may or may not entail adjustments in planned decisions.

For those countries whose currencies participate in the exchange rate mechanism, there is a certain restriction of national sovereignty in so far as changes of central rates can no longer be decided unilaterally, as was the case in the European monetary 'snake' but are subject to the consensus of all participants. The experience with both systems, however, shows that the material impact of this constraint is of limited importance in practice.

Thus, in the framework provided currently by the EMS, policy decision-making rests with several autonomous (national) decision centres. The complex process is characterized *inter alia* by interaction, interdependence, reactivity and competition between national economies of heterogeneous political traditions, institutional structures and degrees of economic development.

Under this system of 'spontaneous' order, a very important, if not the main source of short-term surveillance and sanction is the foreign exchange market and the balance-of-payments performance. If the stance and the mix of policies chosen at a national level are credible to the market, the current exchange rate in the EMS will not come under attack. If the policy cocktail lacks credibility in the market or if the balance-of-payments performance falters, the market will fairly rapidly exert growing pressures on the currency of the country concerned and thus trigger corrective action by policy-makers.

It may be argued that foreign exchange markets may at times be affected by misjudgments leading to a significant overshooting. This has been the case with the US dollar market because of the strategic value and the world reserve character of that currency. In the case of European currencies, however, which have no significant strategic and/or reserve currency role, the foreign exchange markets have in general not developed into lasting misalignments of their respective values. (In this respect it is interesting to note that gyrations of the creation of a single European currency because such a currency would, in the absence of a strong political union, lack the political and strategic format of the US dollar.)

The relative success of the EMS owes a great deal to the discipline stemming from foreign exchange markets, since in the case of some countries participating in the exchange rate mechanism (for example, Belgium in 1982 and France in 1983), fundamental reorientations of policy choices were greatly accelerated through the acceptance of market pressures. In retrospect in would at least seem doubtful, whether, in the absence of market pressures, it would have been possible, by mere analysis and suasion, to scrap a sacred political cow like automatic wage indexation.

Thus it can be said that, in the case of countries whose currencies participate in the exchange rate mechanism, foreign exchange markets have performed a helpful function of discipline and, together with balance-of-payments performances, have provided useful early warning indicators and guidelines for policy-shaping and decision-making.

After the transition to Economic and Monetary Union (EMU) with a centralized monetary policy for a single currency or a set of currencies linked by irrevocably fixed parities, the monitoring and guiding role of foreign exchange markets and balance-of-payments performances will by definition cease to exist.

Decision-making in monetary policy and in certain areas of fiscal and budgetary policies will rest with a central authority. Member countries (EC regions in economic terms) will however retain a still significant portion of autonomy in the field of economic and budgetary policies. The budget of the Community (the central budget) will remain comparatively small. There will be no intra-Community exchange market and balance of payments, for intra-Community transactions will be dedramatized to mere statistics with no effects on foreign exchange reserves.

Under these conditions the adequacy of policies at the central level and of policy combinations between the Community level and national (regional) levels will have to rely solely on a majority based consensus on analysis, on evaluation and on the choice of appropriate means as well as on 'burden sharing'.

Misalignments between centrally decided policies and policies decided at national level, or coordinated but erroneous policy choices at both levels, will no longer be signalled by the reaction of foreign exchange markets. Similarly, regional payments disequilibria will be dedramatized since they are no longer accompanied by a depletion of foreign exchange reserves.

Economic and Monetary Union, as compared to the present European Monetary System, is a more 'constructivist' order which eliminates market effects and is based on coordination and political compromise. Past experience with deliberate political coordination and fine-tuning in the economic area, both in the Community (for example, the common agricultural policy) and in a wider context (for example, the 'Locomotive approach' in 1979 on a Group of Ten level) failed to produce convincing positive results.

Under such a system the identification of misalignments may be delayed either involuntarily or for pertinent political reasons. Regional disequilibria may build up in a gradual way, imperceptibly and easy to ignore in the short to medium term. As a result, severe losses of competitiveness, disindustrialization and unemployment may develop before a new political consensus about the correct diagnosis and corrective action are reached. Coming late, such action has to be more robust and painful than if it had been taken in a timely manner under the more immediate pressure of the foreign exchange markets.

Conclusions

The EMS, and more specifically the adhesion to the exchange rate mechanism, has been and continues to be an efficient factor of convergence by imposing the sanctioning power of foreign exchange markets on policy decision-making.

EMU would eliminate market pressures and would have to rely mainly on a more or less political consensus on analysis, evaluation, the choice of means and burden sharing in the determination of policy mixes at the community level and national levels.

As long as there is a significant need for further adjustment and convergence of economic and budgetary performances of member countries, the framework of discipline provided by the EMS appears to be more appropriate because it is quicker in correcting deviations from the path of orthodoxy of market-oriented economies.

An operational framework for an integrated monetary policy in Europe

C. A. Ciampi

I — Introduction

1. The purpose of this paper is to organize thinking on how to carry out, from an operational point of view, an integrated monetary policy in Europe. The scheme illustrated below is designed to stimulate further reflection and does not pretend to provide a fully-fledged blueprint. The present contribution is a synthesis of two earlier documents discussed in the Committee and incorporates comments and suggestions made by some of the members, particularly Professor Thygesen. The paper focuses on the institutional aspects of the development of monetary cooperation towards full unity and does not address the equally important issue of the market development of the ECU, which has been thoroughly examined by Governor Duisenberg.

2. The paper is divided into two sections. The difficulties inherent in moving towards monetary unification exclusively on the basis of *ad hoc* cooperation among the member countries are examined in the first section, while a possible solution to these difficulties is described in the second.

II — The limits of coordination in conducting a common monetary policy

3. The Werner Report assigns the basic role in the working of a monetary union to the irrevocable locking of parities. It recognizes that a perfect monetary union implies a common currency, but argues that creating a fixed link between currencies can produce an equivalent result. However, the Report suggests that this only applies if the irrevocable locking is akin to the fixed relationship between notes of different denominations of a given currency. In other words, the irrevocable locking of currencies brings about a monetary union only if it implies and is supported by a common monetary policy.

4. The theoretical possibility of achieving 'perfect coordination' of monetary policies through informal arrangements cannot be excluded, but the probability of this occurring in practice is very low. The prerequisites of such coordination are

very demanding and costly: the collection, processing and evaluation of the information needed for the conduct of monetary policy would be cumbersome and inefficient; more importantly, the willingness to take each other's views into account in order to reach a consensus may fall short of what is needed.

5. The first problem in this respect is that exchange rate fixity leaves the level towards which interest rates in participating countries must converge undetermined. Nor is it sufficient to provide unambiguous operational guidance to establish monetary stability as the final objective of the system. The link between this final objective and day-to-day monetary policy is too tenuous, and no econometric model or other formal device could be relied upon to establish it unequivocally. A common judgment, exercised through appropriate procedures, is needed, but this is precisely what is lacking in a system of coordination, and conflicting opinions and policies are likely to emerge.

6. Another shortcoming of *ad hoc* coordination is the difficulty of ensuring continuous compliance with the agreed monetary policy stance. It is conceivable that monetary policies will be forced to diverge, openly or otherwise, from the coordinated stance. For example, monetary policy could be required to support, albeit temporarily, the level of economic activity, or to finance the budget deficit. This would have devastating consequences: as soon as the market realized that the mutual trust and voluntary compliance underpinning the system were in danger, it would test the commitment of monetary authorities to maintain parities, entailing the risk of large capital movements that could jeopardize the irrevocable locking of parities.

7. To sum up, it is not sufficient for member central banks to *declare* that they will pursue a common objective of monetary stability and informally coordinate their action; they must be *seen* to be doing so at every moment; otherwise the market may suspect a policy disagreement, particularly when intermediate objectives are reformulated in the face of changing circumstances.

8. This is why an *operational framework for an integrated monetary policy* is required. Such a framework would ensure that monetary policies which were distinct, though coordinated, would be operationally merged into *one* policy, thereby meeting the conditions for the lasting viability of the irrevocable locking of parities. Any definition of these arrangements, and hence of the minimal requirements of a workable monetary union, must provide: (1) an unambiguous procedure for translating the final goal of monetary stability into specific *objectives;* (2) the *instruments* for ensuring national monetary authorities' compliance with the decisions taken in common. The first issue has been discussed in the contributions to the Committee on the institutional aspects of the ESCB, the second is covered in the following section.

III — An institutional scheme for a common monetary policy

9. This section outlines a scheme based on the creation of a central monetary institution. This, together with national central banks, would constitute a European System of Central Banks (ESCB). In terms of the steps towards monetary union identified in the Report, the scheme fits into the second stage, in which there is still a plurality of currencies not tied by irrevocably locked parities and monetary policies are closely coordinated but not yet completely unified.

10. Under the scheme the monetary organization of the Community would have *three levels:* the central monetary institution, national central banks and commercial banks. At the top, the central monetary institution would only engage in transactions with member central banks; these, in turn, would maintain their present relationships with domestic commercial banks. The central monetary institution would act as the central bank of the national central banks and use its creation of ECU reserves to influence the monetary actions of member central banks. The basic principle underlying the scheme is that there is a link between the ultimate target of price stability, the undertaking to fix parities, the interest rate prevailing in each country and the underlying liquidity conditions, which in turn are determined by the action of each member central bank. This approach, which is based on the 'fundamentals', leads to a system that will allow the central monetary institution to control the liquidity creation of the national central banks as the ultimate source of monetary developments.

11. The ECU would still be a basket currency and only member central banks would hold *ECU deposits with the central monetary institution.* In this latter respect, the situation would be similar to that prevailing domestically, where deposits with the central bank are predominantly held by banks and provide the ultimate means for settling interbank accounts. Of course, in this set-up, commercial banks and their customers would be free, within the aggregate targets set by the ESCB, to denominate deposits and other monetary instruments in ECUs.

12. The scheme involves three fundamental components. The first is an *autonomous balance sheet* for the central monetary institution, in line with the structure of all monetary institutions (national central banks, the IMF, the BIS); this would allow the central monetary institution to take operational decisions, rather than serving simply as a forum for concertation. The second is a mechanism for ensuring direct and *firm control of the supply of ECUs* by the central monetary institution, in strict analogy with the control exercised by national central banks over the domestic money supply. The third is a set of provisions to *strengthen national central banks' demand for official ECUs* created by the central monetary institution by making them a necessary ingredient of the process whereby central banks supply liquidity to the private sector.

13. The balance sheet of the central monetary institution would be based on *capital* in the form of contributions of international reserves by national central banks, along the lines of the proposal of Governor de Larosière. For instance, USD 4 or USD 5 billion of international reserves could be contributed according to a distribution key reflecting the relative economic importance of participating countries. In return, central banks would receive shares of the central monetary institution, i. e. a participation in its capital.

14. Firm management of the supply of ECUs by the central monetary institution requires that all the channels of ECU creation be brought under its direct control. At present, the amount of ECUs created through the swap mechanism depends entirely on exogenous factors: changes in the gold price, the dollar exchange rate and the quantity of reserves. Such swaps will therefore have to be abolished. They could be replaced by an *initial contribution* of international reserves — in exchange for ECUs — by member central banks, amounting, for example, to the equivalent of 3 % of their respective monetary bases.

15. *Credit mechanisms,* the other channel of ECU creation, are similar to the rediscount facilities for commercial banks at the national level. However, while automatic rediscount facilities are generally on a small scale in national systems and the supply of liquidity to commercial banks mainly discretional, the EMS credit mechanisms are mostly automatic and for unlimited amounts up to 75 days. To bring the creation of ECUs from this source under strict control, the central monetary institution should be given the power to grant member central banks discretional credit in ECUs, in the same way as a central bank refinances commercial banks through open market or rediscount operations. The cost of this credit would also be fixed discretionally. In turn, this new mechanism would allow a significant reduction in the scope of very short-term financing (VSTF), for instance by reducing its average duration to 15 days, limiting its applicability to the financing of marginal interventions, eliminating automatic renewals and making it more expensive, in the nature of a Lombard-type facility.

16. The third component needed to complete the scheme, after arranging for an autonomous balance sheet and firm control of the creation of official ECUs, is a specific and *exclusive use for the ECUs* held with the central monetary institution. This is provided by requiring member central banks to hold the ECUs (created through the channels described in paragraphs 14 and 15 above) as deposits with the central monetary institution in the form of both *compulsory* and *free reserves.* The reserve requirement in ECUs would link the supply of liquidity by member central banks, and therefore the aggregate monetary conditions in the Community, to the creation of ECUs by the central monetary institution. In this way, a strong relationship would be established between the action of the central monetary institution and that of each member central bank. Through this link, the stance decided in common within the ESCB would be transmitted to all the members of the system.

17. The system could be implemented in different ways, depending on whether the reserve requirement were applied to the liabilities or the assets of the national central banks, as illustrated in the following two paragraphs.

18. If the reserve requirement were imposed on the *liabilities* of participating central banks, the central monetary institution would have the power to ask member central banks to hold compulsory reserves in ECU amounting to the equivalent of a certain percentage of the total monetary base, or of its increases. The reserve requirement in official ECUs would establish a connection between the supply of central bank money by member central banks, and therefore the aggregate money supply in the Community, and the creation of official ECUs by the central monetary institution. Since central bank money in the participating countries would also be created as a counterpart of net unsterilized interventions in third currencies, indirectly these would also be affected. National central banks would only be able to undertake autonomous foreign exchange operations against third currencies to the extent that they offset the latter's monetary effects by changes in the credit extended to domestic counterparts.

19. As an alternative, the reserve requirement could be applied to the *credit* extended by national central banks to the domestic sector. The total expansion of central bank money in the system would be the counterpart of the credit extended to the domestic sector plus the net effect of unsterilized foreign exchange market interventions against third currencies. The central monetary institution would therefore have to take a stance on the desired overall amount of intervention. This could be achieved by allowing the central monetary institution to intervene directly in the market or by subordinating national central bank interventions to guidelines laid down by the ESCB. With the target rate of domestic credit expansion given, there would be a presumption that these interventions would not be sterilized. It would also be conceivable to apply the reserve requirement to the sum of domestic credit and official reserves in third currencies. In this case, guidelines on unsterilized intervention would no longer be needed.

20. ECUs held with the central monetary institution in excess of the compulsory level would constitute *free reserves*. Central banks would need such reserves to be able to expand their monetary base, settle obligations in the system and obtain international reserves from other central banks (negotiability) or the central monetary institution. The central monetary institution would be under no obligation to buy or sell international reserves against ECUs; it would only do so to the extent that such action was consistent with its monetary objectives, in analogy with central bank behaviour when deciding to intervene in foreign exchange markets. The convertibility of ECUs with the central monetary institution would thus be at the latter's discretion, and would be assured whenever it was deemed necessary to counter a monetary disturbance of systemic significance.

21. As far as the *functioning of the system* is concerned, the governing body of the ESCB would decide each year, in the light of an appraisal of the economic situation, how much money and credit should be created overall in the

Community in order to support economic activity in a non-inflationary environment. This target would then be translated into a figure for the central monetary institution's ECU supply, which would guide the liquidity creation of national central banks.

22. The mechanism described above would be instrumental in achieving the monetary policy objectives set for the Community. If, for instance, it were necessary to make the aggregate monetary stance of the system more restrictive, the ESCB could reduce credit in ECUs to member central banks, increase its cost and/or increase the ECU reserve requirement. Conversely, if the ESCB judged that a more expansionary stance were needed in the aggregate, it could increase ECU credit, reduce its cost and/or decrease the ECU reserve requirement, and the resulting free ECU reserves would support the desired monetary expansion by some, or all, of the national central banks. If, on the other hand, the problem was the tendency for money to expand *in a given country* beyond the stability-oriented common plan, the ESCB could ask for a special deposit of reserves from the central bank of the country concerned. Analogously, if a currency came under speculative attack on foreign exchange markets while the underlying monetary policy was considered appropriate, the ESCB could provide ECU credit and help restore balanced conditions in the market.

23. The foregoing examples appear to imply that the main monetary policy instrument of a system based on ECU reserve requirements has to be a quantitative aggregate, but in fact the scheme can easily be generalized. The ESCB might also be guided in its supply of official ECUs by interest rates. In view of the degree of exchange rate fixity expected for phase two, interest rates in member countries would have to converge within a narrow band. The ESCB could then carry out its monetary policy by focusing on the level of interest rates. For example, if liquidity increased too much in a country, interest rates would tend to fall and pressures would develop on foreign exchange markets. The appropriate response of the ESCB would be to withdraw official ECUs with the aim of inducing the national monetary authorities to rein in the expansion of liquidity. The opposite action would be warranted in the case of insufficient liquidity.

24. While the basic features of a system of ECU reserve requirements for national central banks are relatively simple, the implementation of the scheme would have to take account of a certain number of factors, such as differences in national money multipliers, the effect of realignments and the distribution of reserves among national central banks.

25. *National monetary base multipliers* differ considerably at present, in particular because of the disparities in national reserve requirements in respect of commercial bank deposits. These differences will be reduced by the pressure to converge produced by the liberalization of capital flows and financial services. Nonetheless, the remaining differences would result in a transfer of official ECUs from a national central bank with a low multiplier to one with a high multiplier having an expansionary effect, even with a given total quantity of official ECUs.

This would not be an entirely new problem since national systems often have different reserve coefficients for different types of deposit, so that a shift can affect the observed multiplier. However, the problem would undoubtedly complicate the task of the ESCB, requiring careful monitoring of the distribution of official ECUs and, whenever necessary, intervention to adjust the overall quantity available, in order to offset the expansionary or contractionary effects of transfers of official ECUs between national central banks.

26. As for the effects of a *realignment* on the operation of the scheme, the central bank with a depreciating currency would record an increase in the value of its ECU reserves expressed in national currency and end up with free ECU reserves, while the central banks whose currencies appreciated against the ECU would need to acquire additional ECUs. The monetary consequences of these effects would have to be dealt with by appropriate technical devices built into the system.

27. More generally, there is the issue of the *distribution of ECU reserves among the participating national central banks*. This arises because national central banks are likely to behave differently from commercial banks. National reserve requirements work predictably and affect all banks in the same manner because commercial banks act mainly on the basis of profit motives. Accordingly, in most cases there is an active market for the asset that can be used to satisfy national reserve requirements, with interest rates determining whether any given bank is willing to supply or to demand additional reserves. Especially at the start of the proposed scheme, there is no guarantee that every national central bank would increase its national monetary base in response to an expansion in the supply of official ECUs. Furthermore, national central banks wishing to expand would not be able to count on a market in which to obtain additional official ECUs. In this case, the ESCB would have to guide and adjust the distribution of ECU reserves among national central banks.

28. At an *advanced* stage such as that described above in paragraphs 9 to 22, when responsibility for monetary policy is exercised at Community level, the ECUs held with the central monetary institution would be the *only* asset permitting national central banks to expand their aggregate supply of high-powered money, albeit with a required reserve coefficient that could initially be small. National central banks would not be able to acquire these ECUs automatically from the central institution either through an unconditional right to convert reserves held in other currencies or through access to any of the credit mechanisms. Scarcity of high-powered ECUs would provide effective control over the expansion of money and credit in the Community.

29. At an *intermediate* stage of the process, when national central banks still have primary monetary responsibility, some flexibility in the supply of official ECUs and in the way this is linked to the creation of high-powered national money would allow member central banks to expand or contract the money supply in their countries without being rigidly tied by their ECU reserves. In these conditions, ECU operations carried out by the ESCB using the mechanism

described above would serve primarily to highlight, and in part counter, divergences by individual central banks from the commonly agreed monetary and credit objectives of the Community. The ESCB should also initially take account of the specific needs of each participating country when making and carrying out its plans; its hold on the system's monetary policy would only be tightened gradually. Accordingly, some leeway could be provided by not making the automatic very short-term financing (Lombard-type facility) too strict, in terms of duration and cost, and by granting member central banks the right to exchange ECUs for international reserves and vice versa under certain specific conditions. As gards the link between ECU creation by the central monetary institution and national money supplies, some flexibility could be allowed by fixing ranges for the ECU compulsory reserves rather than a specific level.

IV — Conclusions

30. In institutional terms the proposals presented in this paper involve a very significant step towards monetary union and a loss of monetary autonomy. In practice, however, capital mobility and the exchange rate constraint already drastically reduce the room for autonomous monetary policies: the ultimate responsibility attributed to national monetary authorities is severely limited and each national policy-maker influences, and is influenced by, all the others. Seen in this light, the only innovation in the scheme illustrated above is that the constraint would be explicit and exert an *ex ante* influence on the formulation of monetary policy, instead of being hidden and having an *ex post* effect in the exchange market. Accordingly, the pooling of monetary responsibilities would not so much be a new phenomenon, as the — admittedly important — development of an existing trend.

ð

V — List of members of the Committee

List of members of the Committee

Jacques Delors (Chairman)
Frans Andriessen
Miguel Boyer
Demitrius J. Chalikias
Carlo Azeglio Ciampi
Maurice F. Doyle
Willem F. Duisenberg
Jean Godeaux
Erik Hoffmeyer
Pierre Jaans
Alexandre Lamfalussy
Jacques de Larosière
Robert Leigh-Pemberton
Karl Otto Pöhl
Mariano Rubio
José A.V. Tavares Moreira
Niels Thygesen

Rapporteurs

Gunter D. Baer
Tommaso Padoa-Schioppa

European Communities — Commission

1. Report on economic and monetary union in the European Community

2. Collection of papers submitted to the Committee for the Study of Economic and Monetary Union

Luxembourg: Office for Official Publications of the European Communities

1989 — 235 pp. — 17.6 × 25.0 cm

ISBN 92-826-0655-4

Catalogue number: CB-56-89-401-EN-C

Price (excluding VAT) in Luxembourg: ECU 10